The Ultimate Calling

The Perils and Privileges of the Pastorate

The Ultimate Calling

The Perils and Privileges of the Pastorate

Roland Boyce

Printed in the United States of America.

Unless otherwise noted, scripture quotations are taken from the *1978 edition of the New International Version of the Holy Scriptures.*
Other referenced scripture versions include:
King James Version of the Holy Bible (2001), The Message: The Bible in Contemporary Language (2005), and the Charles Spurgeon Study Bible (2017).

ISBN: 978-1-7369703-0-0

Cover photo: ©boana/Getty Images
Cover and interior design by Rick Lindholtz for On the Tracks Media

On the Tracks Media LLC
onthetracksmedia.com

Dedication

This work is dedicated to the significant people who have loved, cared for, and supported me in my life and ministry: My beloved Joyce, a faithful wife of 51 years, superlative help-mate and pastor's wife, as well as my co-editor; our son, Ryan, our daughter, Alana; our fine grandsons, Easton and Myles; my treasured sister, Char, whose stalwart prayer life has been indispensable to this publishing effort, and to Our Lord and Savior, Jesus Christ, who by His relentless love and grace has called and empowered me to fulfill The Ultimate Calling.

TABLE OF CONTENTS

Dedication i

Acknowledgements viii

Introduction ix

Forward xi

Section One: The Person of the Pastor
(Who the Pastor Is)

1   The Certainty of Call 1

The Holiest and Hardest of Professions

The Inescapability of the Pastoral Call

The Prerequisite of Personal Identity

Expectations: Ally or Enemy?

2   The Imperative of Integrity 16

The Wellspring of the Soul

The Incessant Battle with Evil

The Intrusion of Ego and Power

The Importance of Balance

3   The Life of Devotion 25

The Difference Between Devotion and Devotions

The Intimacy of the Interior Life

The Role of Spiritual Disciplines

The Contrast of Personal and Professional Bible Study

4   The Primacy of Prayer 41

The Basis of Being

Observing the Lord's Model in Ministry

The Dual Needs

Individual and Corporate Prayer

5 Self-care 58

Getting Over the Guilt of Not Performing

The Biblical Definition of Self-care

Taking a Sabbatical

Development of Life Outside the Parish

6 Protecting Marriage and Family Life 70

The Vulnerability of the Pastor as Partner and Parent

The Role of the Spouse as Team Player

Letting the Pastor's Kids be Normal

Riding the Waves of the Adolescent Passage

Protecting the Family Fort

7 The Necessity of Networking 88

Intercession with Intimates

Connecting with Colleagues in the Ministry

The Earthly Trinity

Getting the Next Generation Ready

8 The Supremacy of Shepherding 103

The Biblical Background

The Significance of Suffering

A Spiritual Physician

The Requisites of Shepherding

The Decalogue of Shepherding

Section Two: The Performance of the Pastor
(What the Pastor Does)

9 The Pastor as Coach 126

The Care and Maintenance of the Church Staff

Building rapport with Your Team

The Pastor as Liaison Between Staff and Church Leadership

When it Doesn't Work Out

10 The Pastor as Administrator 139

Administration as a Ministry
The Definition and Place of Authority
Learning to Delegate
Engaging the Volunteer
The Concept of Congregational Co-ministry

11 The Pastor as Vision Caster 158

The Vitalness of the Vision
The Environment of Enthusiasm
The Place of Strategic Planning
The Right to Risk
The Challenge of Casting Vision and Strategic Planning

12 The Pastor as Worship Leader 175

Genuine Worship
Setting the Spiritual Tone
Cultivating the Spirit of Celebration
Making God the Audience
The Service
The Church Gathered to be Scattered

13 The Pastor as Preacher/Teacher 193

Two Essential Elements
The Place of Authenticity and Authority
To Preach is to Teach
The Place of Christian Education
Declaring the Truth
Realistic Expectations

14 The Pastor As Counselor 215

The Need for a Counselor
The Basis of Exhortation/Counseling
The Necessity of Referral
The Role of Client Accountability
Development of Lay Counselors
Land Mines in the Couch

15 The Pastor as Steward..236

Basis of Biblical Stewardship
Total Life Stewardship
The Heart of Stewardship
Investors vs. Consumers
The Benefits of Giving

16 The Pastor As Evangelist 249

Christ in the Market Place
Intentionality in the Life of the Church
Getting Beyond the Walls
Definition Through Demonstration
The Marriage of Local and Global

17 The Pastor as Warrior...266

Ignorance of the Enemy
The Devil and the 'D's: The Timeless Strategy
Our Spiritual Arsenal
Victory in Everyday Life

18 The Pastor as Lifelong Servant 286

Biblical Background on Retirement
Doing Ministry Better
Getting Ready for Modulation
The Art of Finishing Strong
How to Know You Have Reached Your Goal

Endorsements

Guide to using The Ultimate Calling Workbook

At the conclusion of each chapter, there are several questions for you to contemplate personally. The Ultimate Calling Workbook can be used in the following ways:

- For personal study, reflection, and practical application.
- As a syllabus for a class or an elective in a Christian education or a Seminary setting.
- As part of a mentoring relationship with another person presently in ministry or contemplating attending seminary or entering the ministry in the future.

Acknowledgments

Special thanks to my Superintendent, Garth Bolinder, who commissioned the work; my thirteen fellow pastors who read and endorsed it; Pastor Rick Lindholtz, indispensable source of inspiration and assistance in facilitating the ultimate publication; and the great congregations of Milwaukie, Oregon, Stockton, California, Loveland, Colorado, Rockford, Illinois, Carrollton, Texas, Alexandria, Minnesota and Plano, Texas who gave me the opportunity to fulfill the Ultimate Calling, tell my pastoral story, and leave a legacy to those sharing in that calling.

Introduction

The Ultimate Calling is a book written *by* a pastor *about* the pastorate *for* those considering ministry or those already in ministry. It will also be helpful for members of congregations to understand the dynamics of pastoral ministry.

Part One *'The Person of the Pastor'* deals with The Certainty of Call, The Imperative of Integrity, The Life of Devotion, The Primacy of Prayer, Self-care, Protecting Marriage and Family Life, The Necessity of Networking, and The Supremacy of Shepherding.

Part Two *'The Performance of the Pastor'* explores their role as Coach, Administrator, Vision Caster, Worship Leader, Preacher/Teacher, Counselor, Steward, Evangelist, Warrior, and Lifelong Servant.

The work is, in reality, the author's journey through all avenues of the pastorate for over fifty years. He lets you travel with him as he shares his personal experiences and true stories surrounding his encounters with real people, places, problems, the perils, and the privileges of being a pastor. His objective is to help those new to ministry to gain a clear understanding of what they can anticipate as they accept *The Ultimate Calling*, the highest call upon the earth.

Forward

At the time Roland Boyce authored THE ULTIMATE CALLING, he was concluding 55 fruitful years of ministry. His story is exactly the kind of useful reflection that women and men in ministry wish to hear. This book records the burden of a seasoned saint who possesses knowledge that is only gained over decades of experience. It was, in part, that seasoned experience that motivated ministry peers who encouraged Rol to publish this work.

Which immediately asks then for which audience is the book recommended? *The Ultimate Calling* is a book written *by* a pastor *about* the pastorate *for* those considering ministry or those already in ministry. It will also be helpful for members of congregations to understand the dynamics of pastoral ministry.

Because the seasoned pastor has traveled this road before, she or he will recognize the book's nuggets, highlight them and return to them time and again.

For prospective ministry candidates fortunate enough to serve alongside such a seasoned pastor, this book will become their assigned, if not required reading, all eighteen chapters. *The Ultimate Calling* is just the tutorial needed for that man or woman asking themselves the question, "Am I being called by God into vocational ministry?"

The book is neatly arranged around two parts: who the pastor is, part one, and what the pastor does, part two. The busy senior minister can give this time-saving tool to the candidate with instructions about specific themes and be satisfied that the bases were all covered.

In those first eight chapters, the reader will find a treasure trove of insights and suggestions regarding 'Who The Pastor Is.' Boyce patiently paints a mosaic portrait of the minister in a series of scenes ranging from the clarity of calling to issues of character development and best practices for healthy pastoral marriages. Numerous resources and recommendations are offered to aid in more than ministry survival but how to charter a pathway to ministry success.

'What The Pastor Does' is covered in chapters 9-18. For the experienced ministry leader, there are occasions when a fresh or different perspective of the roles and duties of the pastor can be helpful. Boyce does not hold back but reveals antidotes, some personal and others taken from extensive familiarity with pastoral and ministry literature.

Perhaps the most unique contribution to this ministry-calling conversation is what it reveals about Roland Boyce himself. Many of us have known and served for decades with this gracious, humble pastor. We know him for his gifts and passion for serving Christ's Church and her people. When he addresses the full range of hazards, pitfalls, struggles, liabilities, and expectations, we will testify that these are disciplines into which he has lived.

It has been my humble honor as one of the several ministry confidants to encourage Roland Boyce to tell his story. We are all thankful that he has.

Dr. Willie O. Peterson
Dallas, Texas
Assistant to the Superintendent, Midsouth Conference,
Evangelical Covenant Church
Adjunct Professor, Dallas Theological Seminary

1   The Certainty of Call

The Holiest and Hardest of Professions:
The Duality of the Divine Appointment

When I was crossing the bridge from Campus Ministry to the pastorate, I remember interviewing seven pastors in Portland, Oregon. I asked them to tell me the most important thing I should know about the pastoral ministry.

A seasoned pastor offered this admonition. "If you're not sure you're called, don't go into the ministry; it's hard enough when you **know** you are called."

One of the significant aspects of this high calling is understanding the One who extends it.

The highest authority in the universe issues the call. Before time, He knew whom He would call to the sacred task. Inherent within the call is the capacity and the ability to fulfill it. In the words of the New Testament, "The one who calls you is faithful. He will do it." (I Thessalonians 5:24) God does not ask us to do what He cannot enable us to do.

A call to the pastoral ministry is a divine gift; blessed are those chosen to receive it. Though not the easiest of occupations, it is one of the most satisfying and rewarding.

Let's compare the **ultimate calling** to other callings. A physician gives up sleep and regular hours but receives the fulfillment of seeing people become well. A teacher takes on all the challenges of the classroom to make a lifelong impact on the student's life. A road construction worker spends hours in unpleasant weather to create highways that facilitate people's travel throughout the world. Every calling is challenging in some dimension. Every calling has built into it the price and the product of sacrifice. Every calling has some reward. (With the possible exception of phone solicitation.)

Yet, the thing that differentiates the pastoral calling from a secular calling is that the investment renders eternal dividends. Arguably, physicians and teachers perform services that have a lasting impact. The physician cares for the body; the teacher enriches the mind. The pastorate deals with the person's soul, the invisible part of a human being, which affects their relationship with God and eternal destiny.

Christ asked, "What good will it be for a man to gain the whole world yet forfeit his soul?" (Matthew 16:26)

Christ is the prototype, the model, and forerunner in pastoral ministry. He set the standard, established the bar, etched out the pattern of the pastorate in His earthly mission.

The highest calling in the world is to represent the pre-eminent pastor. It was hard for Him; it is hard for us. Yet, it was the price of His sacrifice that earned the divine dividend of salvation for the world. There is no higher honor than representing the God of heaven and the Lord of eternity on earth to achieve lasting results.

Ironically, some called to this highest of occupations have chosen not to enter the race. Instead, they have decided to return to the stands where life looks less challenging and is more comfortable.

I can think of two such men. They received and denied the call to pastoral ministry. God used them in other aspects of the ministry, but they struggled to some degree with doubt and guilt about what might have been had they accepted the specific call.

The Inescapability of the Pastoral Call: Struggling Inside the Center of God's Will

Earlier, I referred to the pastor, who advised me, "If you're not sure, don't do it." Let's reverse the axiom: "If you're sure, you must do it!" In other words, if God calls you to the Christian Ministry in any capacity, you'd better be about answering and following that call from God. We become marked men and women after a manner of speaking.

Jeremiah: "Before I formed you in the womb, I knew you; before you were born, I sanctified you; I *ordained* you a prophet to the nations." (Jeremiah 1:5)

Paul: "I have become its servant by the *commission* God gave me to present to you the Word of God in its fullness." (Colossians 1:25)

By the way, if there is any doubt as to divine calls, the account of Paul's conversion in Acts 9:15 should clarify that. "But the Lord said to Ananias, go. This man is my *chosen* instrument to carry my name before the Gentiles and kings and before the people of Israel. I will show him how much he must suffer for my name." (Could we have blamed Paul for trying to get out of going with God's will?)

He knew that his career as the first evangelist was a done deal as defined in his letter to the Romans. "God's gifts and His call are irrevocable." (Romans 11:29)

When one is called, the calling is not revoked; the mandate for ministry is not withdrawn. Our response to the truth does not change the truth. For example, if I decide to run red lights, the penalties for disobeying the law are the same. My choice to disregard the law does not alter my obligation to keep it; my safety and well-being are both at stake.

Allow me to illustrate my point: My father, one of 12 children, lived under his mother's matriarchy. Mary Miles Boyce, my paternal grandmother had promised the Lord she would go to the mission field. Instead, she married a pastor and had a dozen children. (Perhaps it's fair to say she took on another mission field!) However, to make up for her perceived failure to obey her calling, she insisted my Dad go to seminary and enter the pastoral ministry. For years my Dad was plagued by guilt because, although completing seminary, he did not enter the pastoral ministry. Why? Because his Heavenly Father didn't call him. Instead, he was compelled by his earthly mother. He knew better than to do something God had not called him to do. He wasn't sure; he didn't do it! He was overjoyed in 1974 when I informed him of my intention to enter the pastoral ministry. His guilt was replaced by gratitude. His son was called of God; he wasn't. The Lord called him to use his business acumen to fund those called to the role of pastors and missionaries. If you are sure, accept the call; if you're not, don't. Obedience is required either way.

Our response to the call of God on our life is critical to remaining in the center of God's will. Our refusal to be obedient has a profound impact on all other areas of our life.

During my pastoral pilgrimage, I have often made the statement: "I'd rather struggle at the center of God's will than outside the center." I want my struggle to count for something. It is not if we struggle, but how we respond to the struggle.

We can have second thoughts about this high, holy, and **ultimate calling**, sourced in God's will for our life. So we jump ship. But instead of walking on water, we sink!

Several things happen. We leave the place in which God has called us before birth. We take the path of least resistance induced by the enemy who considers us a threat to his diabolical work. We are merely trading one set of frustrations, challenges, and obstacles for another!

Suppose Christ had foregone the struggle to be obedient and carry out His mission because it was too hard or because of how He would be treated. There would be no redemption, no salvation, no gospel, and no **ultimate calling** by which to declare this message to the world. Think about that! (See 'The Supremacy of Shepherding')

Not only have I wanted to be obedient to my calling, but I have not known what else I would do. We don't usually prepare ourselves for two professions. I am not good with finances, and I cannot fix things. (Ask my wife, who has taught me a great deal about home improvement!)

I was called to be a pastor-shepherd. That is what God created and equipped me to be and to do. I wouldn't be satisfied doing anything else.

But don't think I haven't wanted to hang it up some days. I have considered forgetting the divine call of God. I wanted to quit when it became hard. I wanted out! (Hello, Jonah!)

My call to ministry came during my junior year of High School. I remember it like it was yesterday. God put it to me this way: "I want you to make sharing your witness a profession." I didn't completely understand what that meant, but the Christian ministry concept was formed in my mind.

When attending my ten-year high school reunion, the first question usually asked was, "What do you do?" When I told my peers that I had entered the ministry, more than one person said,

"That figures!" I remember telling my wife, "Well, at least they didn't keel over laughing and say, 'You...the ministry?'" I sensed that my ministry call was already evident to others, even in high school. That's like bringing home the person you want to marry for approval. Though you make the choice, a favorable reaction can be a needed confirmation, right?

My call was confirmed on my pastoral pilgrimage fourteen years later, at a campus ministry retreat. We were to bring back a symbol of what the Lord was saying to us during a discipline of silence. I remember sitting by a giant fir tree and a lake. The Lord brought to mind the portion of Psalm 1 "He shall be like a tree planted by the rivers of water, that brings forth its fruit in its season, whose leaf shall not wither and whatever he does shall prosper." Then He gently said, "If you are true to My Word, I will bless you with success always." We have both kept our promise to each other. This encounter could have taken place in the lives of many people entering all kinds of occupations. Still, the sequence of events was particularly significant at this moment in my life. It precipitated my response to the **ultimate calling.**

I clearly understood that I was called to shepherd, to love, lead, guide, and feed sheep; first, the younger ones, later, the older ones.

I have been confused, lonely, frustrated, disappointed, desperate, insecure, used, and felt taken for granted. I even tried to relocate to another pastorate (twice) amid a pastoral assignment; the Lord would not allow me to do that! Yet, I have never been unsure of my calling. It was and has continued to be clear. The call is, indeed, irrevocable. God won't revoke it; the one who is called ought not to reject it. To do so is to tamper with the Divine; it is to subvert the will of God for our life and the lives of others to whom we are to minister.

It has been a blessing to carry out the will of God. I have loved it. And after all, there's nothing better than doing what you love as a way of life.

The Prerequisite of Personal Identity: Why the Ministry?

How many times have you heard stories about someone who has left the ministry? A fair number of people have entered the ministry for the wrong reasons. There are, of course, many in ministry for the right reasons. They love God; they want to serve Jesus, believe they have pastoral giftedness, and they care for people.

But not everyone who feels inclined to be in ministry is emotionally equipped for that role. People from all walks of life have deficits for which they seek compensation through their relationships with others. This a common phenomenon in the ministry.

Those of us entering the ministry are not called to be perfect, but rather individuals making progress in the process of becoming well spiritually and psychologically. Healthy pastors help to cultivate healthy parishioners! (See 'The Pastor as Counselor')

I came into my adult life particularly sensitive to rejection and criticism, tending to give in too quickly, wanting everyone to like me, and avoiding anything that would rock the boat or disrupt the peace. I feared confronting issues. It was rarely permitted in my home. I was susceptible to pleasing females because pleasing my mother was the dominant force in my life.

So what happens? The male pastor views his Deacon Board Chair as a mother figure. He reacts to her leadership style; he becomes competitive with her to prove his worth and value. The female minister views her Senior pastor as a father figure, weak, easily manipulated, or over-bearing, and highly controlling. Thus, she resents and resists him just as she did her father.

Old patterns of thought and behavior die hard. We tend to repeat in adulthood the ways and means of childhood. Unless these are challenged and changed, they can create problems for leaders, especially in the ministry.

Ministry is a comfortable place to look for and receive personal affirmation, admiration, and approval. After all, pastors are viewed as public servants and the caretakers of people's lives and souls! How could anything be more affirmational than that?

The problem is that the pastor is working with human beings, people with their own identity and security needs; they all have their own baggage. Face it. If all the people we are called to pastor didn't have needs, we would be out of a job! Pastors don't get the luxury of helping perfect people. Shepherds don't get hired to care for sheep that never stray or follow the wrong paths, get stuck in the mud, or walk off cliffs!

The pastor-shepherd is by nature, tender and sensitive. These are necessary qualities for effectiveness in the ministry. Yet those assets can also be liabilities. One who is tender and sensitive can be easily hurt. And the ministry is not a pain-free zone either. (We could only wish!)

A person entering the pastorate needs to have a firm sense of who they are, what they can and can't do, and be willing to give more than they get from others. The pastor should not be defined totally by what they do, how they perform, or whether they can meet everyone's expectations. Pastors need to find their identity and security grounded firmly in who they are in Christ and His call upon their lives.

Ours is a culture that defines us by what we do. How well we work determines how much we're worth! Our parents may have well defined our identity and affirmed our worth by our performance.

Thus, even in the pastorate, accomplishment is the measurement by which many things are determined, including our salaries.

One of the common formalities in meeting someone for the first time is to ask them, "What do you do?" The question implies their occupation. But what if instead, we asked the question, "Who are you?" And what if our response to the question was, "I am a Christ-follower." Who we are in Christ becomes the basis of our identity and security regardless of our occupation.

Those in ministry also need to know what we are called to do in life. We need to know that we matter, that we are people who have worth and value and that we are making a contribution to the lives of people eternally.

Parishioners can demand too much and affirm too little. Sometimes these unreal expectations are simply an extension of their insecurity and inadequacy. They need to have someone else compensate for their deficits. As a result, they withhold appreciation from the pastor. They fail to recognize what is being done and focus on what is not being done. Even the most secure pastor has a hard time performing well in this kind of environment.

Israel became dissatisfied with the leadership of Samuel and his two sons. They were disappointed that God had not intervened, so they rejected Him. The people felt God was not living up to their expectations and they were dissatisfied with His job performance! (Imagine that!)

God understands that pastors are imperfect people who fail and fall short, but still calls them to the sacred task. He allows them to deal with their baggage and even uses their mistakes and failures to relate to and help their people become whole and healthy.

Expectations: Ally or Enemy?

I am a firstborn, oldest son in a family of three siblings. I grew to adulthood during the 50s, primarily when the American Dream came by hard work and achievement, which led to attaining things. The pursuit was compounded by being a male child and a sibling prototype.

As a shy grade school child, I found my identity later in high school as a student leader. Oh yes, and I could cheer, something I led the student body in twice, two years in high school and two years in college. (Unfortunately, they didn't have cheerleading in seminary or...) I chose the course of the theater and student politics. It fit. I wasn't the athlete my father was. I was the dramatist, a different person.

I vividly recall the morning after I played Caligula in a high school stage production when my father announced, "No son of mine is going to be on stage in a skirt." Yet I continued with drama; it aided my career, which would require being in front of people. (I just never wore a skirt on the stage again!)

But upon entering the formal pastorate, I was very achievement orientated. I wanted to please everyone and to be liked! So it doesn't take much to explain my expectations. As the young shepherd, I had visions of doing everything with perfection and not making any enemies in the process. Wow, was I in for a **huge** surprise!

Those entering the ministry may have grown up trying to earn approval and acceptance by living up to someone else's expectations, unsure of being loved, accepted, and forgiven.

Young pastors are nearly always prone to enter the ministry with seminarian stars in their eyes. The fact of the matter is whatever they tell or don't tell you in the ivory towers, you will have to find out about the ministry in the trenches. I went to seminary in the 1960s, the days before Internships. We were released from the safety of the classroom with a diploma and a dream only to be plopped in a pastorate for which we had little, if any, practical experience.

I was called initially to a senior pastor role. True, the campus ministry years had prepared me to work with the adolescent, but the pastorate was a whole lot different than the high school campus.

I was 32, fresh off the campus, and the pastor of a suburban church of under 100 people. I was suddenly preaching every week, counseling people with a host of problems, taking offerings (Yike!), managing church Council meetings, visiting older people in homes and hospitals, and teaching Confirmation. And if that wasn't enough, the Evangelical Covenant Church practiced infant baptism, which made an impression on my Baptist parents. (Although not the kind of impression you'd want to make starting your pastoral career!)

Talk about expectations. My Youth for Christ friends were waiting to see how I would handle adults. My church was waiting to see how this young guy without a lick of pastoral experience would lead a struggling church. My family was waiting to talk with me after I baptized the first baby!

The pastorate welcomed a firstborn, type-A driven, ex-cheerleader, student body president who lacked identity and security apart from performing perfectly. Talk about setting yourself for a hard fall!

I soon discovered that I could be harder on myself than God was! I had to learn that there is a fine line between expecting too much and expecting too little. It's a balancing act. Given my personality, I was prone to expect too much rather than too little of myself.

Expectations can both be an asset and a liability; they can be a strength or a weakness, depending on how we respond to them.

It's not always God or congregations that set the standard and create the expectations. We do that to ourselves. Congregations will let you work as hard and as long as you want to.

More often than not, the pastor has unclear expectations of themselves, but congregations also have unreal expectations of their pastors. This condition often results in overworked pastors and underperforming parishioners, creating pastoral burnout. (See 'Self-care')

Self-expectations become a liability when they keep us from doing the very things we want to do. To put it another way, if I expect myself to do every sermon perfectly, I may make more mistakes because I'm trying too hard. (See 'The Pastor as Preacher/Teacher')

I have often demanded too much of myself and wound up not doing what I wanted to do. My ideality needed to be tempered by reality! I was a perfectionist.

Let me define the perfectionist. A perfectionist is a person who sets unreal expectations for themselves and sets the same for others. They often cannot meet the standard or fulfill those expectations, yet they hold everyone else responsible for doing that. They control people, withhold affirmation, and keep others from getting close enough to see their imperfections!

I consider myself to be a recovering perfectionist. My congregations, my wife, and my children all helped me with my recovery! I have made self-adjustments as well as alterations in my outlook towards myself and those around me. Distorted expectations create tension. Yet, God allows imperfect people to work out His plan.

The real issue is, who knows what to expect in fulfilling this calling? It can be one of the minister's most significant challenges. Such challenges are a part of the job expectations of the pastor. Often it is not the stated expectations but the unstated ones that create the problem.

This was forcibly brought to my attention in a conversation with my chairmen during a yearly evaluation. And I quote: "If you were an NBA coach, we'd probably fire you." Translation: Based on the numbers, attendance, growth, new members, and giving, you are failing. The same church ultimately discovered that it takes more than a coach to make the team succeed; it takes a team willing to play the game under the coach's direction. (See 'The Pastor as Coach')

The religious professional is expected not only to be doing many things but doing them well. They are hired and paid to fulfill multiple expectations from a myriad of bosses. Over the years, I have often said that the ministry is the only place where you have __bosses. (Fill in the blank.) You are selected by the Search Committee, called by the congregation, accountable to the Elders or Deacons, or possibly both! More than one boss, right?

Each of those lovely, God-fearing people often has a different opinion and expectation about what their pastors should do and, more importantly, how they are to do it!

The next chapters will profile the many roles of the parish leader: A balanced individual, self-care expert, model husband and father, a highly able administrator, skilled vision caster, inspiring worship leader, charismatic preacher, riveting teacher, stellar steward, passionate evangelist, and a champion in spiritual warfare. And that's just for starters.

It also helps to know how to run a PowerPoint, the sound equipment, fix the leak in the men's restroom, play on the church basketball team, have ideas for decorating the sanctuary at Christmas, and star in the dramas for Vacation Bible School. (And pastors, remember you need to dress well, drive good cars, and join upscale service organizations, all on your salary, of course!)

Note that an adjective precedes each of these capacities. It means not only do many things. (**What**) It means doing them well. (**How**) The expectations, the printed job description, and the one you're supposed to read between the lines dictate how you function. These are areas that need to be discussed during the interview process.

We can nearly die from trying to meet the performance standards others have placed on us, justifying it as for God and the glory of His work. And death isn't always physical; pastors can die in a lot of different ways. Not death on demand, but rather death *from* demand! (See 'Self-care')

Summary: The certainty of our call to the pastorate must be based on a firm foundation that will help us survive in meeting the challenges of the task. The **ultimate calling**, in the mind of God before time, is irrevocable. It is not **if** one is called but **how** they respond to it. It is ultimately less challenging to obey the call than to disobey it. Obedience is rewarded in the life of the pastor and the lives of those impacted by their ministry. We need to be spiritually and psychologically healthy, entering the ministry for the right reasons and secure enough to serve others. Expectations on the part of both pastor and people need to be realistic to protect the leader and those they lead from being less effective in the ministry.

Peril: Failure to respond to the call to ministry, entering the ministry for the wrong reasons, or not clarifying expectations relating to it.

Privilege: The honor of being selected for the highest calling on earth and enabled to impact people's lives eternally.

Questions for personal reflection: Chapter 1 The Certainty of Call

1. What life event confirmed your call to the Christian ministry?
2. Why is the pastoral ministry harder today than before?
3. What is the potential impact of not accepting the **ultimate calling**?
4. Why is it essential for a pastor to be psychologically healthy?
5. How can expectations in ministry be detrimental?

2   The Imperative of Integrity

The Wellspring of the Soul:
The Person Determines the Nature of the Pastor

In the Book of Proverbs, Solomon defines integrity as a life that is integrated. A synonym for integrated is balanced.

Since the fall of humankind into sin, each of us has lost our balance. Every area of life has become affected. The physical is subject to sickness, suffering, and death. The mental is confused and perverted. The social is dysfunctional and alienated. The spiritual is broken and disconnected. (See 'The Pastor as Counselor')

The Old Testament references this concept of an integrated life in two important texts. Job said, "Weigh me on a set of honest scales so God has proof of my *integrity*." Job confirms a correlation between integrity and balance. (Job 3:16 The Messaage)

Solomon described it in Proverbs 10:9: "He who walks in *integrity* walks securely, but he who perverts his ways shall be found out." (My Life Verse)

The writer of Luke gives a more practical definition of balance and integrity in describing the growth pattern of Christ. "And Jesus grew in wisdom and stature and favor with God and man." (Luke 2:52)

Mentally/Emotionally	(Wisdom)
Physically	(Stature)
Socially	(With man)
Spiritually	(In favor with God)

We now look at these areas in our lives.

Mentally: To stimulate your thinking, to be challenged intellectually, and disciplined in your thought life.

Emotionally: To get in touch with and communicate your feelings, maintain sensitivity to others, and remain psychologically healthy.

Physically: To care for yourself through diet, exercise, sleep, and personal upkeep.

Socially: To cultivate healthy interpersonal relationships with your family and peers and members of the opposite sex.

Spiritually: To establish and maintain your personal relationship with God, beliefs, and lifestyle. To internalize Biblical truth, develop wisdom and understanding of yourself and others.

This fifth dimension is foundational to the other four. *It is the spiritual life of the individual that is a wellspring from which flows all of life itself.* The well needs to be replenished by Christ, the only One to live a life of perfect integrity and balance. (Psalm 87:7b)

"If any man is thirsty, let him come to me and drink." "Whoever believes in me, as the Scripture said, streams of living water will flow from within him." (John 7:38-39). "I am the living bread that came down from heaven. This bread is my flesh. If anyone eats it, he will live forever." (John 6:51a)

We need to eat and drink physically, and we must also eat spiritual manna and drink spiritual water to nourish the soul. God's well is never empty. His manna never runs out. Our wells must be refilled to fill the wells of others. Our hunger must be satiated to satisfy the hunger of others. (See 'The Life of Devotion')

The opposite of integration is disintegration. The opposite of balanced is unbalanced. Our struggle to maintain these essential life elements in ministry is challenged by the evil one, whoever seeks to cause us to lose our balance and violate our integrity. (See 'The Pastor as Warrior')

The Incessant Battle for Integrity and Balance: The Press of the Flesh

To maintain the balance is to walk the tightrope between temptation and yielding to it. The secularization of modern culture intensifies the battle for balance. It becomes evident in the pastorate and society that what a person does emanates from who they are. (See 'The Certainty of Call')

We come to God, who has called us to continuously draw from His unlimited resources to live a life of balance and integrity. Though difficult, it is not impossible; it is **imperative**!

However, there are reasons we fail to draw from the source of replenishment of soul and spirit for ourselves and others.

The Intrusion of Ego and Power: The Enemy of Integrity

Perhaps one of the more subtle seductions in the ministry is that of an ego-driven desire for power.

Satan opposed God and fell from heaven due to the misuse of his authority and power. God had exalted him to a position of power as the highest angel. But he wanted more, as do humans who are infected with the disease of displaced desire.

Such was the case with Adam and Eve. Both had authority and power over the whole of creation in a perfect paradise. But that wasn't enough. They wanted more. It was their complicity with Satan which brought about a loss of balance and integrity in the whole of the human race.

By our very position, we as pastors are given the same borrowed power and authority. Secure people will tend to use it for the benefit of those they lead. Insecure people will tend to use those things for their own benefit. Remember, those who walk in integrity are secure.

Let's use the example of a boss most of us have had. You remember, the one they called Attila the Hun? 'Huns' governed my first two jobs!

Such a person treats employees like peons, humiliating them in public and snarling orders from their office with the tact of a marine drill sergeant. They make crude and cutting remarks about them, ever substituting criticism for commendation; only friendly when drunk.

These bosses have most likely come into the business world with unresolved issues such as anger, insecurity, feeling unloved, unappreciated, and guilty; they retaliate against those who have hurt them.

The result? They take out these unresolved feelings on those who are not responsible for causing them. In time, employees will feel the impact of this treatment and feel less motivated to produce for their employers. 'Huns' misuse and abuse their power.

Pastors and church bosses are not excluded from this problem. They are human. They can use their position to compensate for real or perceived losses in life. They can take out their angst of unresolved issues on others. (See 'The Pastor as Administrator')

Those who misuse their positions of power can produce the following *attitudes*.

Insecurity - Use the church's positions of power to compensate for personal needs.

Dominance - Exercise control over people using their unreal expectations to keep others from seeing them for who they are and contend with others who get in their way.

Accepting no responsibility for their actions - Here is where the term 'Do not touch my anointed ones' is misused, meaning that the pastor or the church leader is above being corrected or held accountable by those they serve.

These attitudes produce the following behaviors.

- Whatever they say must be true.
- They must always be right and in control.
- They can never be criticized.
- They must take credit for everything.
- They punish those who dare to cross them.

These attitudes and behaviors are unbiblical and impractical. They render leaders ineffective.

One of my first church leaders typified the intrusion of ego and power. The man was a twin whose family owned and operated a very well-known company in the city. He was passed over for the company's vice presidency, which was awarded to his twin brother. Shortly after, he became the chairman of our small but rapidly growing church. His security centered in his position. The power lost in the company was compensated for by his role in the church. He entered a realm where he could have power and control over me and the congregation. He attributed what he perceived was wrong in the church to me and sought to undermine my leadership. His behaviors embodied the negative qualities of ill-motivated leadership.

The Importance of Balance: Walking the Pastoral Tightrope

The art of balancing is not an easy one. It is one that needs to be acquired through lifelong effort.

Satan does not want us to keep our balance. He was the one who was instrumental in taking it away and in trying to get Christ out of the way, so balance could not be restored! Thus, pastors and leaders are the very ones he attempts to knock off the wire. He uses the elements of the secular world.

John reiterates this point. "Do not love the world or anything in the world. If anyone loves the world, the love of the Father is not in him. For everything in the world, the cravings of sinful man, the lusts of his eyes and the boasting of what he has and does comes not from the Father, but from the world." (I John 2:15-16)

The word in the New Testament is *cosmos* from which we take our word, cosmetics. It references outward attractiveness, including what we possess and our status. These things which provide status and security can cause us to compromise our integrity and balance. The wants of the contemporary are subtle but no less seductive and destructive. (See 'The Pastor as Warrior')

There is perhaps no clearer picture of Satan's attack on balance, integrity, and the use of power than in Christ's encounter with him in the Gospel of Matthew 4. Note the progression:

Spiritually - Satan tempts Christ to disavow His loyalty to His Father, substitute his purposes for God's purposes and use them as a means to his ends.

Mentally - Satan tempts Christ to think wrong thoughts about God and doubt the consequences of disobedience.

Socially - Satan tempts Christ to gain power over people rather than giving His life for them.

Physically - Satan tempts Christ to let His appetites control Him and undermine His eternal mission of bringing salvation to the world.

Again, it is significant that Satan used his strategy against Christ; it failed. He uses the same strategy against us, but it often succeeds!

Remember, Christ was a leader. To topple Him was to endanger the salvation of others. Our enemy attempts to do the same with Christian leaders. The choices Christ rendered resulted in our salvation and the power to live it out. The choices we make result in the strengthening or weakening of the spiritual relationship in the lives of others. Choices do have consequences, especially in the lives of leaders and subsequently in the lives of their people.

A trapeze artist faced the greatest challenge of his career; the crossing of Niagara Falls on a tightrope. Hundreds of people assembled at the base of the renowned attraction to see this unprecedented feat. Halfway across what appeared to be a routine walk, a car backfired simulating a gunshot, distracting the artist and plunging him to his death in the swirling waters of the Great Falls. Such is a graphic illustration of the impact of distractions on maintaining integrity and balance and precipitating destruction.

Yet, it is easy for ministers to beg off being held accountable for imbalance. Such reasoning includes:

"I don't have time for myself, my spouse, and my family because I am doing God's work."

"I do some things that might be questionable, but nobody knows about them; they don't hurt me."

22

"I can't help but draw close to those with whom I counsel; they feel comfortable with and confide in me, including members of the opposite sex. It's part of my job."

"Sure, I get hot under the collar and let people know how I honestly feel, just like everyone else."

As sensible as these arguments may seem, they tend to be both distractive and detrimental to walking the tightrope. God, by the way, is not impressed by illogical arguments. Healthy people don't make excuses!

It is reasonable that those called to lead with biblical authority are held to a higher standard relative to their attitudes and behaviors. James references this principle in his third chapter. "Not many of you should presume to be teachers, my brothers, because you know that we who teach will be judged more strictly." (James 3:1)

Paul underscores this truth in Acts 24:16, "So I strive always to keep my conscience clear before God and man." America's history reveals that people in places of high authority and power have been known to compromise their integrity. Their leadership was weakened, and their behavior had a negative impact on the nation.

Though human, leaders are called to a higher standard. Who they are and what they do will profoundly impact the lives of those they lead. It is even more critical for those who lead our churches. If leaders lose the integrity battle, how will it be won in the lives of those they lead?

To conclude, we reference an Old Testament giant, David, a man who wanted to emulate God's character as a leader. "I know O God that you examine our hearts and rejoice when you find *integrity*." (I Chronicles 29:17) Though an adulterer and a murderer, David was a man after God's heart because he dealt with and learned from his moral failure and asked God to restore him. David was forgiven, yet the damage to himself and his people was irreversible.

Allowing God to examine us continually enables us to be leaders of integrity and balance.

Summary: Who the pastor is, is precedent to what the pastor does. In a culture that reveres charisma, the God who calls the pastor emphasizes character. Yet, the ego and the quest for position, power, and success can cause Christian leaders to compromise their beliefs and values, which jeopardizes their integrity. They must guard against this by maintaining balance in the mental, emotional, physical, social, and spiritual dimensions of life as mirrored by Christ. The struggle to maintain spiritual consistency coupled with the ministry's merciless demands make life and ministry a tightrope upon which balance is precarious. Leaders must draw upon the resources and model of Christ to maintain a balanced life.

Peril: Neglecting and violating personal integrity and using the ministry to meet your own needs.

Privilege: Being allowed to demonstrate integrity through a balanced life in Christ before your family, congregation, and community.

Questions for personal reflection: Chapter 2 The Imperative of Integrity

1. Explain the concept of who the pastor is as precedent to what a pastor does?
2. How are the terms integrity and balance correlated?
3. What are the enemies of integrity?
4. What can cause pastors to lose their balance in ministry?

3   The Life of Devotion

The Difference between Devotion and Devotions:
Absorbing the Truth

I have a 'Boyceism': "We don't need more devotions. We need more devotion." In other words, I believe that devotion is an end; devotions are a means.

Devotion is hearing from the *source*, God Himself. Devotions are hearing about God through other *sources*. While these sources are of value, they are secondary to the primary source of *being with, speaking to*, and *hearing* from God.

The basis of our personal devotional life is coming into the presence of God regularly. In I Chronicles 18:24, the place of meeting God is called the *inner chamber*. In the New Testament, Christ called it the *prayer closet*. This point in time encounter is known as quiet time.

The life of devotion is also reflected in the words of Isaiah, an Old Testament disciple. "The Sovereign Lord has given me an instructed tongue to know the Word that sustains the weary. He wakens me morning by morning, wakens my ear to *listen* like one being *taught*. The Sovereign Lord has opened my ears, and I have not been rebellious." (Isaiah 50:4-5)

This interaction is absorbing the revealed truth. The early Church Fathers had a synonym for absorption; it was *Lectio Divina*. It is the process of taking one Scripture portion, a chapter, a section, or a verse and making that the single focus of our time with the Lord. The Word and prayer regimen cultivates our relationship with God, which allows us to speak with and hear from Him.

In Santa Fe, New Mexico, there had been a severe drought for several years. Then the city experienced a 1,000-year flood. (People had been praying for rain for an extended time; they just didn't expect it to come all at once.) The hardened soil could not receive it; it overflowed all tributaries and did much damage.

In the spiritual realm, the soul's hardened soil will not allow the water of the Word to be absorbed. The three dimensions of absorption are basic to the life of devotion.

Process/Product: The devotional life is one of absorption, allowing the water of the Word to re-activate the roots of the individual, causing their lives to be rejuvenated. This concept is illustrated in the Psalms, "The righteous man is planted like a tree by rivers of water that brings forth its fruit in its season; his leaf also shall not perish and whatever he does shall prosper." (Psalms 1:3)

Devotional life is more than putting data on your mental hard drive. We live in an impatient culture that directly impacts our devotional life. In an age of ATMs, Wendy's drive-thru, and Lens Crafter's, we expect to see our spiritual life develop quickly. Push the easy button, get the right answer instantly.

The cultivation of devotional life is *incremental*; the building of this spiritual relationship spans a lifetime. Paul describes the Christian life this way, "Therefore if anyone is in Christ, he is a new creation; the old is gone, the new has come." The literal translation reads: old things are in the process of passing away; the new things are in the *process* of coming into being. Simply stated, we are not instantly changed at conversion. (II Corinthians 5:17)

The apple provides a metaphor. How does an apple ripen? It just sits in the sun. It does not ripen in one night. By its effort, it does not find itself a miraculously large, red, ripe, and juicy fruit the next morning. Ripening is a process.

Environment/Event: Paul describes this environment to the Ephesian Church. "See then that ye *walk* circumspectly not as fools, but as wise redeeming the time because the days are evil." (Ephesians 5:15-17 KJV) The word walk implies everywhere we go throughout the whole course of life. In the older translations of scripture, the word conversation denotes the totality of our life. Our spiritual walk does not depend on a point in time alone. It depends upon an ongoing process.

Devotional life is not merely a result of events; reading the scriptures, devotionals, or having times of prayer, as crucial as those practices are. The key is having the scripture in your mind and communicating with God as you travel the freeway or have a flat tire. It is listening to God at 2:00 in the afternoon when you have that board meeting where important decisions are to be made or that after-school conference with your kid's teacher to discuss behavior. It enables you to pray during rush hour when you're a half-hour late for dinner with your daughter's fiancé. (Commutes can provide a perfect place for communing!) Herein is the environment in which devotional life is truly developed. One becomes a living devotional, a person in whose life devotionals are applied.

Formation/Information: We attend another conference, seminar, or workshop, get the latest new book on Kindle, or watch a YouTube featuring Three Minutes a Day to a Dynamic Devotional Life, and we wonder why we remain unchanged.

Spiritual devotion is not merely cognitive or cerebral; it is emotive and volitional. If the information does not *re-form me,* it is of little value. The principles must translate themselves into my daily practices. The information must lead to transformation and motivation.

Paul speaks to the issue in two portions. Romans 12:2 "Do not conform any longer to the pattern of this world, but be *transformed* by the renewing of your mind."

II Corinthians 3:18, "And we are being *transformed* into His likeness with ever-increasing glory." (KJV) The word changed is metamorphazo, to be transformed from the inside out, just as caterpillars are turned into butterflies.

To be informed is to be transformed. James puts it this way in this portion of scripture. One who hears the truth is challenged to do the truth. (James 1:22-25)

What is the essence of devotional life? It is one where we absorb God's truth and His Word and are gradually changed by it. It is the incremental process by which apples ripen and butterflies take flight.

The opposite condition can occur when our spiritual life turns brown, i.e., when our leaf withers for lack of proper nourishment. Having dry times in our spiritual life is permissible; it happens to everyone, including pastors. I should know.

We have lots of company in the Scriptures where people had dry times.

Elijah, in I Kings 19, after conquering Baal's 450 prophets, found himself in a dry time. He wound up tired, hungry, and wanting to die when God found him. He was running for his life from a wicked queen who was out to kill him. He felt that he had failed God and, what's more, was all alone in his work for God. He was ready to give out and give up. The story does have a happy ending. Elijah sleeps, eats, encounters God, regains perspective, and continues his mission as a pastor to the Israelites.

The more important dimension of this encounter is that God understood Elijah's dry time. Significantly, this dry time came after a significant mountain top experience in his ministry. One day the lawn was lush; the next day, it was dry. Spiritual dryness can happen in a hurry. He felt distant from God, who he believed he failed, which left him contemplating his self-destruction. Ever been there?

God met Elijah, permitted him to be down and out, to be dry spiritually. He reached down and brought him out of his spiritual and personal despondency. Through his despair, Elijah developed a new dependency upon his God, who rejuvenated him for the work he was yet called to do. He replenished his inner Spirit. He is still willing and able to do that for a modern-day Elijah, who feels dry, unfruitful, and wants to give up.

John 4 reveals the thirst of a woman who found that physical water could not satisfy her soul's thirst which she found in the Living Water that Christ offered her. She stopped to drink, absorbed the water of the Word; her life was replenished and made fruitful.

But just because Christ provides the living water and spiritual nutrients for our lives doesn't mean we always want to access them. Sometimes we look like people living next to a reservoir complaining that we're thirsty!

The Psalmist put it this way in Psalm 42:1, "As the deer pants for streams of water, so my soul pants for you my God."

Christ, in His Sermon on the Mount, included this beatitude: "Blessed are they which do hunger and thirst after righteousness for they shall be filled." (Matthew 5:6 KJV) Hunger and thirst for God are fundamental to the life of faith and a person's devotion to the Father.

The image is of one in a desert who has wandered for days without water or food. In time, mirages begin to appear. Suddenly the wanderer sees water and food that aren't there. Thus, the body's appetites go unsatisfied; the physical nourishment for the body is unavailable. There are so many lesser things in this age we look to in an effort to quench our innate hunger and thirst for God besides God himself. These are the mirages that provide no replenishment.

The spiritual wanderer, however, never faces that crisis. Though they may have wandered in the dry wilderness for a long time, the source of replenishment, God Himself, is never a mere mirage. The God who provided manna and unpolluted water for His people knows how to provide spiritual nourishment for the soul. The wanderer is never disappointed; the search is never for nothing.

The Intimacy of the Interior Life:
Knowing and Hearing God

Knowing and hearing God is at the center of devotional life. But who can hear God? The Psalmist said, "Only those with clean hands and a pure heart." Quite a mandate and standard! (Psalm 24:4 KJV)

When we think of people knowing and hearing from God, we think of Moses in the Old Testament and Paul in the New Testament.

The Old Testament records the lives of those who encountered God before Christ came. The veil had yet to be rent in two, giving them free access through a new and living way.

These people knew they needed God, their lives were in crisis, and leadership was threatened. Their desperation led to dependence.

It was God or nothing; they were out on a limb with only Him. Their crises brought them closer; they had no other options. They chose to trust the best one!

Unlike their modern counterparts, they didn't have a large staff to consult. There was no local Bible book store selling Chuck Swindoll videos or church management helps from John Maxwell. There were no satellite conferences or popular sermons they could download.

We believe we can live the Christian life and do the ministry's work by ourselves, on our own. In essence, we can be practical atheists. "The fool says in his heart, there is no God." (Psalm 14:1a) We trust God in theory, but in actuality, we may trust other sources.

The life of devotion is the vital link between our personal and our professional life. It represents the hinge uniting the two major sections of this book: *Who the pastor is* and *What the pastor does*. There are no shortcuts to understanding and following God's direction. The only standard that governs our call is *knowing* Him and *hearing* Him. In the age of Google, this is a problematic mindset to cultivate, much less practice.

There is nothing intrinsically wrong with human resources. I believe God has anointed and used many of His followers, ministers like ourselves, to help us know God and hear what He wants for us. But we must always be cautious of listening to a human voice above the voice of God Himself.

I believe that God has a plan for every life and every church. God never uses a single prototype for either one. He has never cloned a life or ministry.

One of the dangers in the church world is looking to the experts and emulating their success. As in devotional life, we are anxious for shortcuts and quick fixes in our life and ministry.

You can be the Billy Graham of your denomination, preach to thousands, have it televised or open a theme park named after your ministry and still not be intimate with your God. We can come to depend on ourselves rather than our God. It is such a subtle temptation. History records many people in ministry who stopped seeking and hearing from God, who instead coasted on their charisma and accomplishments.

As I write, the headlines carry yet another story of a woman bringing allegations against a prominent, internationally known pastor whose life has disgraced the church and the cause of Christ. Paul warned, "So if you think you are standing firm, be careful that you don't fall." (I Corinthians 10:12) This pastor became a spiritual domino that caused others to fall.

Truly successful men and women in God's work are those who consistently seek after, know, and hear from the Living God. They learn to listen and be led in order to lead. We turn to the Living God who instructs, teaches, and counsels us. "Let your eyes look straight ahead, fix your gaze directly before you. And make level paths for your feet and take only ways that are firm. Do not swerve to the right or the left; keep your foot from evil." (Proverbs 4:25-27)

I believe that intimacy with God includes both the head and the heart from which come the real-life issues.

Brother Lawrence, a lay brother in a Carmelite monastery in Paris and author of the *Presence of God*, developed his interior life by attempting to practice God's presence wherever he was. (He did it washing pots and pans and peeling potatoes.) He is a modern example of one who maintained intimacy with God as a way of life, drawing near, speaking with, listening to, and doing what his God instructed him to do. Wise men still seek Him!

The Hebrew word that best describes the term intimacy, yada, was first used in Genesis 4:1. This Word is used in the context of the union between the first man and the first woman. When the transcriber of Genesis uses this word, it implied the intimate connection between the sexes. It conveys the highest degree of closeness possible between two humans. It is expressive of the full commitment of both partners and the basis of procreation. It was referred to in Genesis 2 when God pronounced that the two would become one flesh. In the New Testament, Christ used this term in Matthew 19 and Mark 10. More literally, the term means to be glued together.

This word is descriptive of the relationship between humans and God. Ours is to experience the ultimate intimacy made possible by Christ's redemptive work to restore our relationship with God. This spiritual intimacy correlates to physical intimacy in that it represents the closest relationship between the human and the Divine. It is based on God's full commitment to man and man to God. This is the basis of spiritual procreation, which results in the new birth.

Moreover, God used the metaphor of marriage to describe the union between Himself and Israel and Christ's union with the church. Herein is a righteous love affair of the highest and holiest order.

Worship music resonates this spiritual love affair. "In the Secret" by Hillsong and "Open our Eyes" by Bob Cull express the renewed desire for intimacy with God.

These songwriters convey that the central aspects of worship is the relationship of the worshipper to God. To know Him intimately is to truly glorify Him. What the religious leader experiences themselves can be transferable to others. (See 'The Pastor as Worship Leader')

The term Christian used first in the New Testament translates as Christ in One. The Infinite God possesses us through the indwelling Christ. *Devotion is intimacy with the Infinite.*

As we get to know God, we can develop the capacity to listen and hear Him, much like a child learns to respond to their parent or a pet to its master.

Herein is where the tributaries of devotional life converge. The person who develops the interior life of knowing God disciplines themselves to hear God speak through His Word in various ways.

David expresses these sentiments in Psalm 27. "One thing I asked of the Lord, that I will seek after: to live in the house of the Lord all the days of my life, to behold the beauty of the Lord, and to inquire in His temple. Hear, O Lord, when I cry aloud, be gracious to me and answer me. Come, my heart says, 'Seek His face'! Your face, O Lord, do I seek. Do not hide your face from me. Do not turn your servant away in anger, you who have been my help. Do not cast me off; do not forsake me O God of my salvation!" (Psalm 27:4-9) David was not intimidated by his intimacy with the infinite.

With the coming of Christ in the New Testament, we can come far differently to God than before. God has come in person; the relationship between Himself and humanity is restored. Hebrews explains: "Therefore my friends since we have confidence to enter the sanctuary by the blood of Jesus by the new and living way, let us draw near to God with a sincere heart in full assurance of faith." (Hebrews 10:19,20a,22 NRSV)

"Therefore, since then we have a great high priest who has gone through the heavens, Jesus, the Son of God, let us hold fast firmly to the faith we profess, let us then approach the throne of grace with confidence so that we may receive mercy and find grace to help in time of need." (Hebrews 4:14,16) Christ, who is intimate with God, makes it possible for us to enjoy the same with Him.

Moses was intimate with God in Exodus 33. He entered into the Tent of Meeting, his inner chamber-prayer closet where he would commune with God. They enjoyed a holy conversation. God spoke, Moses listened; Moses spoke, God listened. It is described as "The Lord speaking to Moses face to face as a man speaks with his friend."

The New Testament reveals another man who enjoyed an intimate relationship with God. *Paul* states his utmost desire to know God. "What is more, I consider everything a loss compared to the surpassing greatness of knowing Christ, my Lord. I want to know Christ and the power of His resurrection and the fellowship of sharing in His sufferings." (Philippians 3:8,10)

However, it is essential to remember that these two men were every bit human and imperfect and did not always hear their God. Moses lost his temper and took matters into his own hands. Paul contested with Silas over John Mark. Both situations affected not only the two leaders themselves but the people they were called to lead.

This section closes with a passage centering on the life of a father and son. David, the father, admonishes the son, Solomon, the King elect. "And Solomon, my son, know the God of your ancestors intimately. Worship and serve Him with your whole heart and a willing mind." (II Chronicles 28:9 KJV) Remember how that went for the royal offspring? He was wooed away from his intimacy and devotion to God. His life and his people became out of control and went astray. As the leader, so the people.

The Role of Spiritual Disciplines: Learning Internal Control

Spiritual disciplines are a way by which we continue to pursue devotion to and have intimacy with God.

The concept of discipline, for the most part, is countercultural. Ours is an age where people are not given to exercise, enamored by junk foods, obsessed with video games, less likely to read, and attracted to quick-fix diets.

Yet discipline is a fundamental part of all aspects of human life. Try getting a degree from law school, for example, not showing up for a class or passing the Bar Exam. Qualifying for the Olympics doesn't belong to overweight people, with the possible exception of Sumo wrestlers. Discipline is systemic to success! The two terms, disciple and discipline, are corollary.

The writer of Hebrews, in chapter 12:11, reminds us that "No discipline seems pleasant at the time but painful. Later on, however, it produces a harvest of righteousness." Simply stated, our pain can be productive!

Like the runner who puts in their mile, the dieter who eats a balanced diet, the pianist who carves out daily practice time, the person of faith strives to integrate specific regimens into their life.

The Ten Commandments reflect the correlation between the Word and the internal control of our life. Exodus 20:20 states, "Do not be afraid. God has come to test you so that the fear of God will be in you and keep you from sinning."

The writer of Psalm 119 endorses this reality. "Your Word have I hidden in my heart that I might not sin against you." (Psalm 119:11)

When I am God-governed, I will be self-governed. The spiritual disciplines help me maintain a higher and healthier quality of life and helps others achieve the same.

Three of the most dangerous areas where there is a lack of control are alcohol, adultery, and pornography. The stories are too familiar but always tragic in the church and Christian ministry.

Rarely do these addictions appear suddenly; they are a residual of long-neglected needs in one's life and failure to live under the control of God, the Holy Spirit.

For instance, if someone is addicted to pornography, both integrity and inward control are compromised. The sexual desire can be a fire raging out of control fed by over-activated lust and fueled by magazines and the Internet. The person has unlocked the Pandora box of passion. The Ten Commandments and the Scriptural principles don't control them outwardly because nothing is controlling them inwardly. (See 'The Pastor as Warrior')

Some Christ-followers have no self-control; they live more under the control of their old nature than their new nature. The scriptures identify this condition as carnal. The field of aviation can illustrate it. The old life is like gravity; the new life is the law of aerodynamics. The carnal Christian is more under the gravity of the old nature than the new nature's aerodynamic. (Romans 8:5-8) "Those who live according to the sinful nature have their minds set on what nature desires; but those who live in accordance with the Spirit have their minds set on what the Spirit desires. The mind of a sinful man is death, but the mind controlled by the Spirit is life and peace; those controlled by the sinful nature cannot please God."

Their union with God has ceased to be intimate, their interior life is in disarray, and their lifestyle exhibits a lack of integrity and balance.

Yet, we as pastors are prone to be undisciplined, often rationalizing our behaviors by making excuses. Additionally, the undisciplined pastor fails to offer a model for emulation. Paul, for instance, in Philippians 3:17, seems almost overconfident in saying: "Join with others in following my example, brothers, and take note of those who live according to the pattern we gave you."

Paul expected to live up to the standards himself and thus calls others to do the same.

But this is the same person who in Romans 7 confessed his struggle to do the right thing and not do the wrong thing. However, he set an example of his maturity in recognizing how hard it is to maintain a new life in Christ.

For Christ, there was no compartmentalization of the spiritual from the practical, the sacred from the secular. Christ allowed the truth to extend to every part of His life. He is the only truly disciplined human being; He is the only perfect example!

Three instances underscore compartmentalization.

One evening while walking through a store, I spotted my music minister looking at a magazine of dubious ethical content. He happened to look up and see me. I called him later to encourage him to use better judgment.

In another instance, a fellow pastor friend of mine relayed a story of an encounter with one of his elders who informed him that how he ran his business had nothing to do with his personal faith.

One of my parishioners attended a morning Bible Study with a friend from his church. Afterward, the guy took him to his office. However, upon arriving, the business manager began to interact with foul and crude language with his employees. My friend was amazed and asked the man about it. The man didn't seem to think there was a problem.

These instances also underscore the interconnection between intimacy and inner control. The life of the Christ-follower is to be one of inter-connection, not disconnection. *A lack of devotion creates disconnection, which can result in disobedience.*

The Contrast of Personal and Professional Bible Study:
Fed to Be Feeding

One of the elements of spiritual discipline is reading, studying, and meditation on God's Word.

The potential problem is substituting professional study time for personal quiet time. The contrast is between looking to the Word for yourself instead of looking to the Word for others.

In my early years, my study time was substituted for quiet time, a tactical error. I assumed that the reading and studying the Word in sermon preparation was personal time with God. He was trying to tell me that the preparation of a message was never to be a substitute for the preparation of myself. The quality of the messenger would determine the quality of the message. (See 'The Pastor as Preacher/Teacher')

The sword of the Spirit, which is the Word of God, explores us in every aspect of our being. (Hebrews 4:12,13). In short, He must work *to* me before He can work *through* me.

I have a confession to make. I believe in devotional life; it is necessary to the pastor's life and ministry. However, prescribing these practices can come off as idealistic and somewhat intimidating. Thus, I hope not to have come across as one who has all the answers or that I consistently do these things well. I continue to struggle with these very same areas. I rarely miss my time with the Lord at the beginning of my day. Sometimes I feel like I am merely going through the religious motions out of a sense of duty rather than the desire. Yet, the most crucial factor in quiet time is sustaining intimacy with the Lord and absorbing His Word. Of all the disciplines, the spiritual ones are perhaps the hardest because they have the greatest effect on our life and ministry. They are the very things our opponent seeks to disrupt and destroy. So if I were to encapsulate the entire chapter in a phrase, it would be:

"Above all else, guard your heart for it is the wellspring of life." (Proverbs 4:23)

Summary: The pastor's devotional life is systemic to carrying out the call of ministry. It is an attitude before it is an activity, the cultivation of a constant sense of God's presence, and absorbing His truth. It is an ongoing process that develops an intimacy with God who can be known, heard, and with whom we can speak. From the pastor's interior life comes an understanding and practice of spiritual disciplines to maintain self-control by internalizing the Word to feed ourselves, then our people.

Peril: Hearing the wrong voices rather than God's voice allowing your heart for the Lord to be drawn away from Him through the challenges of life and ministry.

Privilege: Allowing God to speak to you so you may speak to others through His Word.

Questions for personal reflection: Chapter 3 The Life of Devotion

1. What is the difference between devotion and devotions?
2. Why is the devotional life a gradual process?
3. How does spiritual discipline build internal control?
4. What is the difference between devotional time and sermon preparation?

4   The Primacy of Prayer

The Basis of Being:
Declaration of Dependence

Prayer is that mysterious means that allows us to commune and converse with the Creator and Caretaker of the world.

It is a primary means by which we can enter into a deeper life with our God who has everything, yet desires to communicate personally with the creatures He has made in His likeness.

The cross is emblematic of this relationship between the Divine and daily life. The vertical (spiritual) intersects with the horizontal (practical); it is the basis of our total being.

The scriptures bear witness to this reality in Paul's letters to the Ephesians when he writes, "But now in Christ Jesus, you who were once far away have been brought near by the blood of Christ. For He, Himself is our peace, who has made the two groups one and has destroyed the barrier, the dividing wall of hostility." (Ephesians 2:13-14)

The writer of Hebrews concurs. "Therefore, since we have a great High Priest who has gone through the heavens, Jesus, the Son of God, let us then approach the throne of grace with confidence, so that we may receive mercy and grace to help us in our time of need." (Hebrews 4:14,16)

Prayer is our personal connection with an all-knowing God. *It is a divine dialogue.* Yet, the prospect of this connection can be a bit daunting when coming under the scrutiny of the omniscient One. To know Him intimately is to be known by Him. We may come as errant children who expect to be punished rather than those forgiven by His grace.

David pleaded for God not to reject him in the Old Testament. (Psalm 27) In the New Testament, Christ reassures us with His welcoming words, "No one who comes to me will be cast out." (John 6:37)

We can come out of a sense of guilt and obligation. Ours can be an attitude of *having* to go rather than *wanting* to go, performing a religious ritual rather than drawing close to the Lord. (See 'The Life of Devotion')

In today's world, we don't come to God with too much fear, but actually, too little. People in the Old Testament came with an aura of fearfulness. They often came to God as an autocratic, distant, and cold deity. In the New Testament, people entered into the presence of God and felt welcomed. The completed work of Christ makes it possible to fear God with a healthy fear, one which allows us to come to a holy, righteous judge who forgives us, cares for us and desires intimacy with us. Thus, our fear of God must be a balance between too fearful and too friendly.

We feel we shouldn't bother the God of the universe with our petty problems. We reason we should be able to figure certain things out by ourselves and only come to God with the BIG issues. Yet, He never makes us feel rejected or awkward coming to Him. (James 1:5)

We are often too independent, too busy, and too preoccupied to accept God's invitation to come into His presence and maintain a prescribed prayer life. He has made accessibility possible anywhere, at any time, and under any circumstances. (Acts 17:24-28)

We wrestle with a central question on the subject of prayer in the Sermon on the Mount. If God knows everything already, then why do we need to pray? The Father wants to know that we need Him as children need a parent. In this context, we are called to ask for daily bread, personal forgiveness, the capacity to forgive others and to be delivered from temptations.

Any parent wants to know that their child needs them. Yet, unlike the human parent who desires the child to become independent of them, our Heavenly Parent wants us to be increasingly dependent upon Him. (Paradoxical!)

Prayer has been defined as centering. We must be careful, however, to distinguish this activity from secular meditation. The former is to focus on the truth of God and His Word. The latter is to simply open our minds and allow us to focus on ourselves.

To center ourselves is to give our full attention to Him, a God who is all-powerful and all-personal. The prophet Isaiah describes God this way, "I live in a high and holy place but also with him who is contrite and lowly in spirit, to revive the spirit of the lowly and revive the heart of the contrite." (Isaiah 57:15)

He desires to be at the center, not the periphery of our lives. God rejects outward religious ritual in favor of inward holiness, a life of Godliness marked by humility, honesty, sincerity, contriteness, and true devotion. (Micah 6:8) The Pharisees simply went through the motions to impress people rather than access the God to whom they prayed. (Matthew 6:5)

The life of prayer directly affects us and our relationships. One who listens to and hears God is better able to listen to and hear others; spouses, children, staff members, and congregation. When we seek and receive direction from God, we are better able to offer guidance to others. We can't give to others what we don't have ourselves.

One of the residuals of the prayer life is the model it provides to those in the pastor's charge. If prayer is given primacy in the parish leader's life, it will be obvious; the non-primacy of prayer will be equally apparent. Christ taught, "I tell you a truth, no servant is greater than his master, nor are messengers greater than those who sent him." (John 13:16)

Psalm 37:4 exhorts, "Delight yourself in the Lord, and He will give you the desires of your heart." I call this developing *holy habits*.

Once again, the imagery of Psalm 1 comes to mind. Herein the roots of the tree go down as far as necessary to reach the water. It also has important implications for the ministry. For example, the rootedness of our relationship determines the spiritual power generated through a fruitful life. (Psalm 1:1-3)

History records the role of prayer in the life of Martin Luther, who prayed for three hours a day to accomplish his gigantic labors. The depth of the roots (devotional life) supplies the tree's strength (ministry) needs.

Throughout history, great men and women of God have struggled with times when they felt that God had abandoned them. This mindset came from either their failure or God's testing upon their lives. God understands our mental and emotional frame of mind. He is always present with us even when we are not fully present with Him.

Christ Himself understood feeling distant from His Father, as recorded in Psalm 22. His own Father could not look upon the sin borne by His Son on the cross.

Christ was compelled to converse with His Father for guidance in life and ministry. *His was a declaration of dependence.* (Hebrews 5:7-9)

Observing the Lord's Model in Ministry:
Lord Teach Us to Pray

The Lord gave us a model of prayer at strategic times in His life and earthly ministry.

• At the inauguration of His ministry	Matthew 4:1-11
• After a rugged day of ministering	Mark 1:35
• Before choosing the 12 disciples	Luke 6:12
• After healing the leper	Luke 5:16
• After hearing of John's death	Matthew 14:13
• After feeding the 5,000	Matthew 14:23
• Before revealing Himself as the Messiah	Luke 9:18
• With those He was discipling	Luke 9:28-29
• Before teaching the Lord's Prayer	Luke 11:1
• Before He endured the cross	Luke 22:39-41

Christ's prayer life centered on two things: Sustaining an intimate, dependent relationship with His Father and the continual intercession for others. The presence of prayer in the Master's life also impacted the crowd's reaction to His Sermon on the Mount. His authority was borne of authenticity. Christ's prayer life intersected the whole of who He was and what He did on earth. He sets forth the pattern for us.

What did His disciples first ask Him to teach them? To preach, heal, perform miracles, administer the synagogue services, and manage difficult people? No! It was to pray. All other areas of the ministry would emanate from this divine-human connection.

Christ taught His disciples a model prayer. Christ modeled the prayer of first looking towards God, then within Himself, and to others around Him. It is a prototype of our daily prayer life.

Upward

Adoration for who God is.

Praise for what He does.

Adoration and praise are powerful; they redirect our focus, prevent inwardness and preoccupation with what isn't. It rejuvenates the heart with new hope. It looks beyond the problem to the provision.

Inward

Confession for who we are, what we do and don't do; our omissions and commissions. The concept of confession means to agree with God about our sin.

Supplication for things we need. God's resources can be trusted to supply everything we need.

Outward

Intercession for what others need. The intercessor serves as a go-between with God and others.

Intervention for the church and the needs of our world. We can claim God's promises to manifest His power through deliverance.

The pastoral roles of the **ultimate calling**, coaching, administrative leadership, vision casting, leading worship, preaching-teaching, counseling, stewardship, promoting evangelism, and doing spiritual warfare all receive special unction through prayer.

As Christ claimed God's resources (**Upward**) for His own needs (**Inward**), He focused His attention on the needs of others (**Outward**). Note there was no confession; there was no sin, but there were definitely temptations!

Intercessory prayer becomes intrinsic to the pastoral ministry. As

I progressed in my spiritual life and the pastorate, my prayer focus changed. It modulated from my needs to the needs of others. I continued to praise the Lord, claim His forgiveness and resources for my needs.

It has been said that the most effective way to intercede for others is to say the name and let the Lord fill in the blank. He knows exactly what they need.

We state the Name _____. He identifies the Need _____.

Another system of intercession is utilizing such Scriptures as Ephesians 3:14-19 and Colossians 1:9-14. Insert the name of the person you are praying for in the place of the person for whom Paul interceded.

My system of intercessory prayer involves praying for certain groups of people each day of the week. I have prayed for them by name for years and thus have them memorized. I have a small prayer log that provides a monthly listing of needs. Keeping track of prayer requests is vital because, after every name, there is a need. In Ephesians 1:16, Paul reminds us of the importance of thanking God and praying for the people to whom He ministered. (See 'Supremacy of Shepherding')

The prayer of intervention has also become increasingly important in the instability of our world. We need God to manifest Himself in extraordinary ways that give us the promise of deliverance and hope.

In other words, prayer needs to permeate all aspects of the pastoral ministry. I made it a habit to pray for people in various ways, integrating the upward, inward, outward paradigm.

This prayer life enabled the Master Pastor to enter His earthly ministry with zeal, consistency, concentration, endurance, and power.

When we pray the way Christ did, we will receive the blessings He realized in His life and work. And we can pray anytime, anywhere, entering into a holy conversation and divine dialogue with the God who is everywhere present.

The Dual Needs: Direction and Protection

Most of us have been taught to pray for direction. One of my Old Testament favorites is Psalm 32:8, "I will instruct you and teach you in the way you should go. I will counsel and watch over you."

Here is God's personalized involvement in the lives of those He has created. The direction is critical, especially for us referred to as sheep, described in Isaiah 53:6a as "All we like sheep have gone astray." We need the Good Shepherd to help us to stay on the right path.

The great people of scripture also indicated their need for direction; Abraham, the patriarch, Isaiah, the prophet, Paul, the pastor. Each needed direction for themselves and God's people.

The New Testament reminds us that the Holy Spirit, who now resides in us due to God's completed work in Christ, will guide us into all truth. He will make the principles of the Word able to be understood and applied. (John 16:7-8,13-14)

Thus, the direction is not merely conceptual; it is highly practical. For example, in the ministry, the pastor needs guidance for the following:

- Establishing parameters in ministry relating to self-care.
- Managing marriage and family.
- Building relationships inside and outside the church.
- Dealing with difficult people.
- Determining how to administer the church.
- Casting vision.

- Leading worship.
- Knowing what and how to communicate the Word of God.
- Fulfilling stewardship in life and ministry.
- Carrying out the mission of the church locally and globally.
- Engaging in spiritual warfare.

Each of these areas requires clear direction, which needs to be determined individually and corporately. A wise pastor seeks direction by including others in the process, promoting ownership on the part of the congregation. (See 'The Importance of Networking')

Life teaches us that direction does not come easily or quickly. It does not always come at a point in time but more as the product of an ongoing process. Yet, we are impatient people. (See 'The Life of Devotion')

But needing direction is not the only thing that drives prayer. The need for protection initiates it. We need the Good Shepherd to prepare a table before us in the presence of our enemies and walk with us through the valley of the shadow of death. (Psalm 23)

The Good Shepherd gave His life to care for the sheep. He protects them from predators. Protection is ours to claim by the power of the One who promises it. Spiritual enemies endanger the sheep. The Apostle Paul warns the church of that in Acts 20:29 during his farewell address to the Ephesian Elders. Warning: "I know that when I depart, savage wolves will come in among you and not spare the flock." The animal metaphor is also used to describe Satan as a roaring lion. (I Peter 5:8)

Ephesians 6 tells the believers to take up the whole armor of God, to stand firm, to put on the military equipment, and to pray in the Spirit. Prayer is an essential part of the arsenal needed to protect ourselves. (See 'The Pastor as Warrior')

One of the portions illustrating this principle in practice is II Chronicles 20:12, where King Jehoshaphat is confronted with armies of three pagan countries advancing on Jerusalem. Amid the conflict, he mobilizes the people to pray. "For we have no power to face this vast army that is attacking us; We do not know what to do, but our eyes are upon you." It is a picture of a pastor and people praying for direction and protection in crisis.

A pastor is assuredly a person who must face and withstand attack. The enemy is intent on rendering us powerless to nullify our life and ministry. His purposes are never altered nor his strategies ever changed.

What are the areas of our life that need protection?

- Marriage and family from forces within the culture.
- Guarding the integrity of belief systems and morality from compromise.
- Church staff and congregation from discord and disunity.
- Distraction in the pursuit of the mission.

This kind of protection comes from proactive prayer. It is intended to be preventative for the individual and the congregation.

In one of my parishes, we had an incident with two of our young people who attended the same college. As a result of a change in their relationship, the young man became aggressive and demonstrated behavior considered to be potentially dangerous. Thus, we had two families whose children could not be together and were not allowed to be within 90 feet of each other for a year! Family 'A' could attend church anytime, which included holidays when their daughter was home. Family 'B' resultantly did not participate in the church during those times. (They came to separate Christmas Eve Services.) The civil war prospect was real; people would take sides, lending their support to the child they believed was right. But we went to prayer. The war never happened. We got through the year with planned absences and purposeful avoidances.

One of my church leaders made a statement I have never forgotten. "When it comes to Satan, prayer keeps him at the edges because he can't get through to the center." He was right!

The church leader must set the example. They must be convinced that prayer is vital to the direction and protection of themselves and the congregation. Prayer is the only entity that no opposition can withstand or overcome.

Individual and Corporate Prayer: The Spilling Over of the Well

The metaphor of the well and water serves our purpose. The prayer life of pastors and their congregations can impact the life of the community, the nation, and the world.

One of the most meaningful but often confusing passages of scripture differentiates individual and corporate prayer. "For where two or three come together in My name, there am I with them." (Matthew 18:20)

The logical question: Is Christ only in the midst of a group and not with an individual? Answer: He is present with each person individually, yet He is even more powerfully present in corporate prayer.

There is extraordinary power in corporate prayer. Here we seek the Lord and together agree in prayer over matters of our life and church life. We become more united in shared ministry.

Throughout history, God has called His people together to pray.

- When Solomon dedicated the temple. II Chronicles 7
- When Hezekiah faced the Assyrians. II Kings 19

- When Nehemiah and Ezra returned to rebuild the walls and temple in Jerusalem. Nehemiah 9
- When the church faced persecution after Pentecost. Acts 4
- When Jewish authorities jailed the early disciples. Acts 12

God's presence was noticeable among His people. God descended upon the place of worship, revival came to the people of God, opposition to the church was withstood, and disciples were delivered from jail.

But God's people didn't always remember to seek Him with all their heart, soul, mind, and strength as He had commanded them.

Their wells were not always overflowing because their devotion to God had dried up. The power of God did not always fall; the skies were bronze. No water, no wells.

In this crisis, God admonished His people and leaders in II Chronicles 7 to Humble themselves, seek His face, turn from their wicked ways, then He would hear from heaven and heal their land. God responded to their imperiled condition. He used the crisis to bring them closer to Himself. Crisis often brings us closer.

God doesn't discount the place of strategies, methods, and programs. He simply declares that they are not more important than His people seeking Him, confessing their sin, and being obedient. Then He unleashes the fullness of His power in their presence.

Effective prayer often includes fasting. Fasting is one of those topics we don't talk much about in a land that loves eating and drinking.

Fasting is more than giving up food. It breaks the routine through abstinence from anything, like television, shopping, playing video games, surfing the Internet, or even coffee. (How would we possibly function without our daily visit to Starbucks? Gasp!)

Fasting, in essence, is saying to God, "I am serious about what I'm asking; serious enough to give up something I enjoy for something that is ultimately more important." I tried to exercise this discipline on Saturdays in prayer for the country and Sundays.

Two things result from fasting. You allow yourself to focus on other items you may have neglected. (Reading God's Word instead of checking your Facebook page for likes!) You learn to appreciate the things you have given up. (Just think of the reward of that first Starbucks Latte after six weeks.)

It reminds me of an older gentleman in one of our pastorates who said. "I've given up fasting for Lent!" (He missed the whole point!)

It is believed that Christ addressed these two areas in Matthew 17:21 when He explains that something could only happen by the practice of the twin disciplines of prayer and fasting. Both are expressions of devotion to God and the determination to know His will personally and corporately.

Our denomination's School of Prayer defines the prayer life of the church this way:

Closet	The Individual
Cell	The Small Group
Congregation	The Large Church Group
Concert	The Large City Group

Individual prayer spreads to the city, community, and country as water overflows from the well to the reservoir. What begins inside extends outside; what starts at the center extends beyond the edges.

What does this mean for the pastor? Prayer must have precedence in the whole of a pastor's life and ministry. It allows God's presence to permeate the atmosphere of the church.

Prayer affects the church **within**.

- Members pray after entering the sanctuary to claim God's power upon that service.
- Worship leaders pray before services to be united in leading the congregation.
- Individuals pray with others after services as they attempt to apply the Word of God to the real-life issues they face.
- The church comes together at midweek meetings to pray for its needs directed by the leaders themselves.
- Congregational boards and committees pray before meetings to better facilitate their agendas and decision-making.
- Small groups pray as part of their Bible studies and support groups to deal with personal needs.
- Prayer teams undergird special seasonal events and community outreach efforts.
- Youth meet for breakfast or Meet at the Pole to pray for each other's challenges.
- Young parents pray together to share their children's needs as part of their fellowship time.
- Older folk have prayer time for their various needs during their monthly lunch at the church or a Care Center.

Prayer affects the church **without**.

Pastors, youth leaders, music ministers, and other staff meet regularly to pray. Churches of the same denominational fellowship gather to pray perhaps quarterly.

Christ-followers from a variety of backgrounds meet to pray at city-wide prayer concerts. They come to pray for their churches and their city, their leaders and challenges, their country, and the world.

The following format was used in our local church and city-wide prayer gatherings.

- Everyone praying out loud together simultaneously.
- Half and half: Some people pray audibly; others pray silently. This encourages people who are uncomfortable praying out loud or feel they must compete with someone else who prays better. (A very real issue in cultivating group prayer.)
- Scriptural proclamation: Reading or reciting the scripture together as it pertains to the area being prayed for, which can be integrated into any season or concert of prayer.
- Testimonials: People share their needs and real-life answers to prayer.
- Topical praying: The leader announces a topic, i.e., government leaders, and the whole group prays for them.

Individual prayer focuses on the upward and inward elements; corporate prayer directs its attention to exterior parts of intercession and intervention.

For many years, I served a pastorate in a medium-sized city where a small group of churches began to pray once a quarter. The format was simple and uniform. The people celebrated worship with songs interwoven with concentrated prayer segments led by different religious leaders from the community. The segments were usually about 15 minutes, ended with singing, and included prayer for churches in the city, the city itself, the nation, and God's mission throughout the world. The last I heard, this group had conducted 35 such concerts over nine years!

The impact was measured by the participation of city churches and governmental leaders who regularly submitted prayer requests. The local media highlighted the gatherings on more than one occasion. Prayer had gotten the city's attention. It had gotten

God's attention. Things happened unexplainable apart from prayer!

I must share one extraordinary story. In this city, a school board was divided and continuously in conflict during an especially tense time of teacher contract negotiations. A woman from the community had situated herself outside the meeting room to pray for the outcome. A school board member who was set to vote against the raise changed his mind and voted in favor of not freezing wages, primarily due to hearing this woman's prayer.

The church needs to make a prayer presence in the city where it is situated. And the pastor needs to be one of the pivotal people who makes that presence a reality.

Trace the prayer pattern: The pastor sustains a consistent prayer life. The pastor encourages the congregation to pray. The church joins with other churches to pray.

Here's a simple object lesson. It involves three mixing bowls, each a different size. I asked three people to hold the bowls as if they were suspended in the air. I pour water over the first bowl, which spills over to the second, and the second, which spills over to the third. The symbolism is immediately evident.

Bowl 1 - The individual in prayer.

Bowl 2 - The church in prayer.

Bowl 3 - The community in prayer.

Such is the nature of prayer in the life of the pastor, the church, and the community.

Summary: Prayer needs to be a top priority in the pastor's life, reflected in its centrality in the whole of their ministry. In essence, it is a declaration of dependence; it is where the vertical meets with the horizontal. Pastor and people need to develop an on-going awareness of their need to depend upon a power beyond themselves. Christ modeled dependency upon His Father for ministry resources, direction and protection, and intense intercession for His own and those He came to save. The leader's prayer life will spill over into the lives of those they lead within the church, the broader community, and beyond.

Peril: Depending on our resources for success, praying only in times of crisis and failing to mobilize the congregation to pray in various ways.

Privilege: Instructing our people to pray by precept and example and witnessing the power of individual and corporate prayer in the life of the congregation and the community.

Questions for personal reflection: Chapter 4 The Primacy of Prayer

1. What is divine dialogue? What are the challenges to it?
2. How did prayer impact Christ's ministry?
3. Explain the importance of prayer for direction and protection.
4. What are the benefits of collective prayer?
5. How can you promote the local church's prayer involvement in the broader community?

5   Self-care

Getting Over the Guilt of Not Performing:
Countering the Culture

The mantra of this performance-driven society is to work yourself to death.

The doing syndrome is based on working to prove your worth and value as an individual. Thus, self-care seems to be unnecessary in the modern social paradigm.

I, by nature, was not given to self-care. During the early years of the ministry, I would take Saturdays off. I couldn't take Mondays off because I spent the whole day thinking about what I had to do on Tuesday. But my Saturday was preoccupied with Sunday. So, I wasn't of as much value as I might have been to my family or congregation.

It was a conundrum. Not only taking time off, but how much work I needed to do to succeed in my calling. This way of thinking is inculcated into many pastors that make self-care a difficult subject to broach.

The term workaholic has been used to describe people who are addicted to work. The difference between this addiction and others is that it is acceptable to both the secular and Christian cultures.

Did you catch the cartoon where a stern-faced CEO is staring down a somber-faced employee with the caption, "It has come to our attention that you have a personal life!"

We've all heard employees complain about how they felt they needed to sell their soul to the company store.

The admonition against gaining the whole world but losing our soul applies to self-care. If we make great strides in the ministry at our expense, we may pay too high a price for success.

How could hard work be wrong? On the surface, it looks like an asset, not a liability. But upon closer inspection, working too hard can often be unhealthy.

The person is controlled by a skewed work ethic and a false sense of performance approval. We appear truly committed and successful when we work hard, right?

One of my favorite cartoons runs like this:

Frame 1- Workaholics Anonymous

Frame 2- Out to lunch

Frame 3- Back in four minutes

The images are illustrative of a driven culture, one obsessed with two excesses: labor and leisure. Work, work, work so we can play, play, play. The problem? We don't do either of these well!

Here's a question: Why do we work and play so hard but continue to find so little satisfaction with either?

People can become educated, prepare for a career, and work until retirement without any sense of any real purpose apart from doing what is socially acceptable and, of course, what generates income.

For the average person, a job has only to do with now. It has an immediate reward. The more you work, the more you will be rewarded. And for people addicted to the office, time to play is viewed as unnecessary and a mark of laziness. In other words, you're not worth much if you're not working harder to make more money than the next guy.

Pastors are not exempt from falling into the work trap. I wasn't. Often we feel that we are required to work harder than other people because our job is a mission with eternal implications.

However, the ministry's demands can become counter-productive if the pastor does not have reasonable expectations about how long they work or how much they do. (See 'The Certainty of Call')

As the old saying goes, "All work and no play makes Jack a dull boy." It also makes them insensitive to their own needs, their family, an out-of-balance life, and even subject to illness. Caring for yourself is not a sin. Not caring for yourself could be. (See 'The Imperative of Integrity')

The Biblical Definition of Self-care: Setting Down Limits

In viewing the Lord's life and ministry through the prism of the gospel, we see the very basis of self-care.

Christ knows we need re-charging, and He tells us how to do it. In Matthew 11:28-29, we read, "Come to me all of you who are weary and burdened, and I will give you rest. Take my yoke upon you and learn from me, for I am gentle and humble in heart, and you will find rest for your souls."

In other words, Christ enables us to do everything better if we let Him help us maintain a proper perspective of our work. In Mark 6:31, the eyewitness account records, "Then, because so many people are coming and going that they did not even have a chance to eat, He said to them, Come unto me by yourselves and get some rest." It sounds like something most modern ministers could have written! (Lunch on the run, anyone? I usually skipped them, not good!)

The narrative of Genesis 2:2 tells us that God rested on the seventh day from all the work He had done. He wasn't tired; He wanted to make a statement and set an example.

The theme of resting continues in the Epistles, namely Hebrews 4:9-10. "There remains then a Sabbath rest for the people of God, for anyone who enters God's rest also rests from his work, just as God did from His. Let us, therefore, make every effort to enter into that rest."

It seems evident that both God and Christ intended to model the importance of resting from their work. God took a break from creating; Christ took a break from ministering. He became human during His time on earth and thus able to identify with our need for physical rest. If they rested, shouldn't we?

The concept of rest in scripture not only runs counter to our culture; it runs counter to our self-concept. Admit it: Like Nissan, "We are driven!"

But Jesus could have been driven, too. After all, He had less time to get the job done. He had only 33 years. Yet, the intensity of His work made His need for resting even more necessary.

Yours truly often had a hard time working too hard and struggled with resting too little. Often the excesses go together to produce a person stressed out from working too hard and yet feeling guilty for taking time off from their self-imposed regimen.

Let's put it another way: *We need to work at resting!*

On our 30th Anniversary, we made a long-awaited road trip to the East Coast during the Fall; we had allotted three weeks. At the end of the second week, I was done with vacationing and rarin' to get back to the pulpit. So, much to my wife's dismay, we packed the bags and headed for home. In retrospect, I realize now that it was an unhealthy reaction to time off. And insensitive to my wife, who wasn't ready to return. I felt guilty taking any more time away and felt unproductive by not working. (I had a work addiction, but I am in recovery!)

Yet, as people have trouble working too much, they also have trouble playing too much. They can be obsessed at both ends of the spectrum. Both can become addictive; both can cause an unbalanced life.

Unlike work, play often lacks definition and a purpose. For many, play is merely having fun, which they view as the purpose of life. We identify that as hedonism, making pleasure the highest good and purpose of human life.

The average person equates having fun as the only way to rest and relax. If that hypothesis holds true, then why do so many people come home needing a vacation to rest up from their vacation? They come back from many activities, tired and dissatisfied, and I might add, wanting more of the same to find fulfillment.

The scriptures define relaxation differently. The purpose of a time out is to restore ourselves in every area of our life; spiritually, physically, intellectually, and emotionally. It is to be an R and R; Rest, and Renewal. Notice the term renewal, RE-*NEW*-AL, to be made new again and again. I define renewal as RE-CREATION. *Real recreation is meant to re-create us.* Such is the rest that leads to restoration. It is God's version of a vacation.

Many people have quiet times, read a book, or spend quality time with loved ones on vacation. But many simply want to get away and exchange one hectic routine for another. Their focus is on the quantity of time rather than the quality of it.

My Father's idea of an ideal vacation was to drive, drive, drive, see as much as possible, and return home exhausted. (So I carried on the family tradition by driving 7,000 miles on our honeymoon and coming home the same way.)

Biblical R and R is for renewal and restoration of body, soul, mind, and spirit. It is more than just doing nothing. It is the kind of rest that genuinely refreshes and replenishes all aspects of our life.

Sabbath (Shabbat) in the Old testament means an intermission. We could compare it to halftime intended to give the players a break from the game. Sabbath means taking a break from the game of life. Another definition of the word is to discontinue or stop doing what you do most of the time.

This struggle for balance is exacerbated by church members who can be hypocritical when it comes to time off. Sometimes what they insist on for themselves, they disallow for their pastors. They will let their leaders work as much as they want. After all, they get the best of that deal!

To get away for R and R through a day off, a vacation, a sabbatical, to play or enjoy a hobby is a good thing for you and the people you lead. One of my hobbies is baking, and by the way, I can turn out a batch of cinnamon rolls in two hours and immediately enjoy the results!

Pastors are not indispensable; they do not have to do everything! They are human beings with the same needs as everyone else. The truth is, they will work better when they play better. They will be more effective if their whole life is not confined to their job or measured by the time they spend at church.

A television commercial depicted a family heading out for a Saturday excursion. As they leave home, the little girl spots men and women going to work and finally asks, "Is it Saturday?" Her father responds with a smile of pride and contentment, "Yes, it is." He had chosen not to work this Saturday. And his daughter notices!

Pastoral time-outs benefit the church in another way. People tend to appreciate and take up the slack for their pastors in these seasons. We call this the ministry of absence.

Taking a Sabbatical: Finding Another Day Off

One of the problems for pastors is that they work every Sunday. (Well, almost!) In the words of the little girl, "Pastors have an easy job; they work one day a week for only an hour!" Right!

I have told people over the years that when it comes to preaching on keeping the Sabbath, I'm a hypocrite! Where do I get off telling them to honor the Sabbath when I don't?

The early Christian Church chose Sunday instead of Saturday to be the Sabbath; either way, the clergy had to work on the Lord's Day. No Blue laws for the church! It's open every Sunday.

So we have a problem here. How do those who teach others to obey the Law of God get away with breaking it? Let's just say that God makes an exception for those in the pastorate and the church ministry. The Son of God worked on the Sabbath because He was doing God's work.

Congregations accept and appreciate that their pastors serve on the Christian Sabbath; actually, they come to expect it! They don't consider ministering on Sunday to be a violation of the Sabbath. After all, it is God's Work; He legitimizes it.

By definition, a Sabbath needs to be different. A change of routine allows rejuvenation in all areas of life, especially in the spiritual realm. Nonetheless, the day free from weekly obligations should be enjoyable.

My Dad came from a family of 12 brothers and sisters. His Dad was a Baptist pastor. So, their Sabbath prohibited everything from reading the comics, playing sports, and anything except sitting in church for hours. (Not the right prototype!) Sunday can and ought to be a Fun-Day.

Many people have to work on a Sunday and therefore cannot attend worship services. For them, their Sabbath must be another day or time.

The rule then becomes that it's not always Sunday, but any day can qualify as a Sabbath. If you work on Sunday, why not pick another day for your Sabbath? Easy to suggest, hard to implement, especially for pastors!

The regimen of the ministry, however, can make this problematic. I know from personal experience. Here's why. I began ministry wondering if people would think I was not doing my job when they didn't find me at church during the week. When my wife took a part-time job, I finally settled on Saturdays as a day off and focused less on the next day! But then, frequently, the weekend became a time for church activities like weddings, men's retreats, dinner groups, and a myriad of other things. Thus, Saturday was often not a complete day off either.

There is yet another issue. Do we as pastors and staff have a day that is a true Sabbath? Part of our problem is that we think our Sabbath rest must only be one day, two weeks of vacation, or a Sabbatical every seven years. The secret is learning to take little Sabbaths and a time-out along the way. In one church, the staff called it Dawg Days. (A **D**ay **A**way **W**ith **G**od.)

Many facilities provide the minister with an opportunity to get away for a couple of days or longer. Such an opportunity offers the chance to withdraw from our routine to spend quality time alone with God, catch up on personal reading and formulate goals and objectives for the future. Information regarding retreat centers is available on the website: Retreathood.com or by contacting them at info@retreathood.com.

To rest is to break our routine. It is a form of fasting. Many pastors take all their vacation days at one time and consider that their only time away. But there can be other shorter times apart from that. Pastors of smaller churches face the obstacle of pulpit supply in the absence of other staff who could fill in, or the church does not have a budget that allows for it. Sabbatical times should be beyond the scope of a family vacation. Perhaps this can be negotiated at the time of the call predicated on an understanding of pastoral self-care.

Of my pastoral tenures, I was only in one church long enough to earn an extended sabbatical, which generally comes every seven years. The length of it varies from several weeks to several months. It is most often used for independent study, enhancing the pastor's devotional life and ministry to the church. Some have traveled during this time, perhaps to a place where they could combine study and vacation. The church leadership was unfamiliar with the concept and reluctant to grant me a block of time. I should have educated them about the dual benefit of self-care for myself and them. However, given my temperament and anticipatory mindset, I would have counted the days until I had to return to work, thus diminishing the break's value anyway. (I hadn't completed recovery as yet!)

Development of Life Outside the Parish: Establishing Normal Socialization

Part of self-care often overlooked is having friends like everyone else does. (See 'The Importance of Networking')

However, the reality is that pastors have to be careful with the people in the congregation they befriend. For instance, some pastors have been known to form friendships with the more wealthy folk in the church for obvious reasons. In one of our churches, these people were considered the country club clique of which we were never formally a part. We developed a close friendship with the church chairperson and his wife. They had come to our old home in Oregon and helped us in our move to California. I remember them cleaning bathrooms, packing boxes, and escorting us across the border. We came to love and enjoy spending time with them socially. But, there was a small pocket of people in the parish who became jealous of our time together and wound up monitoring our house to see how often the chairman's van was parked there!

Our children would ask us, "Do you guys have any friends?" We honestly had to admit we didn't have any friendships outside the church, at least. (And after the California experience, we weren't sure we should have any inside the church either!)

Pastors usually have ambivalent feelings about non-church friendships for several reasons. One is that they may feel guilty for not spending all their time with their parishioners. Or they don't know any people outside the church with whom they would enjoy building a relationship.

The simple truth is pastors are people, and people need friends. Why should those in the pastorate not have the same freedoms that others have when it comes to friendships? The answer is, they should!

There is a need for normal socialization in the ministry, which provides contact with people outside the congregation. Building a friendship with people other than those we serve not only broadens our circle of friends but provides a new fresh perspective on life. It reminds us why we do ministry.

I chose to be involved in the Kiwanis social service club, several leadership programs sponsored by the local chamber of commerce, community theatre, and several musical productions. These activities provided ways to be an ordinary guy who just happened to be a pastor. These also allowed me to be Christ in the marketplace and challenge people's negative impressions of the church and clergy!

We discovered that we could still relate to people different than we were. Then our kids said, "We can't believe you became friends with those people...but good for you!"

Friendships are an essential part of our self-care. When pastors take care of themselves, they can better care for others.

Summary: In a culture that puts a premium on work determining our worth, taking time to care for ourselves is counter-cultural. Ironically, the same society that lives to party and vacation doesn't know how to rest! Self-care requires definition, guidelines, and boundaries to counter the work urge. Sabbath rest was ordained and modeled by God and Christ for spiritual and personal R and R, true Rest and Re-creation; it is designed to be restorative. Since pastors work on Sundays, they need to take time other than the Lord's day for rest as others do. They are encouraged to form social connections with people inside and outside of the parish, enhancing their care for others and providing a model for the congregation.

Peril: Neglecting care for yourself by not sustaining a balance between work and rest and not developing close friendships inside and outside the church.

Privilege: To model the work-rest balance for family and congregation, be restored through time off and personal renewal, and build social connections.

Questions for personal reflection: Chapter 5 Self-care

1. Why is rest a counter-cultural concept?
2. In what ways do pastors struggle with work and rest?
3. How can pastors have a Sabbath apart from Sunday?
4. Why are friendships important to self-care?

6   Protecting Marriage and Family Life

The Vulnerability of the Pastor as Partner and Parent: The Triangle of Tension

Taking care of ourselves is a precedent to caring for our marriage and family. We who are in the ministry must be especially attentive to this responsibility. What better way can our enemy lessen our effectiveness than to go after our marriages and families?

In I Timothy 3:4, the criteria for an effective church leader is that "He must manage his family well and see to it that his children treat him with respect." Paul poses the question, "If anyone does not know how to manage his own family, how can he take care of God's Church?" Intimidating, isn't it?

In Titus 1:6, a leader is to be "A man whose children believe and are not open to the charge of being wild and disobedient." (So about now we're asking, did these guys have any children?) It is essential to realize that managing your own home does not mean it is perfect and with no problems!

However, church congregations put pressure on a pastoral marriage and family by having unrealistic expectations for them, just as they do their pastors. They ignore the reality that when pastors put their primary relationships first, they are more effective in caring for the church family.

Pastors need to draw boundaries about what is expected of us, our spouses, and our children. My wife and I learned and implemented this principle s-l-o-w-l-y. (See 'Self-care')

The Role of the Spouse as Team Player: The Non-paid Position

The minister's spouse deserves special care, yet they tend to be overlooked and taken for granted. It takes a unique person to fill this strategic role.

My wife has often told the story of how she didn't want to come to Bible School because she was afraid of two things: one, becoming a missionary or, worse, becoming a pastor's wife. Yet, if ever there was a woman suited for the co-calling, it is Joyce Boyce. She has been an extraordinary co-partner in the pastorate. But not all spouses exemplify this spirit.

I know of situations involving two churches we served. One was a small town in Colorado. A potential candidate's wife made it very clear that she wouldn't live in the small podunk town if they were called there.

The other was the wife of a man I followed in our second pastorate who disliked his sermons so much that she went to another church! (It reminds me of the cartoon showing a pastor's wife with a TV in the second row. A parishioner remarked, "I guess she's heard all of his sermons before!") These spouses were not the paragon of supportiveness! They became detriments instead of assets in the ministry. Pastoral spouses can make or break the ministry.

On the other hand, I know of a female senior pastor whose husband stayed home and cared for their two young children; a supportive team-mate in the work. Role changes have become more common in the contemporary parish.

Spouses struggle to define what they do. Churches need to remember that they are not getting two for the price of one. They are not hiring the spouse. Yet, a congregation can have expectations of what the other half is to do. Besides caring for the home and family, attending every church activity, serving in multiple capacities, this person is to be the model of stellar spirituality! They can feel pressured by the unreasonable demands of others. It is a bit like the President and the First Lady. Each has a different role to play, but both are expected to perform individual tasks even though only one is elected to office!

Caring for our spouse is one of the most critical components of the ministry in a calling that continually demands us to care for everyone else. This expectation directly impacts the pastoral couple's ability to act and serve as a team based on a strong, healthy marriage.

The pressure of maintaining a marriage is captured in several witty quotes I have spotted. "I'm not bossy; I just have more good ideas." "We've had a lot of problems in our marriage, and most of them are your fault." "My wife always lets me have the final word: yes, dear."

Making a successful marriage requires hard work, especially in the ministry. It's more challenging in the parish because the expectations are usually greater.

The pattern for the marriage is a reciprocal relationship defined in Ephesians 5:21. It mandates that each partner "Submit to one another out of reverence for Christ." The reciprocity takes place as a man *cherishes* the woman and a woman *supports* the man. Cherishing is the synonym for loving and honoring; supporting is the synonym for obeying and submitting. (Ephesians 5:25-30,33) A cherishing husband will nurture a supportive wife. A supportive wife will nurture a cherishing husband. It is a never-ending cycle; it spans a lifetime.

72

Men, one of the ways you can cherish your wife is to recognize and appreciate her intuition. One of the great assets my wife has given to me in ministry has been her wisdom and insight.

A flashback to the pioneers describes it well. The husband provides the incentive, "Let's go West and conquer new frontiers!" And the wife says, "The back left wagon wheel is loose!" She is an indispensable entity.

I have always made a particular point to honor my wife in public. I have referred to her as my beloved and shown her appropriate affection. We have kept the cherish-support cycle going through the 50 plus years of our marriage. We have honored and submitted to one another, the basis of cherishing and supporting one another. This cycle also fortifies the marriage and guards against potential allegations of indiscretion with members of the opposite sex.

Care requires giving time and attention to our mate. The care of our mate is central to the marriage and the family's health and staying power. I often recollect my conversation with a 70-year-old widow who was giving me advice as a single man, "If one has enough horse sense to treat their spouse like a thoroughbred, they will never turn them into an old nag." (Sound advice from a sage.)

The issue of personal security is central to a strong, healthy marriage. There must be a modicum of self-security present in the two adults who enter into a marriage. It is a reserve out of which each replenishes the other's needs in every dimension of the relationship. The reserve is primarily spiritual, psychological, and emotional. My marriage mantra: If my wife's needs are met, all my needs are met. Conversely, when a husband's needs are met, all her needs are met.

When marriages struggle and flounder, it is easy for partners to focus on Me rather than We as the security source. As the We weakens, the Me surfaces in a variety of ways.

The most robust union is the marriage of two givers, both able to give from their spiritual, emotional, and psychological resources to the other. A less healthy marriage is a giver and a taker, the seedbed for co-dependency. The weakest union comprises two takers, each drawing more from the relationship than what they put back into it.

Marital discord between couples may result from both having unreal expectations coming into the relationship. Failing to maintain healthy habits in the marriage can compound incompatibility. These conditions may be present before entering the ministry and simply be brought to the surface by the demands of marriage.

Marriage problems are not a blowout as much as a slow leak. A word to marriage partners: Watch for leaks!

Essential to any marriage is the couple having adequate time for each other. It is so easy to minimize and disregard this need. The story is told of a pastor's wife who wrote her name in her husband's calendar at the same time every week. She was desperate for time with him; she decided to take the initiative!

Often your spouse may feel they are in competition with y-o-u-r ministry. Pastors are encouraged to make their spouse feel part of the ministry other than through service in the ministry itself.

The ministry context can also make it more difficult for couples to admit and get help for solving their problems. It is hard to come home from a day of dealing with everyone else's problems only to be confronted by your own.

Remember, it is entirely permissible for any couple to seek help and needed counsel. This help can come through Marriage

Encounters, Marriage Enrichment opportunities, or professional counseling. (See 'The Pastor as Counselor')

Letting the Pastor's Kids be Normal:
Projecting Unreal Expectations

If marriage in ministry is challenging, how can we not expect it to accelerate when the circle expands beyond the two of you?

Foundational to partnering and parenting are the issues sourced in our family of origin. The anger and hurt of current or past experiences keep us from healthy relationships within our family and our church family. It is important to remember that much of what was done to us was not our fault. We can't change that. What we can change is how we respond to it.

Fostering a normal growing-up experience for kids in this culture, especially within the church context, is challenging. Children in the pastorate can often feel they compete with a second family. And in the glasshouse of the pastoral home, the challenge of raising kids is more complicated.

The central issue in pastoral families is expectations. Children of pastors and missionaries are often referred to as PKs or MKs. I've always disliked these terms. The label seems to set them apart in a way other kids aren't. We don't call lawyer's kids LKs or teacher's kids TKs. These terms seem to deny them normalcy, causing them to incur more pressure in the course of growing up.

Our children confessed that they did not feel other people expected too much of them; the real pressure was self-imposed. They did not want us to look bad if they messed up. Whatever the source, demands imposed on the pastor's kids are real and can often be detrimental to their personal development and faith.

In school and the church, we asked that people be fair in their treatment of our children. Even so, parish children can feel the pressure to perform from what they perceive is life under surveillance and a higher standard for them in the church and public arenas.

We came to realize that guilt is also a prominent factor in pastor's children. They not only face the issue of failing their parents but also the congregation and even God. They can feel they are never good enough, which may affect how they see themselves. Such was the case in the one-hundred-year-old church we served, where a whole next generation of kids was virtually lost, consumed with inadequacy, guilt, and rejection.

Other elements in parenting can be viewed through the prism of the pastorate.

Time

Giving time lets a child know they have worth, value, and security and that they are more important to us than the congregation. We made a concerted effort to spend time with our two. Quite frankly, if I had it to do over again, I would have arranged my schedule differently, especially in the evenings and weekends. But we attempted to have a weekly family night and a date with each kid regularly. Most people have a two-day weekend; pastors usually get only one day, so it's hard to get away like everyone else. On your deathbed, you probably won't be saying, "I wish I'd gone to the office more often." It is also tempting for parents to replace the giving of time with the giving of things.

It seems to be a real problem for parents in The Netherlands who are too busy to read to their children and outsource the task. A company called Sprrokiebel (Dial-A-Fairy Tale) offers ten-minute recordings of classic fairytales like Little Red Riding Hood, all for only $7.00 a call. (Such a deal...but a bad one!)

Intimacy and Closeness

Touch and affirming words give your child a sense of belonging, understanding, acceptance, and accessibility to you. Our family expressed love, verbally and physically. Bedtimes provided special moments of communication, as did working through times of crisis, like running an injured pet to the vet.

Area of Openness

Honest sharing provides a secure environment where kids can be themselves, share needs, feelings, opinions, and ask questions. Some of the questions kids have to deal with are: "Am I accepted as a pastor's kid?" "Is there is a place for me to doubt and even question my faith?" "Can I make alternate choices from those my parents want me to make?"

We allowed them to express negative feelings and question why we did things a certain way or disagree with our beliefs. Although we expected compliance, we endeavored to give rules with reasons.

Freedom to be Themselves

We faced the subtle temptation to make our kids conform to what we believed they should be. We mused over how they could perform well at work, be on time, be neat, accept responsibility, and then display the opposite at home. We finally realized that they needed home to be a safe place where they did not have to perform. (What's worse, a messy bedroom or a messed up life?)

We also tried to honor our kids as individuals and rear them accordingly. One size does not fit all. We encouraged them to use their natural abilities and interests, and we celebrated when they did things better than we did! (An indirect compliment.)

Unconditional Love

Pastors and missionaries often struggle with this issue in their professions. It is vital to protect them from unreal expectations and resist labeling, criticizing, and rejecting kids who fail to meet them. They need to know that the love of God and their parents are without conditions and that someone will have their back even when they fail or go in the wrong direction. We learned to guard against preaching about loving others then failing to practice that same love for our own family.

It helped to remember that the person who knows the most about parenting is God, the Super Parent. When it comes to the challenges of raising kids, we know how He feels. After all, He has to raise us! (Talk about kids who don't conform to expectations, color outside the lines, crush hopes, and break hearts!) God, the Father, knows all about raising children; He can help us raise ours.

The promise of Proverbs 22 is that if we train our children in the rudiments of faith and appropriate values, they will eventually return to them, though it may be when they are older. (We may not live long enough to see it happen, but...)

We gradually learned that God gave us the exact children He wanted us to have. He used them as an anvil to shape us as parents. My wife and I would be a lot less than we would have been without children.

Riding the Rapids of the Adolescent Passage: Unavoidable Transparency

I remember reading an article about the different stages of raising an adolescent. The parent learns that rearing teenagers is like nailing Jell-O to a tree. That describes it pretty well. It was a word picture I'll never forget!

This dilemma is pronounced during the child's passage toward adulthood, the mysterious transition we call adolescence.

Before the Industrial Age, this categorization did not exist. The first nineteen years of life were considered a continuation of pre-adulthood, not a separate age grouping. The result has formed a sub-culture with its own rules, styles, language, music, and heroes. It is a cultural cocoon that isolates and alienates teenagers from their families and the culture at large.

Of course, is it easy for most of us to think that kids today have never been worse than they are in this generation. But someone else felt that way about the kids of their generation.

"Children today are tyrants. They contradict their parents, gobble their food, and tyrannize their teachers!" Socrates (399 B.C.)

A modern philosopher has captured the essence of this transitional stage in life. "Hire your adolescents while they still know everything!"

A friend of mine in ministry had a teenage daughter who was not a conventional person. She was a bit different from what the congregation expected. It was a church that never had a pastor with older children, only the cute nursery kiddos that everyone loved, mostly before they learned to talk or have an opinion. But when she began to express her individuality, this congregation was merciless in their treatment of the young woman. She later left the church and turned her back on her faith.

Sometimes getting a kid to adulthood is even harder when you are the pastor, and it's *your* kid! Nice Christian people in your church can complicate the process!

Not all the reasons for a teenager's behavior revolve around being raised in a religious home. It can be the condition of the home and the family itself. It is easy to blame others or the kid themselves rather than take a closer look at the marriage and family unit. (Ouch!)

Such is illustrated in the life of our former pastor. The dominant characteristic of his family was dysfunctional, before we knew or used the term. The home was reasonably sound spiritually but not psychologically, something which impacted each of the five children. Christian? Yes. Healthy? No.

Parents play a significant role in the psychological and spiritual environment of the home and family life. The two are corollary. A spiritually healthy home is more likely to be a psychologically healthy home. The integration of personal faith, the freedom to fail and be forgiven, permission to question, and being accepted and loved when not living up to the expectations of others will impact the child's development.

As our children entered the adolescent phase of their lives, my wife and I had no idea what was ahead or how we would navigate it. We reminded our kids that this stage of life was new to them and us! (Both of us asked for a little slack from each other!)

We offer some discoveries that might be helpful as you ride your rapids. They are not intended to tell what to do or how you should do it, but provide some observations that may help you figure out the situation yourself! (With God's help, of course.)

Observations and guidelines for parenting adolescents:

Observation: Rearing our kids today vs. generations past is way more complicated. Everything is up for grabs; spirituality, moral values, sexual identity, marriage. We really can't compare things today with how they were when we were kids. It is like comparing apples and kumquats. Take learning to drive, for example. My Dad learned to drive when he was eight years old on a tractor; that was 1923! By the time I needed to learn in 1959, my Dad had no memory of how he had learned and had no patience in teaching me!

Sometimes we forget what it was like when we were the age of our kids. We need to realize today's teenage world is entirely different and much more complicated than the one in which we lived. (I recommend the book: **Crazy-Stressed** by Michael Bradley)

Guideline: Recognize that teenagers are growing up in a drastically different world than the one you grew up in.

Observation: We remember two families in the church we attended before we were married. Two families each had two boys. One family had no rules; the second one had too many. The result was the same in the four boys. They were rebellious toward authority and resentful toward the church. The key is balance, hard to maintain in reality. (Another tightrope.)

Guideline: Be more controlling in the early years and less as they mature and learn to apply self-control.

Observation: We learned that our personal issues from the past needed to be improved. Admittedly, I had an anger issue leftover from childhood that manifested itself in unhealthy ways. With time and counseling, I came to a balance between holding the anger in and showing it. This was especially important in reacting to my children and parishioners. We had traits we hoped they would emulate, and others we hoped they didn't.

Guideline: Take a good look at your strength and weaknesses, admit them, seek to work on them and ask for forgiveness when you fall short.

Observation: We often said we'd rather have our kids fail in our presence than in our absence. We did not want them to give lip service to belief, then have it all fall apart when they got beyond the reef of home and church. Dealing with it now was better in the long run than dealing with it after they left home. But families and congregations have ways of postponing kids having to deal with their issues. Healthy children need a safe arena to test beliefs and life principles.

We often want to avoid the danger zones, which causes kids to fake it till they make it; it sets up the double-life syndrome. The hypocrisy can precipitate the breakdown of faith in the adult years and produces prodigals, some of who never come home.

We realize now that a certain degree of failure happened at home. But wouldn't you know, our young adults waited on some things until they were beyond our reach. They were on their own then and responsible for their own choices.

Guideline: Have reasonable expectations. Give them the freedom to fail, question, and let them face the consequences of their choices.

Observation: Having been reared in conservative Christian homes, we were firm disciplinarians with definite views on how faith was practiced. When our kids challenged us on how we were taught to think about many things such as faith, curfew, politics, music, etc., we viewed that as disrespect for us. All we knew was how we had been raised, and it was hard to think we were good parents if we departed from that standard. Yet, we did the best we could with what we had. There are no guarantees. We were Christians, in the ministry, and with good intentions. So, we believed that we would be great parents with those things going for us and have foolproof kids with few problems. (Parent Utopia!)

Guideline: Resist feeling blame, guilt, and self-pity if your kids don't turn out the way you hoped.

Observation: As we looked back over our parenting career and our children's pilgrimage to adulthood, the Lord gave us a surprising discovery. We knew our intentions and efforts to be the best Christian parents we could be. But we also came to realize that the situations and outcomes could have been far worse if it had not been for our faith and dependency upon the Lord. This realization was a source of great relief and encouragement.

The pastor-parent can feel tremendous guilt, blame, and self-pity. We lamented, "We did the best we could!" Sometimes children simply choose a different road.

Guideline: Be thankful for the person God has allowed you to become and the things He prevented from happening because of your faith and obedience to your calling.

Protecting the Family Fort: Seeking Help From Others

The family is under attack in our culture today, especially the Christian family. There are modern philosophies that undermine traditional values and historic Christian faith. There are increasing numbers of forces antagonistic to parents, encouraging others to make critical decisions for them.

Commitment to traditional marriage has changed dramatically. Divorce is promoted, as is pre-marital sexual involvement, cohabitation before marriage, and lifestyle choices, which undermine traditional values and become the new norm.

Many today deal with the blended family issue, where one parent is usually invited into an already established family unit. The merging of separate families, often brought about by divorce and re-marriage, exacerbates the challenges of growing up. It can be a hard road, but a truly united and committed couple and family can survive.

Gone are the days when you could pretty much count on most of the people down the street to support your belief systems as well as the rules for responsibility and accountability. These are the perilous days of which Paul spoke to Timothy. These are hard days to maintain a marriage and a family. Note these words in II Timothy 3:2, "People will be lovers of themselves, lovers of money, boastful, proud, abusive, disobedient to their parents, ungrateful and unholy."

The pastor must ever remain alert to the enemy's constant, unrelenting attempt to injure and impair the marriage and family. To paraphrase the words of Luke 9:25, It is not God's intention that a minister gains the whole congregation or community and loses their family in the process. The family must continue to be a priority despite the culture's intention to undermine and vilify it.

One of the keys to this process is allowing other believers to come along-side pastors and church staff to guardian their marriages and families. Often the very people committed to the same objective can support, understand, and intercede with us.

At the lowest point in parenting, I came to the pulpit devastated and hurting beyond anything I had ever felt before. Yet, in our struggle, people saw realness. They saw us try to cope. They surrounded us with empathy. They learned from us, and we learned from them. In those times, we needed to find perspective, something which came from both God and others.

It's also made easier by having church leaders who allow you and your children the freedom to fail and those who have gone before you, who are there to pray and walk you through your valley.

It is often at these most challenging times in the parenting process when we are most vulnerable and transparent. We need others to help navigate us through these troubled waters. This navigation comes thru collective prayer. (See 'The Primacy of Prayer')

My wife and I prayed over our children before they were born, and we are still praying for them as adults.

Prayer helps us to keep priorities in place. It is so easy to misplace them, especially in the child's early years. I recall as a teenager staying at the home of a woman in Winona Lake, Indiana. Her mother was a neighbor of Billy Sunday, a world-renowned evangelist. Sadly, she told the story of how Mr. Sunday traveled the world and preached to thousands. Yet his children all forsook their childhood belief primarily because they failed to see their famous father's love and passion for the ministry translated to them in real life. As adults, these misplaced priorities distanced them from their father and their faith.

Prayer is both preventative and remedial. In one of our ministries, my wife co-founded a Mother's Support Group for the express purpose of praying openly, honestly, and consistently for one another's children. We see the results of those prayers in their adult lives today.

Prayer underscores our need for help from others. Pastoral parents need others to pray at the time when they feel most helpless in life and ministry. There is probably nothing healthier, more helpful, or hope-producing for pastors and their people than to form support groups with the express purpose of sharing and praying for one another in mutual parenting struggles. Intimate intercessors can be of particular assistance. (See 'The Importance of Networking')

Caring for ourselves and our family in ministry is nothing short of a tightrope, one we fall off many times. But when it comes to walking that rope, we need to be sure we fall on the side of protecting those at home even more than those in the church and asking our congregations to understand and support us in doing that!

It is essential to remember that we may have more than one church in our pastoral career. We will likely have only ONE family and only a brief time to bring those closest to us to maturity and prepare them for life. *The family is our more significant ministry!*

Succeeding in this endeavor was primarily the result of prayer and a parent network that rode the rapids with us. Our children both survived and avoided even greater danger because of the protection afforded them by congregational support.

Despite the perils of the pastoral home, our two adult children seem to be reasonably well-adjusted. They have not forsaken the faith, been mad at God for calling us into ministry, or retained hostility towards the church, although they have not always been comfortable with or involved in it.

I share an unforgettable conversation with a deaconess in our second pastorate. I posed a question to her when our kids were still in grade school. "What would happen if my kids ever really messed up?" This mother of three grown sons, all of whom had encountered troubled marriages and disrupted lives, looked at me with a broad grin and a sparkle in her eye and responded, "You'd be more valuable to us than you are already!" (Amazing insight.)

We referenced that comment many times as our kids got older and made decisions that disappointed us. It relieved us of the very real pressures of performing perfectly and meeting a whole host of expectations. It helped us to realize that our struggles made us stronger and of greater value to the ministry.

Summary: Being a pastor, partner, and parent is a challenging role because the pastor is, in a sense, married to the ministry and has a second family to care for. The pastoral task, coupled with the pressure to be all and do all in the ministry, tends to compete with the care of our marriage and family. Boundaries need to be drawn to protect the marriage and family from the demands of the pastorate. The spouse often can be presumed to be an unpaid staff member who feels conflicted with home and family responsibilities and estranged from having close personal friendships. Maintaining some degree of normalcy and privacy is challenging for families. This is especially true for children who feel scrutinized and expected to be above average, heightened by the adolescent passage where transparency is inevitable. Pastors need prayer from others in the task of parenting. However their children turn out, pastors will be of more value to the congregation for having gone through the process.

Peril: Sacrificing a marriage and family on the altar of the ministry and failing to establish boundaries to protect our primary relationships.

Privilege: Helping build strong and healthy marriages and families within the congregation as you come alongside each other in the process.

Questions for personal reflection: Chapter 6 Protecting Marriage and Family

1. Why is a healthy marriage important in the ministry?
2. How are kids in ministerial homes affected by unrealistic expectations?
3. Identify the elements of effective parenting, especially during adolescence.
4. How can others in the church help a pastor with their marriage and family?

7   The Necessity of Networking

Intercession with Intimates:
Partners in the Pastorate

A pastor is only as strong as their prayer team. I didn't always believe that, so I didn't have one. In the early enterprising years of my ministry, I thought that I could do it alone. The concept of needing a network was alien to my autonomy.

Network is a noun; flank is a verb. A network flanks a leader. Synonyms for flanking: supporting, protecting, undergirding, and interceding.

Having a team of prayer intercessors is imperative for survival in life and ministry. It is not a sign of weakness to have a need, but rather a mark of strength to own the need *and* let others help you meet it. It permits them to do the same.

The term intercessor is taken from the Latin word pontificate, a term closely related to the word Pope. It translates *bridge-builder*. I like to define it as one who bridges troubled waters. In life and ministry, the waters are not always tranquil. The prayers of God's people can help quiet them.

This ideal sounds good, but it's challenging to actualize for two reasons. Sometimes people don't want to get close with, know, and pray for their pastor. They want to keep them on a pedestal from which they can be toppled. After all, if they get to know them, love them, and care for them, it's harder to oppose them.

Some pastors don't want to get close to their people. They are power-driven, governed by ego, or have a distorted work ethic. They wish to work independently of other people. Thus, a congregation can choose not to get close to their leaders, or leadership can keep them at a distance. Both attitudes violate biblical principles.

The scriptures are replete with examples in both Old and New Testaments of a network of intercessors. Old Testament: Moses had two mighty intercessors. David had three other team members who cared for and defended him. Daniel also had three in his support system.

New Testament: The chief example of a network comes from Paul. One has only to read the credits at the end of most of his writings to know that this great apostle believed in the necessity of having a network. (Romans 16, Philippians 4, Colossians 4)

Perhaps the best example of a network is the one Peter had. He had Christ as his chief intercessor. Peter struggled with his faith and allegiance to Christ, who reassured him that He would pray for him. We can only imagine what it was like to have Christ as our chief intercessor to intercede for us. But that's exactly who the Son of God is and what He does!

There are three categories of intercessors: remote, casual, and intimate.

The *remote intercessors* are usually not in the congregation and often live somewhere else, like retired church members.

The *casual intercessors* could be considered anyone in the congregation who prays for general needs, staff, events, and special outreaches.

Intimate intercessors are characterized by having a prayer gift and capacity with the particular assignment of praying for their leaders. Their selection is a dual calling, first by the Lord and then by the church leader. A chief intercessor comes from this group.

In our fourth pastorate, a woman in her seventies approached me, telling me she was quitting all her ministries shortly after we came to the church. A bit alarmed, I asked, "Why?" She responded, "Because the Lord told me I was to pray for you." She became my chief intercessor. I confirmed her call with tears and a huge hug.

It wasn't until the third pastorate that we formed a personal team of people to regularly pray for us. We learned slowly about the necessity of having a network in place.

The intimate prayer team fulfills a specific purpose, praying for things that the remote and casual intercessors often don't know. Example: I called my team when I had a critical appointment. I didn't disclose the details; they didn't need to know them; they would be on their knees at 3:00! I never had a meeting that did not go well when I had my team praying for me. They were able to pray for situations in the church that could not be shared with the general congregation.

This close-knit team prayed for my personal and family needs. More than once, I asked the group to pray for a health need or a crisis with one of the children. Again, with no questions asked, they were there for me, for us. And they guarded confidences.

Sometimes my teams met together; sometimes, they did not know the other team members. This precludes elitism or the formation of a pastoral clique.

One of the important things is communicating with team members and updating them on what was happening in our life and ministry. It also allows them to share their prayer needs. After all, turnabout is fair play. If they pray for us, we need to pray for them.

One of the prime prerequisites in establishing a prayer network is for pastors to recognize the need for this ministry, be vulnerable, and ask for help. A self-sufficient pastor is, as they say, an oxymoron, i.e., a jumbo shrimp!

In his writing to the Thessalonian Church, Paul instructed the congregation, "Now we ask you to respect those who work hard among you, who are over you and admonish you. Hold them in the highest regard because of their work." In simple terms, get to know your leaders because if you know and care for them, you will have a much easier time esteeming and supporting them. (I Thessalonians 5:12-13)

Leaders suffer a dilemma faced by the whale. A mother and baby whale ascended and descended in the water. One day, the baby whale asked the mother, "Mother, why is there is so much noise when we swim above the water?" To which the mother replied, "Because when you're on top, you get shot at!"

The ministry is challenging enough without people who are supposed to be your allies if they become your enemies. If the church people don't know their pastors, what they do, or what needs they have, they will be more prone to make assumptions about those things. This mindset may cause them to depreciate and often become critical of their pastor.

How many pastors have wrestled with this thought: "If they only knew what it takes to do this job and how much my family sacrifices for me to do it!"

This principle connects with earlier themes of this book. Pastors feel they need to perform for approval and acceptance and thus are reluctant to utilize others in the ministry. Pastors are also apprehensive about sharing private things about themselves and their families because doing so might allow the information to fall into the wrong hands. (See 'The Certainty of Call')

It does not mean that people follow or support their leaders blindly in a spirit of over-compliance. Instead, congregations can seek to befriend, support, encourage, and help their pastor, creating trust based on the leader's heart and motive.

The writer of Hebrews put it this way: "Remember your leaders, who spoke the Word of God to you. Obey your leaders and submit to their authority. They keep watch over you as men who must give account." "Obey them so their work will be a joy, not a burden, for that would be of no advantage to you." (Hebrews 13:7,17)

But church people don't always behave like it. They can become adversarial toward the people who love and try to protect them. People who fire on their pastors shoot themselves in the foot, figuratively speaking. They do not make pastoring a joy. (See 'The Pastor as Vision Caster')

Pastors need their people to care for them through encouragement and gratitude for who they are and what they do. (And not only during Pastoral Appreciation Month.)

In the New Testament Church, two of their apostle-pastors, Peter and John, had just had a run-in with the religious authorities who took a shot at them. These two dear servants of the church needed prayer surrounding them and divine guidance going before them. Their network was in place. (Acts 4:27-30)

I liked to say that my prayer network is like a Spiritual American Express Card, and I didn't leave home without it!

Connecting with Colleagues: Making the Journey Together

In addition to a prayer network, a pastor needs the support of pastoral peers. These people can be both inside and outside the congregation, including the local church teammates and fellow pastors from other churches.

Men, by nature, do not connect easily. We are loners. Women, in essence, are joiners; connection seems to come more naturally for the female. Thus, women in ministry find the networking concept easier to incorporate into their ministry paradigm. Despite their male persona, men need to become intentional about opening up, sharing with, and being accountable to others.

And if sports-loving men disdain the idea of having a support team, perhaps they should consider the world of professional sports. I spotted a bumper sticker recently, "Even Tiger Woods has a caddy!" In other words, even the best need someone to help them. (Can you just imagine Tiger carting around his own clubs?)

To enter into these kinds of relationships, men need to move past their innate inhibitions and non-disclosure to deal with their fears and needs.

In the hit animated movie, *The Incredibles*, the male lead turns to his newly found family with these words, "I can't lose you again because I am too weak to stand alone." To which his wife responds, "We'll stay with you so you won't have to."

As I look back over the years, I am grateful for those men and women whom God brought into my life so that I wouldn't have to stand alone. They are significant enough to be named and recognized for their contribution to my life and ministry.

I had pastoral peers in ministry who were a vital part of my network. John Johnson in Milwaukie, Oregon, Tom Glossi in Loveland, Colorado, the late Chuck Reagan in Rockford, Illinois, David Bird in Carrollton, Texas, Tracy Weaver in Alexandria, Minnesota, and Eric Torrence in Plano, Texas. I met with them regularly during my pastoral assignments. We shared insights, prayed for and with each other, found humor amidst the challenges, cried together, and maintained accountability for our lives.

Pastors and spiritual leaders need the stamina to deal with pressures, attacks, and temptations. It is important to remember that the evil one often causes us to weaken in the face of temptation when we're in isolation. Like the king of the jungle, Satan is called a roaring lion. A lion will lure its prey away from others, so he is better able to make the kill.

It is true: no man is an island; no man stands alone. It took me a while, however, to understand the truth of that principle practically.

I was not close to my father, who did not know about closeness with his father. I had always excelled in student leadership in my high school and college years. Later, I realized that this allowed me to stay distant from other people by being up in front, something which the pastoral ministry allowed me to continue.

Only by trial and error did I realize that I could not lead alone; I needed other people to help me. I needed to network with people, especially my peers in ministry, which illustrates the principle of *inter-dependence*.

It is not only biblical but a practical concept. After all, who knows better about the challenges of the ministry than those actively involved in it? This network gave me insights on living and ministering that I otherwise might not have had. I am richer for having been relational.

One of the other critical dimensions of connecting with colleagues is accountability. I have known those who profess to be only accountable to God as an excuse for not being in an accountability relationship with someone else. The truth is that we need to be responsible to a God we can't see, and also to our brothers and sisters, we can.

Some people call these individuals accountability partners or spiritual directors. Adjectives that align with these people are safe, dependable, indispensable, protective, and constant.

One of the pastorate's technological gifts is CovenantEyes.com, which provides an electronic means of being held accountable for choices we make in everything we read online, and what we do on our computers. Pastors can check on each other using a rating system that flags unhealthy behavior patterns.

Those who know you well can tell when you're not leveling with them. You can't deceive or play games. They love you too much and care too much about your ministry to let you get away with it. If you cheat the system, you cheat yourself.

Accountability partners draw encouragement from the reality described by the writer of Corinthians, "No temptation has seized you except what is common to man." In other words, we all live in the same world, and we are susceptible to the same temptations. What works on me may not work on you, but the bottom line is: we are all tempted by something. (I Corinthians 10:13a)

Often a foothold becomes a stronghold. What begins as a casual look at a magazine in an airport turns into gazing endlessly at a computer screen in our basement. The first look turns into obsessive lust. "But each one is tempted when, by his evil desires, he is dragged away and enticed. Then after desire has conceived, it gives birth to sin." James 1:14-15. "Do not give the devil a foothold." Ephesians 4:27 (See 'The Pastor as Warrior')

God may be watching, but our accountability partner is looking us in the eye over breakfast, asking the hard questions. The way we answer may make all the difference in how we decide to live our lives, even though we may resent it at the time! It's pretty hard to sit across from someone you know who understands what you're going through. No matter is too small. What matters is your integrity and the impact of your ministry. If you care about those things at all, you won't try to bluff your way through breakfast!

The journey is too hard to make it alone. We need those who can make it with us. As pastors who tend to go it alone, we need to learn that lesson early and well. Your prayer network and your accountability system can make the difference between running the race well or being disqualified. You can't run and win this race without the rest of your team.

The Earthly Trinity: Three Essential Teammates

The late Howard Hendricks, a professor to pastors, originated the pastoral network paradigm: Every pastor needs three types of people in their life. A *Paul*, a *Barnabas*, and a *Timothy*. I learned to incorporate them into my life and ministry.

A *Paul*: A seasoned person of God. One who has put a lot of miles on the spiritual odometer. This person most usually would be older than the pastor, one whom God has indicated to be the right person. (One time, that person was confirmed to me as I was meeting a group of senior church members during a candidating weekend.) This individual has often traveled the roads you have yet to travel. *Wise* is their signature quality. For six years, I regularly met with eight older men in various homes.

A *Barnabas*: Most usually a peer in age; the kind of person you can golf with, grab lunch on the run, or call on the spur of the moment. While your Paul is your older brother, your Barnabas is a buddy. Given that the two of you are pretty much at the same station in life by age and experience, they are there to provide friendship, socialization, and empathy, all qualities of the biblical Barnabas. *Encouragement* is their signature quality. In one pastorate, I met with ten non-clergy peers in my home regularly.

A *Timothy*: This individual is usually younger than yourself. In nearly every case, this person approached me, asking about the possibility of my serving as their mentor. I have always entered this relationship with a sense of equality. Age and experience were not prominent factors. After reaching adulthood, age is inconsequential; the playing field is level. I considered myself a co-learner, one not having all the answers. I considered it a two-way relationship where both of us could learn from and teach each other. This inter-generational connection is also essential in developing a spiritual progeny. *Teachable* is their signature quality. In another pastorate, I met monthly with 25 younger men, divided into two teams who met at my home and the church.

My *Paul* - Spiritual Directors/Accountability Partners

These men were senior in age to me, with older children, often retired, those who walked before me as professionals and parents.

In Milwaukie, Oregon, such a man was the late Bob Jones, businessman. In Stockton, California, Jim Fox, Liverpool Lab, in Loveland, Colorado, Carl Buchannan, a retired airline pilot. In Rockford, Illinois, the late Bill Mapelsdon and Mike Anderson, both business professionals. In Carrollton, Chuck Lamb and Dean Anderson, my Chair and Vice-Chair, respectively. In Alexandria, Minnesota, Chuck Erickson and the late Lloyd Anderson, a retired businessman. I will ever be in their debt.

My *Barnabas* - These spiritual brothers, both fellow pastors, and friends shared life with me in the trenches.

Rick Lindholtz, Alan Eagle, Bob Linscheid, Chuck Wahlstrom, John Smith, David Ed, Roy Christman, Tim Musselwhite, Tom Miller, Bob McCrae, David Aherns, Dan Craig, Darren Olson, Mike Cunningham, John LeVahn, Steve Eng, Tim Schmoyer, David

Dean, Al Carlson, Steve Olson, Mark Olson, Dave Lambert, Jim Baer, Dan Miller, Paul Seelhammer, Sven Swanson, Tim Hurlbut, Keith Martinson, Bill Fletchner, Gordon Nyberg, John Failor, Kent Ward, Don Michael, and Carl Mason.

My *Timothy* - These men were my juniors, many of them laypeople who possessed a teachable spirit and showed great promise with significant ministry potential.

Ron, Mike, Bob, Joe, Seth, Bill, John, Tom, Dave, Jim, Steve, Phil, Denny, Gary, Bruce, Mark, Darren, David, Tim, Tony, Scott, Jeff, Larry, Ryan, Craig, Brent, Eric, Blaine, Bruce, Carl, Paul, Steve, Mark, Dan, Terry, Tyrone, Chris, Ed, Marshall, and Cody.

Networking allows the leader to connect with the prayer partners, mentors, pastoral peers, and apprentices. My personal ministry and that of the church were shaped and sustained by these connections.

Getting the Next Generation Ready: Mentoring Potential Leaders

The pastor who is intentional about establishing networks in their ministry models the necessity of needing others to help them. It also equips others to help in ongoing ministry.

This commitment is enunciated in Paul's counsel to the younger Timothy in his second letter, "And the things you have heard me say in the presence of many witnesses entrust to reliable men who will be qualified to teach others." (II Timothy 2:2)

Over the years, I have received word of individuals who took on increased responsibility in the ministry. I believe that networking was a part of the preparation process. Specifically, four men have gone into the ministry, several men have become elders, 11 have become staff members, and four have become church chairpersons. I was always training my congregational members, albeit vicariously, for the ministry's next phase. (See 'Pastor as Lifelong Servant').

Pastors usually serve for a season. God uses their unique gift mix to complete a specified season of ministry. Each pastor prepares their congregation for the next stage. This reminds me of a dear woman, Pearl Schloman, who was a member of the first church we served. She was irate that another church had extended a call to us to be their new pastor. She kept up her tirade until finally, I said, "Pearl, thanks for loving us so much and thinking the church cannot go on without us, but if we stay when we are supposed to go, we'll mess it up!" Her response? "I'll help you pack." She finally got it. God had called and used us for a season but appointed another pastor to take the church through the next phase of ministry.

The correlation between pastoring and parenting is evident. To be a parent is to rear a child to adulthood. To be a pastor is to raise a spiritual child to maturity in Christ. A parent seeks to leave a legacy. A pastor aims to do the same. The impetus for *The Ultimate Calling* has been to leave a legacy to those in the ministry.

Paul describes this process. "Teach the older men to be temperate, worthy of respect, self-controlled and sound in faith, in love and endurance." (Titus 2:1-2) "Young men, in the same way, be submissive to those who are older. All of you clothe yourselves with humility toward one another." (I Peter 5:5)

Let me explain this practically. First, the older congregation members are charged with training the younger members. Secondly, it is incumbent upon older men and women to live exemplary lives and elicit the respect and trust of those younger. (Titus 2:2-5)

The young and old are to be humble before God and each other. Everyone can be a co-learner to learn from someone else, no matter their age and stage in life. To prepare the next generation of leaders is a biblical mandate in the Old and New Testaments. Moses trained Joshua; Paul trained Timothy.

At various points in my pastoral pilgrimage, I approached older church members in the congregation to mentor a younger member. But I was met with various excuses. "I am not a theologian; I don't know the Bible very well." "I have issues that would make me ineffective; I would be uncomfortable opening up to another person." "No one ever mentored me. I wouldn't know how to do it."

My response? You don't need to be anything but yourself, and you don't need to do anything but share your life experiences. Just being in a younger person's life will make a difference; give them someone to talk to and pray with who has gone before them in life.

What is true for older men and younger men is equally valid for older women and younger women. This is part of imparting the truth to each generation.

On the reverse side, I have had younger members decline the offer to be mentored. They felt they didn't need an older person's counsel and guidance from a different generation and who wouldn't understand them.

In a culture where many young people have not had the nurture and direction of their parents, men and women in the church can play a vital role in their development.

Modern-day pastors have a chance to invest in this ministry's dimension during the entire course of their ministry. (See 'The Pastor as Lifelong Servant')

After we complete each phase of the pastoral race, there will always be those who remain on the track, those we have helped to continue building up the church. We want to equip them to cross the finish line successfully. Networking is essential to this process.

The amazing story is told of Jim Redden in the 1972 Olympic Games. After long months of preparation, the day had come. Shortly after the starting gun, Jim fell sprawled on the track, the victim of a torn hamstring. Staggering to his feet, he determined that he would finish the race; he had no chance of winning. Suddenly up in the stands, a man busted past security guards and ran onto the field. It was Jim's father. He whispered to his son, "You know, son, you don't have to do this." "Yes, Dad, I do." "Well then," the father smiled, "we're going to do it together." So together, before thousands of people now standing to their feet, yelling words of encouragement, father and son went the distance and crossed the finish line, together!

So is the race of life, especially the race we run in the ministry. We cannot run it successfully alone!

Summary: Being a pastor can be a lonely assignment, not one to go solo. Pastors need to enter into partnerships with those inside and outside the congregation, especially prayer partnerships. Some pastors and parishioners resist allowing others to network with them. Yet this is a biblical concept imperative to an effective ministry. There are essentially three types of prayer circles; remote, casual, and intimate. These lay team members come alongside their pastors regularly. Pastors are encouraged to pray with pastoral colleagues, who can provide empathetic support and intercession. Pastors need to connect with accountability partners; an older Paul, a peer Barnabas, and a younger Timothy. Networking prepares the people you are serving and future leadership after you leave.

Peril: Not letting others into your life and ministry as a needed resource; intercessors and accountability partners.

Privilege: To model inter-dependency upon others and prepare your congregation for their ministry's next phase.

Questions for personal reflection: Chapter 7 The Necessity of Networking

1. Why is it beneficial to have prayer teams?
2. How can colleagues in ministry aid the pastor?
3. Why have a Paul, a Barnabas, and a Timothy in your ministry?
4. What is the role of older men and women in preparing the church for its next phase of ministry?

8   The Supremacy of Shepherding

The Biblical Background:
A Look at the Supreme Shepherd

We are immediately drawn to two images. The sheep and the shepherds, to view the pastoral ministry through the lens of shepherding.

A *Dallas Morning News* headline captured my attention: *Training Preachers for Pastures*. What caught my eyes were the words, preachers for pastures. The pastor is called to shepherd sheep. Pastors are under-shepherds; they are under the authority of Christ whose life and ministry they are to emulate.

Isaiah uses the term in his writing, "All we like sheep have gone astray. Each of us has turned to his own way." (Isaiah 53:6a)

The scriptures refer to people as sheep because they act that way. For instance, sheep follow herd instincts and don't have a reputation for being the brightest animal. They wind up in dangerous situations, get caught in brambles, become lodged on their backs, wander off frequently with little sense of direction, and they encounter the most significant threat, being attacked by predators. Quite simply, sheep are stupid and needy.

I read an amazing story about sheep the other day. Nearly 1500 of them jumped off a cliff in Turkey. First, one sheep jumped to its death. The stunned shepherds who had left the grazing flock watched as each sheep did the same thing. Only 450 of them died since the cushion saved the rest for those who jumped after them! (Any questions about the IQ of sheep?)

However, pastor-shepherds can quickly recognize these qualities because they are sheep themselves; they understand the conditions in which sheep find themselves. And no one who has ever been a pastor would deny that the care of sheep is difficult. (Now we know how the Chief Shepherd feels!)

In Jeremiah 23, the prophet describes bad shepherds and good shepherds. The former do not tend and care for the sheep; they serve themselves instead. The good shepherds know, hear, and follow Christ Himself, who is introduced to us in Psalm 23 and John 10. Peter describes Him as both shepherd and guardian of the flock entrusted to His care.

Christ is also an under-shepherd, a human being who subjugated Himself to His Father. Therefore we are called to be under-shepherds of Christ.

What correlations do we find here between the shepherds of the pastures and the shepherd of the pews? Shepherding involves getting to know the sheep who become familiar with their shepherd's presence and voice. Theirs is a close relationship. Shepherds rescue the sheep from those who would lead them astray and kill them. Shepherds lay down their life for them.

I remember watching my denominational president leave a meeting after his election. He was immediately amidst the delegates. I watched him walk through the crowd touching people as he inter-faced with them; it was natural, comfortable, effortless. He was a shepherd amidst his sheep.

Under-shepherds sacrifice for their sheep. Pastors don't go to the cross as Christ did, but they sacrifice differently. Those sacrifices come in taking phone calls at all hours, including on your day off, taking walk-ins in the middle of preparing a sermon, coming to a church activity on the weekend, supporting the family for long hours as their loved one faces surgery or after a funeral service when no one stays in contact with the bereaved.

The shepherd is the most nuanced term that can be used to define the role of the pastor. It is not coincidental that the words pastor and pasture are semantically related. It identifies the under-shepherd who understands how to deal with human-sheep in the places where they live everyday life.

During a trip to the Holy Land, I saw Bedouin shepherds tending and protecting their sheep on the hillside between Galilee and Jerusalem. Men of meager means cared for their sheep as their ancestors had done since biblical times. Steeling themselves against the elements and giving constant attention to wandering flocks, these sheep-tenders epitomized the pastor's role, whose charge is human flocks.

Prerequisite for shepherds: Love the sheep! Nothing is more important, nothing! Resumes, degrees, educational credentials, letters after your name, lofty grade-points are not as important as loving the sheep.

When being considered for our second pastorate, I was part of a conference call with the Superintendent, who asked, "And what gifts do you think you bring to this assignment?" He said this in a tone that made it sound like going there was my idea. I replied, "Well, I'm not overly-confident of any of my gifts, but one thing I know, I will love the people." What I remember most was his response. "Oh good, that's what they need." (Like it was some rare and unique capacity the pastor would bring to their congregation!) In my way of thinking, this attribute is essential, not exceptional.

The earthly pastor-shepherd is given the **ultimate calling** to help the sheep follow the Supreme Shepherd.

The Significance of Suffering: The Value of Life Lessons

In Hebrews 5:1, the writer describes Christ as the High Priest. "He was taken from *among* men and appointed to *represent* them in things pertaining to God in order to offer gifts and sacrifices for sins." Christ bore the crosses of everyday ministry in preparation for carrying the ultimate cross, by which He bought salvation for all.

The writer goes on, "He is able to deal gently with those who are *misguided* since He Himself is subject to *weakness*." (Hebrews 5:2) In other words, Christ could identify with the people He represented. He became one of them.

Suffering and weakness are themes that contemporary culture does not face or deal with well. Christ experienced our pain so that we could help others deal with their pain. "That's why He had to enter every detail of human life. Then, when He came before God as a high priest to get rid of other people's sins, He would have already experienced it all Himself, all the pain, all the testing, and would help where help was needed." (Hebrews 2: 17-18   The Message)

Thus, for the Chief Shepherd and High Priest, whom we represent as members of the clergy, suffering is an unwritten part of the job description.

We have only to look at Jesus, who is seen throughout the scriptures as one familiar with suffering. The Old Testament reveals this in Psalm 22 and Isaiah 53 and New Testament portions, Philippians 2, Hebrews 9, and I Peter 3.

During this initial writing, *The Passion of the Christ*, produced by Mel Gibson, debuted. It gave the world perhaps the most vivid portrayal of the suffering Savior. For one, I will never read the narrative in the same way again; I will see it cinematically.

As we focus once again on Hebrews 5:7-8, we are captured by these words, "Who in the days of His flesh, when He offered up both prayers and supplications with loud crying and tears to Him who was able to save Him from death and was heard in that He feared. Though He were a Son, He learned obedience from the things which He suffered." (KJV) In other words, God became human flesh to relate to the people He came to serve. And God preserved Christ in His suffering, using it for the ultimate salvation of the world

Granted, Hebrews 4:15b tells us that "He was in all points tempted like as we are, yet without sin."(KJV) The term does not mean He was tempted in the same areas, but with the same magnitude. Yet, the difference between His temptations and ours is that we give into them, and He didn't!

Similarly, pastors may not experience every temptation their parishioners go through. Nor have they passed all the temptation tests; they have, however, experienced temptation and testing. It allows leaders to relate to those they lead.

The apostle Paul viewed suffering from a positive perspective in his epistle to the Corinthians. "In all our troubles, my joy knows no bounds." (II Corinthians 7:4b)

He validates the reason for suffering in II Corinthians 1:3-4. "Praise be to the God and Father of our Lord Jesus Christ, the Father of compassion and the God of all comfort who comforts us in all our troubles so that we can comfort those in any trouble with the comfort we have received from God."

What Christ has gone through allows Him to experience what we go through. *As for Him, so for us: What we go through, we learn for two.*No experience is ever wasted.

Even believers in Christ can naturally wish to get a pass on suffering. It is out of place in a culture that is enamored with comfort and avoiding crisis. Sometimes it looks like we think we can simply leave the comforts on earth for the conveniences of heaven. Yet, for followers of Christ, the comfort of heaven is the only one that is assured. Pastors are indeed not exempted.

We usually don't understand why we're going through something at the time; only later do we see it retrospectively. The axiom is true: Hindsight is always 20/20! In hindsight, our pain is validated and productive.

Personally, my family and I have been spared a lot of things in life and ministry that others have endured, especially in terms of health, kids, and congregational crises.

That is not to say we didn't have our share of challenges. My wife was diagnosed with an auto-immune disease, which, in rare instances, could have been fatal. Through adolescence, our children's pilgrimage was not without its genuine tensions. Having led six unique congregations was difficult and not without exhaustion and pain.

A pastor may experience pain in the ministry. This may mean having something hurtful said about you or other family members, meeting with opposition when you try to cast vision, or lead people in a mission that requires change. It can mean betrayal at the hands of those who are so-called friends, those who take issue with you or dislike your leadership.

For example, my wife and I learned not to stay with church families during the candidating weekend. These initially charming hosts somehow felt they had a special relationship with the pastor, which gave them clout in getting their way later on. They became adversarial instead of allies. (So, we asked to be lodged in a motel instead of a private home.)

Yet, suffering has its residuals. Suffering allows for transparency in the pastor's life. Here is the opportunity to let people inside and outside the parish know that we are people with needs who need help. We become less of a threat, we become more approachable, and those we lead are allowed to become part of our struggles. We not only give services *to* them but receive services *from* them.

In our era of ministry, pastors were not given to being transparent in the way they are today.

THEN - Pastors were put on a pedestal; they were considered holier than thou. They were warned not to parade their problems from the pulpit. They did not want to appear unable to resolve their issues.

Part of the no-fault pastor's image was the uniform, the robe, the suit, tie, and of course, the pocket hanky. It served as a sort of barrier to keep pastors removed from their people. Indirectly, they withheld permission for the congregation to be transparent and open.

NOW - By the very nature of the culture, people are forced to be open about their issues. A pastor who is open and honest is not considered a liability but an asset to his understanding of and willingness to deal with people's real needs. The informal dress motif is complimented, i.e., shirts worn outside, without ties, sometimes jeans and tennis shoes. (My Conservative Baptist grandfather, who was a preacher, would have had heart failure!) In today's culture, realness enhances both reverence and relevance.

Allow me to introduce you to my friend, Igor. This precious brother is a pastor in Ukraine. The church I was pastoring was instrumental in building the only Evangelical Church in Kalinovka. He had only been pastoring for four years when we met. Igor was not seminary trained but rather a lay leader and a recovering alcoholic. How many churches in this country would allow a person only four years old in the Lord, with no formal training, and a recovering alcoholic to pastor a church?

Yet, this humble man with the most exuberant heart for God had all the qualifications to identify with the people he led. He was not a threat to them; he was a friend. He is the pastor-shepherd who can lead them through familiar paths, ones through which His Shepherd has led him!

No pedestal, no performance, no pocket hanky. Igor was in the trenches, in work clothes, transparent by necessity, the epitome of the contemporary pastor.

A Spiritual Physician: The Rx for Restoration and Healing

The pastor is called to represent the Great Physician, who came to care for those who were sick, not those who were well and had it all together.

Doctors and pastors have something in common in the recovery process. They both bring health and wellness to the people for whom they care. Pastors are spiritual physicians.

While serving as a volunteer chaplain at the local hospital, I was making my rounds in a sports coat and light tan colored slacks and just happened to be carrying a clipboard. The Catholic Father was also making his rounds. When he poked his head in the room to visit with one of his parishioners, he remarked, "Oh, I'm sorry, I didn't know you were with your doctor" and left hurriedly. (So, I looked like a doctor. I just didn't have the paycheck to match the image!)

But there are similarities between the two professions besides being on call day and night. Spiritual physicians help people get well, but their prescriptions are of a different kind. Their medications don't come from bottles; they come from Bibles. They prescribe spiritual diagnosis and treatment. They often deal not so much with physical maladies but those of a spiritual and emotional nature. These may be harder to deal with, but then the pastor has an edge. Our leader, the Chief Physician, is perfect and has all the answers! (Try to find a medical school headed by someone with those credentials.)

Spiritual physicians deal with parishioners who are getting well all their life, recovering from the sickness of sin with which they were born. Getting them well is often a long, slow process, requiring more than a couple of visits to the study or a quick prescription of Bible verses. The ability of the doctor to identify with the suffering of the patient is essential.

Spiritual physicians cannot have a lack of concern for their people. And a suitable bedside manner is non-optional.

Under-shepherds are to guide and care for their sheep. Care is manifested through preaching and teaching, regular intercession, faithful care as extended through phone calls, personal notes, and being in their homes and hospital rooms.

I recall a former associate pastor who was often heard singing in hospital rooms where he visited. Swedish hymns were his specialty. Parishioners loved to have him come, pray and sing with them. He had a rare and remarkable gift of compassion. But, comrades, take heart; you don't have to sing in Swedish to demonstrate compassion for sheep.

It is inconceivable that any man or woman could believe themselves called to the Christian ministry if they didn't have a genuine concern and desire to care for people.

The Great Physician gives us a model. Much of His earthly ministry was centered on healing people. He cured physical illness, spiritual disease, including dealing with demonic conditions that impaired the person's quality of life. Eyewitnesses recounted that He taught, and He touched the sick. He confirmed His Word through His work. As was His, so ours is the task of bringing about restoration and recovery.

The cure for the spiritual disease brings about a change of heart, mind, and spirit, based on the patient's willingness. No patient has been turned away, the spiritual diagnosis is never wrong, and the treatment costs nothing, except for the willingness to follow the regimen to become well.

I can confirm that there is no greater source of joy and satisfaction than seeing spiritually sick people become well, broken people become whole, and impaired people become healthy. It matches the biblical criteria. (Luke 4:18-19)

One of my pastorates was in a reasonably large city with an older congregation. Judging from what appeared to be a high degree of spiritual maturity and the low number of counseling agencies in the area, I concluded that this was perhaps a problem-free bunch of believers.

That's what they wanted people to think. However, during my time there, I dealt with every type of problem, especially pornography, amongst the men. The people maintained a problem-free profile to keep others from getting close enough to see what they were really like! This attitude restricted the church from realizing its full potential; it couldn't relate to real people with real problems. I observed that the higher the socio-economic status and the wealthier the community, the greater the tendency to project the all-together image, which often hid sin and prevented people from getting help for their problems.

The Requisites of Shepherding: Lead, Feed, and Meet the Need

Christ typifies the Good Shepherd who does these three things: He *leads, feeds,* and *meets the needs* of His sheep.

LEAD: Biblical leadership is mandated and to be modeled by leaders who have gone before us. Though human, men and women are put in place to lead God's people. Where would God's people have been without Moses, David, Paul, and of course, Christ Himself? In each of these leadership roles, it is not so much a matter of *if* men and women are to lead congregations, but *how* they lead them.

We live in an age that is resistant to authority. Parishioners have the right to question and hold their leaders accountable. Pastors have the responsibility to treat their congregations with honor and respect.

Peter sets down the criteria for leadership in I Peter 5:1-3. "To the elders among you, I appeal as a fellow elder, be shepherds of God's flock that is under your care, serving as overseers not because you must, but because you are willing, as God wants you to be; not greedy for money, but eager to serve; not lording over those entrusted to you, but being examples to the flock." This admonition applies to both Peter, the pastor, and the elders, his church leaders.

Biblical leadership emanates from following God and then leading others, again, led to lead. The order dictates the outcome. Follow God, lead others.

Servant leadership is a term we have heard increasingly in the life of the church. It is an outworking of being led by God the Father, Christ the Son, and the Holy Spirit. This leadership is characterized by humility, sacrifice, sensitivity, honesty, openness, compassion, integrity, and consistency. (I Timothy 3,

Titus 2 and I Peter 5). It was instituted by a shepherd who won the right to be followed by displaying a godly example. The term servant appears 850 times in the scriptures; the term serve appears 1153 times. Christ came not to be served but to serve, the prototype for all leaders of His church. (Mark 10:43-44)

Pastors also serve by leading with divine authority. It is a loaned authority, one given by God to those who lead. It is derived, not earned, but bequeathed. It is not provided for the pastor's benefit but the benefit of others and administered with integrity. (See 'The Imperative of Integrity')

However, as in feeding and meeting the need, pastors who lead will always need the cooperation and help of those they lead.

The writer of I Thessalonians (5:12-13) charges church members "To respect those who work hard among you, who are over you in the Lord and who admonish you, hold them in highest regard in love because of their work." And in Hebrews 13:17, the church is commanded: "Obey your leaders and submit to their authority as those who must give an account. Obey them so their work will be a joy and not a burden, for this would be of no advantage to you."

But, sheep are not always prone to follow the Chief Shepherd or His under-shepherds. Not all sheep want to be shepherded. They resist authority; they undermine those who govern them, which harms themselves and the church.

Shepherds are called to lead the sheep who are held responsible for supporting and following those chosen to lead them. People who are not held accountable may perpetuate unhealthy attitudes and immature responses, which hinder the work of the church.

There are people in our churches who have authority issues yet unresolved in their adult life. Perhaps unintentionally, they project them onto those who lead them.

In my estimation, these church members can project their guilt and pain onto someone in leadership, most often their pastors. For the pastor who strives to please everyone and perform well, this can be disillusioning! I frankly was stunned by the actions of parishioners. My term for them is detractors; they detract from their leader's welfare, the church's health, and the fulfillment of God's mission.

Certain traits characterize these detractors: They are often people in power who have been in the church for a long time and are used to having their way. Not unlike the New Testament Pharisees, they become combative when their territory is threatened. They can be hypocritical. They get you to believe they are spiritually mature, but their behavior betrays that. They may appear to be supportive and even offer a word of encouragement to a pastor, but do just the opposite in private settings. Their objective is power and control.

I was informed of such a person in another church who took issue with hiring an ethnic music pastor. A wealthy church member had not only forced the music minister to leave but persuaded 20 families to turn against the pastor. They made their case known by withholding their money, always a chief tactic.

I have a question. Are these people an asset or a liability? Quite frankly, they are the latter. Are their intentions intended for the welfare of the Church? Hardly!

Frankly, the ministry is hard enough without having to deal with these kinds of people. But these are, nonetheless, the people we pastors have to shepherd and care for. Paul calls it forbearing one another, something which they can make very difficult! I have also asked myself, why do these people get away with this?

They get away with it because the church is an easy place to do this. These detractors need to be dealt with, but they intimidate people, so no one will dare do that. When we fail to correct these actions, they harm the congregation; it enables them to continue to behave in unhealthy and unacceptable ways that injure the mission of the church. We, as leaders, are responsible for dealing with these difficult people. Pastors must take the risk to confront these few for the welfare of the many; shepherds are to protect their flocks.

But, the pastorate is not a popularity contest. It's not likely that you'll get points for holding people accountable for immature attitudes and behaviors.

I had such an individual in my third pastorate. He felt that I was not treating a young pastor on the staff fairly. Based on this inaccurate perception, he mounted an all-out war against me. However, upon hearing him criticize another staff member in public, I called him in for a conference. I confronted him, citing his indiscretion of talking behind a staff member's back. I knew he had done the same thing to me. I did what I considered was my role as a leader. I made it very clear that this was not a personal affront to me, but was in fact, detrimental to the congregation whom, as a shepherd, I was bound to protect. And although I paid for that confrontation for the duration of my time there, I was willing to pay the price to do it. (Tough work).

Here are my perceptions. Detractors are older; they have been Christians for a long time and thus perceived to be wise and spiritually sensitive. Funny thing, often, the individuals you would think are the most spiritually mature are sometimes the least; they may be 70 years old chronologically, but much younger spiritually. They only *look* mature; they don't *act* maturely. It's like they are stuck both spiritually and psychologically and have come into adulthood with unresolved authority and power issues.

We often make the mistake of thinking that if a person becomes born again through a spiritual conversion, this will automatically solve all their problems. I believe it's reversed. When psychological problems block the grid, they distort authentic spiritual conversion. Thus, their faith becomes toxic; a person distorts their faith to justify their way of thinking and behaving. They feel they are entirely in the right because of their spirituality, which, unfortunately, has not penetrated the layers of untreated emotional issues.

Too, these are the very people who can attract others to side with them in church conflict. More often than not, they criticize, attack, and go to war with the pastor and church leaders.

Unfortunately, our churches have many people just like this. I have known more than one. They are people who make leading difficult and challenging. They fail to do for their leaders what the writer of Thessalonians and Hebrews commanded them to do.

I made an intriguing discovery, however. All these people had certain things in common.

- Most of them had come from other churches where they had problems with leadership and people in general. They simply brought the baggage from their past with them.
- They attacked our ministry, my family, or me personally. All three of those things happened when I encountered my first detractor.
- They took little or no responsibility for their actions. They focused the blame on the pastor or others.
- They had the clout to get other people to go along with them and support their cause.
- They had unrealistic expectations toward their pastoral leadership. When things didn't go their way, they retaliated.

Tragically, some detractors never resolve their baggage issues but instead continue to project their way of doing things on the pastor and other people. They either leave to find the next perfect church or stay or may run the pastor out of town.

It has been said that if you find the perfect church, don't join it; it will no longer be perfect! A good rule for congregants and those in leadership.

Not all detractors are old and seasoned members; some are much younger. My term for these folks is *entrepreneurial idealists.* These people are in the idealistic stage of their life, usually with new careers and young families. They are usually perfectionists, wanting everything to be a certain way, their way, the right way, right away! They have a minimal margin for failure and almost no tolerance for anything that falls short of their standard of quality. You name it; they've got a way to do it that will work, a way they are sure you've never thought of. (God just told them, of course.)

Frankly, these people drove me nuts! They were ever criticizing, rarely commending anything in the church. They were obsessed with having it done differently; thus, better. *'If only we'* was their mantra. Although willing to help with the ministry, they become unhelpful due to their critical attitudes and their adamant position on how things were to be done.

Let me tell you the story of my first run-in with an entrepreneurial idealist. This young man, in seminary at the time, became involved in our church. He had charisma and a charm that was disarming. People were drawn to him; he found followers easily. He had all kinds of ideas as to what the church should be doing. All this was based, of course, on his vast two years of experience. (In the classroom, no less!) It was never said openly, but I always felt that he wanted to be the Lead Pastor, which he became in a subsequent call. Ironically, a call that made a big dent in his idealism.

He and his family visited our home after we had taken another pastorate. After dinner, he said he owed me an apology. In so many words, he confessed that he had probably been a source of frustration to me and asked my forgiveness. It was granted, of course. His idealism had been tempered by the realism of being in the pastorate himself. He was already becoming a better leader because he had learned how to be a better follower.

Let's face it, we may be competent and cooperative and possibly exceptional in some areas, but not everyone will rise up and call us blessed. It has been speculated in a given congregation, one third will love you, one-third will not like you, and one-third won't care. (How heartening!)

In every pastorate, prominent people and church leaders themselves were resistant to authority and unsupportive. I have reflected on the life and ministry of Christ Himself. The common people received Him gladly; the Pharisees killed Him! There are modern-day Pharisees among us still.

However, the Lord taught me in dealing with older and younger detractors to look beyond their fault and see their needs. I came to realize that they had been deeply hurt and wounded. They, in turn, hurt other people.

Part of my call to shepherding required me to be strong enough, tough enough, and secure enough to take difficult people in stride and help them resolve their issues. I might have been the first person who dared to do that! More than once, the Lord reminded me that He put those people in my life and ministry because He knew that I would care for them in the right way. He would teach me new lessons about Him, them, and myself.

To my question, "Why me?" "Why them?" "Why here?" "Why now?" God answered, "Why not?"

A young son about to be disciplined asked his father, "Who

disciplines you?" The wise father responded, "God does. I am accountable to God for the way I take care of you."

Our Heavenly Father holds us accountable for the care of our congregations. There are two reasons: first, because we love the sheep, and secondly, we know we are accountable to the Shepherd who entrusted them to us.

FEED: Christ compelled Peter to feed His sheep in John 21. The feeding of spiritual sheep was also eluded to in several passages of the Old Testament, including Psalms, Jeremiah, and Ezekiel.

To feed congregational sheep means to give them spiritual nourishment dispensed through the preaching and teaching of the Word as well as through exhortation-counseling.

Feeding is defined differently by different people. How many times has a pastor heard this statement? "We aren't attending this or that church anymore because we aren't being fed." I view that statement often as an excuse that allows members not to deal with the real issues. Not being fed, which sounds spiritual, keeps them from being honest about the real reason for their departure.

However, it would indeed be simplistic to indicate that anyone can be fed if they attend a church where the Word is preached. Styles, personalities, and approaches all influence how people hear and learn.

Feeding does require preparation on the part of the pastor. The seminary I attended strongly suggested that 30 hours a week should be spent on sermon preparation. Further, you should block all calls until noon and not be interrupted in the study. It didn't take me long to realize the major priority would be challenging given the demands of a parish and often being the lone preaching pastor. Yet, our primary task as those who are to feed the sheep is to present the Word of God correctly, clearly, and consistently.

120

All the other aspects of ministry hinge on this component. The pastor who honors this priority will see God's blessing on the other ministry elements.

To feed our people is a sacred and solemn task, one for which we as a pastor-teacher are held responsible more than in any other profession. It is to rightly divide the Word of truth, as Paul described it to Timothy. (II Timothy 2:15)

But, feeding is also a matter of participation on the part of the parishioners. People who don't open their Bible all week or don't bring it on Sunday, though some might choose to view it on their Bible App, are often not serious about the Word. Instead, they depend on the preacher to feed them once a week rather than feeding themselves. Many times they are most likely the people saying they're not being fed. (See 'The Pastor as Preacher/Teacher')

MEET THE NEED: Like feeding, meeting the need can be a matter of perspective and opinion. More than one disenchanted church member can opt to change churches because their needs aren't being met.

Early in our first church, a couple threatened to leave the church for several reasons. One was that I was not feeding them. For example, they took issue with my using the word *accountable*, showing emotion in the pulpit, and my negative referencing of people who stayed home on Sunday night preferring to watch Disney instead of attending service. (On that last one, I'll admit my overzealousness in the early years.) Additionally, his wife complained that I had failed to visit her in the hospital, especially at the birth of her first natural-born child; the couple had two other adopted children. They threatened to leave because I failed to meet their need. (Sometimes, these are the unreal expectations foisted on pastoral leadership.) Meeting needs is a complex task!

Meeting the need can range from preaching and teaching to officiating at weddings, speaking for the Ladies Tea, leading the Men's Breakfast Bible Study, giving the invocation at graduation, visiting parishioners in the hospital, doing pre-marital and regular counseling, playing on the softball team, and having people in for dinner. It is pretty much being on call 24/7. Of course, the temptation is for the pastor to try to meet everyone else's need but their own, failing to exercise self-care. (See 'Self-care')

As noted, meeting a congregation's needs is like performing for multiple bosses with divergent expectations. (See 'The Certainty of Call')

Meeting the needs is also a two-way street. People are responsible for using the resources provided to them. The pastoral office is that of being a shepherd of sheep. Yet, the sheep also have a responsibility to God and each other in being led, being fed, and having their needs met.

Here are some guidelines for those called to the task of sheep tending.

The Decalogue of Shepherding: The 10 Commandments of the Pastorate

Thou Shalt Be Godly: Sheep desire that their leader is a person who seeks God and attempts to reflect His character, although imperfectly.

Thou Shalt Be Transparent: Sheep want realness and authenticity in their leaders who consider honesty a strength, not a weakness.

Thou Shalt Be Accessible: Sheep respond to a shepherd who is approachable, who can come alongside them and make them feel comfortable.

Thou Shalt Be Trustworthy: Sheep react better to a shepherd who can be trusted to keep confidences and commitments, return phone calls, show up on time, and follow through on what they promise to do.

Thou Shalt Be Yourself: Sheep follow a shepherd more easily when they don't try to be someone they're not and who can laugh at themselves and enjoy life.

Thou Shalt Be Honest: Sheep respect a shepherd who will level with them in love, hold them accountable, and is open to evaluation and suggestions.

Thou Shalt Be Accountable: Sheep expect their leaders to live by the same standard they set for others, who play by the same rules.

Thou Shalt Be Humble: Sheep identify with shepherds who have a realistic view of their God-given abilities, lift up others instead of themselves, and who can admit mistakes and ask for forgiveness.

Thou Shalt Be Appreciative: Sheep find it easier to work with a shepherd who values them and thanks them for their ministry.

Thou Shalt Be Faithful: Sheep look to their shepherds to carry out their tasks consistently, stay the course when it's hard, be loyal to their spouse and family, and model integrity-balance in their lives.

And one more thing. The eleventh commandment in the pastoral Decalogue is:

Thou Shalt Be Detailed: Keeping track of details is crucial to effective shepherding. At the end of every detail is a person with a need, a comment, suggestion, complaint, or a prayer request. Keeping track of details is not something you learn in seminary; you learn it in the school of experience. People need to be noticed, heard, and paid attention to. We need to be reminded to call them, set up appointments, answer their questions, pray for and with them. Keeping track or losing track of those details may very well make or break your ministry.

I carried a small notebook with me for that very purpose. Writing down a prayer request, an idea, or a number I needed to call was critical. I'm still a notebook guy, but cell phones provide an even more efficient way of doing it. The practice is called the *Ministry of Details.*

Pastor Peter reminds us: "For you were like sheep going astray, but now you have returned to the Shepherd and Overseer of your souls." An overseer pays attention to details. (I Peter 2:25)

The **ultimate calling** of shepherding sheep is one of the most significant in terms of its objectives and outcomes: to save the world, eternally through the Lamb of God, the Supreme Shepherd. We are part of a select few called and chosen by the Chief Shepherd to be under-shepherds in the noblest and most rewarding profession and the highest calling on earth.

Summary: The pastoral call is sourced in the Supreme Shepherd, who laid down life for His sheep. The metaphor of a sheep describes them accurately as requiring an immense amount of care. Christ, the High priest, was taken from among men and experienced immense suffering during His time on earth. This enabled Him to sympathize and empathize with our weaknesses and our needs. What He went thru He learned for two, just as modern-day spiritual shepherds do. As shepherds, we are fellow sheep; we are like ones we have come to help. Shepherding involves leading, feeding, and meeting the flock's needs given to the pastor's charge. Leading is more challenging when authority is resisted and often opposed by those so-called mature believers who have become detractors.

Peril: Failing to lead, feed, and meet the congregation's needs by failing to follow the Chief Shepherd closely and carefully.

Privilege: Following the Chief Shepherd, who provides the ultimate care for the congregation with the help of a healthy and supportive church leadership.

Questions for personal reflection: Chapter 8 The Supremacy of Shepherding

1. What model does the Supreme Shepherd offer to under-shepherds?
2. Why is sacrifice an essential element in pastoring?
3. What does it mean to lead, feed and meet the need of the congregation?
4. Give a synopsis of how to deal with difficult people.

9   The Pastor as Coach

The Care and Maintenance of the Church Staff:
How to Build a Co-ministry Team

In a modern church era, we have come to view the pastor as a coach and the church staff as a team. A coach is less a boss or a president who stands over, but one who comes along-side those they lead.

Traditionally, a leader is often standing above; those led are often seen as standing under. There is a biblical precedent for these terms. To obey, in the language of the New Testament is to listen or stand under. The Lord is the leader, and we obey Him. He is our superior; we are His subordinates.

Though Christ is over people, He is, nonetheless, alongside them. He is both president and coach. His followers are considered sons and daughters, friends, joint-heirs, and associates. (John 15:13-15, Galatians 4:1-7)

Consider this concept from the standpoint of the NBA. The winning coach knows his team, makes suggestions, is down on the floor with them, earns their respect, communicates effectively with them, and appreciates their contribution to the team. The link between a sports team and a church team is evident in all aspects of networking. (See 'The Importance of Networking')

Here are the characteristics of a winning coach:

126

- Comfortable in getting close to players.
- Open to assistance and counsel.
- Knows they do not have all the ideas.
- Earns and sustains respect.
- Learns through defeat.
- Concerned for the personal development of the individual as well as the success of the team.

Coaches respect people and build strong interpersonal relationships with a company of equals, recognizing each with a specific calling and capacity to succeed in the team effort.

Thus, the first requirement of a coach is getting close to their team. You can't regulate the game and the players from the premium box seats. Some pastors, however, find it easier to rule from above rather than to relate alongside. It takes a secure person to get close.

A good coach knows the capacities of their players and helps them to realize their full potential. Coaches recognize that they cannot win the game alone; they recruit individuals who know how to play their respective positions. The coach is there to coach, not play for them.

A good coach affirms and appreciates the team members. They believe their members have worth and value, motivating them to do their best for the coach and the team.

When a pastor employs the coach-team concept, the whole working environment changes. The staff becomes a team. The game becomes a co-ministry. The congregation becomes a co-ministering unit. The game is not winable unless the whole team is involved in winning it! (See 'The Pastor as Vision Caster')

When you *know* you count, you make what you *do* count! And it does. Thus, the team leader determines the morale of the players and the team's ability to win!

Building Rapport with Your Team: Trust vs. Micromanagement

I did not attempt to micromanage my teammates. We hired carefully, so we believed they were competent to carry out their tasks, trusting them to complete their work without constant supervision. I chose to convey confidence in them and their performance, which made a difference in how they viewed themselves and the quality of work they produced.

My largest team was three specialists, one general secretary, one bookkeeper, a senior visitation couple, and two custodians. Each person had a particular area. I made it a point to spend one-on-one time with each employee outside of the weekly staff meeting.

The team environment was cultivated during these times. Personally, I felt that they were necessary, underscored by giving them time, attention, and affirmation. They believed I wanted to know them as people and pastoral teammates. We developed trust and rapport with each other. This work environment made them both better people and better employees.

In business and industry, close relationships are often discouraged and considered unattainable. The closest you get to spending time with your manager is at the annual Christmas party.

But in ministry, the friendship factor is one to be carefully considered. An effective church leader is encouraged to know and get close to the people with whom they co-minister. Yet, there must be an appropriate distance between them.

Let's look at what the friendship factor isn't. It isn't designed to remove all distinctions as to position. The pastor is the
128

administrative lead person; proper respect is yet a requisite between them. However, the team should also be free of cliquishness or elitism.

Let's look at what it is. It is a typical social link between peers who need to be friends with their ministerial cohorts. It represents a commitment to each other's personal and professional growth and provides an environment where people enjoy working and playing together.

There is also a fine line between too much trust and insufficient supervision, resulting in frustrated team members who were not given enough oversight, support, or direction. Ideally, you find the balance between over-management and under-management. Although the staff is not to be micromanaged, they need to be held accountable for setting personal/professional goals and complying with expectations.

We had the annual review based on the team member's self-evaluation followed up by my assessment. But, this annual review was predicated on informal assessment all year long. We didn't store up all the sharing of problems, concerns, or recommendations for the one trip to the principal's office. We came to this time as friends and teammates, not merely as boss and employee. The coach who knows their team and comes alongside them will not depend on an annual report/salary review to understand how the team members are doing. Frequent visits and short accounts work better.

And remember, your staff members are all different and may require an individual approach. However, measurement tools can be used to determine individual and collective characteristics that affect group dynamics and performance. The Myers-Briggs Type Indicator and DiSC Personality profile are excellent assessment tools in determining the temperament, leadership style, response patterns of individuals personally and as team members.

I also did not allow inter-staff conflict to go unchecked. Believing that the pastoral team is a microcosm of the whole congregation, in-house fighting must be dealt with quickly and effectively. Part of the coach's responsibility is to keep the team from becoming adversarial within its ranks. I remember several times when it was necessary to be the coach and the referee to help settle a dispute between teammates.

Sometimes the conflict was between the teammate and the coach! I insisted on resolving disputes expeditiously. The game cannot be won if the team forgets who their real opponent is; it is not each other. The coach reminds the team of the goal and game plan to attain it. Both require mutual respect, unity of spirit, and good sportsmanship.

The church provided continuing education opportunities to help team members remain current in their field and improve personal and professional capacities. If possible, this was included in their salary/benefit package.

Opportunities were provided for our team to be together apart from ministry functions. Certain activities enhanced the building of friendships and having fun as ministry peers. We celebrated birthdays with staff members. They were allowed to pick out the place; teammates signed the card and helped with the tab. We attempted to have socials at various times of the year, usually in homes, often on holidays such as July Fourth. We included spouses who could sometimes feel out of the loop when building close friendships within the church. (See 'Protecting Marriage and Family Life')

Of course, there are always ministerial meetings of various genres allowing team members to get together with other pastors. Such groups within or outside your denomination may include senior and associate pastors, youth, music, Christian Education directors, and office personnel. These connections also provide an opportunity for support, encouragement, and accountability.

Building personal relationships within the pastoral team and with others is based on intentional friendship building. This environment provides spiritual inspiration, mutual support, doing everyday life together.

One thing that fosters this environment is personal attentiveness to what is happening in your team member's life. I remember a couple in our Colorado church that thanked me one year for sending them an anniversary card because they would both have forgotten it if I hadn't.

Developing this relationship with your team in ministry requires such things as stopping by to see how they are doing. (One of our denominational presidents made this a morning ritual with a staff far larger than most churches.) It includes sending notes of affirmation or a phone call on special occasions. I often made posters for my staff, placing them on their door for everyone else to see or a welcome sign for someone returning from a mission trip. It also means ensuring that your staff is taking adequate time off. The pastor and team show an interest in each other's life in and outside of the workplace.

Perhaps most of all, being a friend is being there for another person in their time of real need. Meeting the congregation's needs is part of what pastors do, so it should naturally include their team members.

Since my ministry's early years, my objective has been to be viewed by those I worked with as loving, available, open to input, caring, fair, and fun-loving. You'd have to survey the 49 staff I have coached over 55 years. I hope that despite my humanity and blind spots, I came close to being the right kind of coach. I still pray for them to this day, and I will consider them friends and teammates for life.

The Pastor as Liaison Between Staff and Church Leadership: How to Have Your Teammate's Back

One of the pastor's essential roles is to represent the pastoral team to the church leadership. I consider it as walking another administrative tightrope. It's easy to fall off on one side or the other. For instance, you can give too much or too little support to either staff or church leadership. Such can be problematic.

What does it take to walk the tightrope?

Remaining objective is a priority. It is easier to be on your staff's side because these are the people in the trenches with you every day; the natural inclination is to protect them. Yet, they need to be assessed neutrally. They also need someone who will represent them to the leadership in the best possible light to ensure they will be treated with sensitivity and fairness. The ministry is challenging enough without losing the support of your coach or your church leadership.

It requires immediate follow-up and feed-back. I made it a practice to relay information to the staff as soon as possible after meeting with the church leadership. It is especially important when it deals with attitude and performance issues. No staff person should be left waiting for information; they need to hear it from their pastor-coach first.

However, representing each group to the other does not mean that they should not have direct interaction with each other. In this sense, the pastor becomes a bridge-builder, one who promotes direct dialogue and conciliation. The pastoral representative builds a relationship between the church staff and the church leadership, which engenders mutual respect and cooperative effort.

Board and staff must remember they are on the same team; they are not adversaries; they are allies. The devil likes nothing more than to promote in-fighting between people within rather than fighting the real enemy without!

Following this principle is especially important when a team member is under attack from the congregation. I recall those times in my pastoral career; when a youth pastor was raked over the coals at a congregational meeting, a music pastor was accused of questionable behavior by a parishioner, and a secretary was performing unprofessionally. At times like these, an individual in ministry needs support from their pastors and church leaders. They who are the dispensers of services to others need someone to dispense assistance to them. Coaches protect their team members and attempt to work out the conflict with the church leadership and congregation. To do less puts the entire team and congregation at risk.

When It Doesn't Work Out: Terminating a Teammate

Ever fire someone? Most people wouldn't include that on their bucket list. And if you think it's hard to do in society-at-large, try doing it in a church!

I vividly remember the first person I fired some 45 years ago. The termination involved an older couple (with grown children) who had left a secular job to head up a group home for delinquent boys. They had taken a pay cut and moved on-site. Now we were going to fire them for the inability to meet the objectives of the rehabilitation program. We met, I did it, they were very distraught, angry with me and everyone else and left under protest.

Actually, in my ministry career, I have participated in four firings.

All involved either incompetence, immorality, or incompatibility with people. Firing someone with diplomacy is an art form, one I'm not sure I had perfected.

One of the challenges in dismissing a church staff person is determining the truth and what should be done in the situation. The situation is made more problematic in a religious organization. When a person leaves under healthy conditions, God usually calls them on. When the church dismisses them, there usually isn't another call waiting. Too, you also think a church can resolve any problem itself. After all, if a church doesn't know how to develop people to function effectively, who does? Sometimes it may require the counsel and intervention of a Superintendent or someone outside of the congregation. Firings are never uncomplicated!

This brings up an important point. How far does a ministry manager go before they let someone go?

During my preparation for pastoral ministry, I asked a seasoned pastor what he would do in the situation of having to fire a staff member. His assessment proved to be very helpful. "Never sacrifice the congregation on the altar of an employee." Translation: Don't keep a person on too long if what they are doing is adversely affecting the rest of the congregation.

People can take extreme positions in this process. Every staff person is well-meaning and should be given every opportunity to stay on. no matter what the situation. Or a person who is not performing should simply be fired as any secular employee would be. (This is yet another tightrope in ministry.)

People called to the ministry can fail to function. They may even start well, but things change. Even gifted individuals may find the demands of the job are outside the scope of what they are equipped to do or even enjoy doing. They may find it far more demanding than they thought it would be. Not unlike a marriage, dating, courtship, and engagement may be fun, but the test is doing life together.

Yes, we should be committed to helping our staff develop spiritually and professionally. But the broader charge is to serve the congregation. A word of caution is in order, however. Congregations have earned a reputation for mistreating staff members and letting them go without objective decisions. The dilemma leaves a person confused, resentful and may cause them to leave the ministry permanently.

I have always had a high commitment to the personal development of those around me. I would be more likely to go the extra mile with a team member before escorting them out. But there is a limit. In other terms, when the rate of exchange between what the church is getting and what the individual is giving is not equal, then it's probably time for a change.

There is another important consideration. Letting someone go must be precipitated by helping the person know and, if possible, make the changes necessary in their performance. It is essential to thoroughly document the concerns that ultimately may have led to their termination. Every person deserves to receive the help required to improve, and if there is no improvement, they should know the specifics of why they are not being kept on the staff. These are not unreasonable demands. Yet, the church needs to handle the dismissal with grace and encouragement, giving the person the best reference possible to help them find another place of service.

The process may be arduous. One incident comes to mind relative to the termination of a worship leader who had questionable organizational skills and even less ability with inter-personal relationships. It became evident that this person probably wasn't going to work out. But, making a move to facilitate a change had to be prayerfully and carefully strategized. Part of this decision's delicacy was due to the potential impact on the congregation, which was divided on this issue. Letting him stay seemed safer than letting him go.

The anticipated fall-out with him and with those who loved and idealized his ministry was high risk. Would you believe we waited an entire year? And the outcome? He self-terminated. He finally realized that things weren't working out and decided it was time to go. This situation, however, is the exception, not the rule.

I wish I could tell you that a termination always works out nicely, but I can't. Even the certainty of call and the highest of intentions won't pre-empt someone from failing to perform adequately and having to be let go. Sometimes a lack of competence comes in other forms, either personally or professionally.

The church is not spared from letting people go. Of course, it is presumed that the church will do everything possible to alert the staff member to the problems and resolve them. In so doing, they are called to hold people accountable and responsible for personal maturity and professionalism in the discharge of their calling.

Galatians 6:1,2,4-5 gives us potential guidelines for dealing with a team member who faces termination. "Brothers, if a man be overtaken in a fault, ye who are spiritual, restore such a man in the spirit of meekness, considering yourself, lest you also be tempted. Bear ye one another's burden, and so fulfill the law of Christ. But let every man prove his own work, then shall he have rejoicing in himself alone and not another. For every man shall bear his own burden." (KJV)

What is the pattern? The person struggling in some area of their life and ministry is to be treated with humility and courtesy. Every effort should be made to help them succeed or help them clearly understand why they didn't. A critical component of the procedure is helping the individual to learn from the situation to improve performance in the future.

But breaking up is very hard to do, especially in a church. Yet not to break up at the proper time or do it improperly may well be more formidable. What seems to be more painful and poses a greater risk initially becomes less painful and far less risky later. Letting someone go can provide a teaching moment for them and for the church, which in the long haul produces benefits unseen at the time.

Remember that former music pastor? In the years that followed his self-termination, he came back to see us. He shared with me how he had grown through the experience and thanked us for our patience and support in the process. In essence, his pain had been productive. God provided work and resources for him and his family. He had entered a new profession, construction of all things, where he was happy. He also found out why he often struggled with his interpersonal relationships; and found a new outlet for his musical skills. A challenging and risky decision and accompanying pain had resulted in something useful: a repaired and redirected life. Breaking up in this situation was the right thing to do.

Summary: By its very description, the term coach is a person who involves themselves with their players. It takes secure and mature people to come alongside others. Ideally, the pastor functions more as a coach, one called to care for and maintain a co-pastoral team. Pastors spend time building friendships, demonstrating trust and support for teammates, and encouraging them to use their skills without micromanaging them. The coach also serves as the go-between with the staff and the church congregation and leadership, fostering good communication. The coach has the back of his teammates, representing them well and caring that they are treated fairly, which is even more critical and vital in the termination process.

Peril: Ruling over rather than coming along-side teammates and congregational leaders or diminishing the importance of each person's capacity, underutilizing their contribution to the mission.

Privilege: Creating a positive environment for staff and congregational leaders to work cooperatively to make their ministry succeed.

Questions for personal reflection: Chapter 9 The Pastor as Coach

1. How is a coach different from a president?
2. How do you make staff members teammates?
3. How do you have your teammate's back?
4. What factors need consideration in letting a teammate go?

10   The Pastor as Administrator

Administration as a Ministry:
The Management of God's Work

Meeting the needs of a local congregation alone is like trying to service an entire Walmart store without any other personnel on duty. Even with other church personnel managing the ministry, it can be a full-time challenge for anyone in ministry, especially Lead Pastors.

The Lead Pastor is a General Practitioner, and the rest of the staff are specialists: music, youth or family ministry, visitation, Christian education, etc.

KEY 1: Everyone in the ministry is an administrator; each staff member and church leader administers someone.

A recent development in the church is to hire an administrative/executive pastor. This person is both a general practitioner and a specialist. I would have welcomed such a person in a couple of my larger assignments; I functioned in both roles as lead pastor and pastoral administrator.

Definition: The word administration/administrator is the composite of minister and administer.

There is a biblical basis for the pastoral administrator; it is a natural outgrowth of their role as an undershepherd and spiritual director. Shepherds have sheep to oversee, and coaches have players to mobilize. Pastoral administrators have congregations to administer.

Herein is an intrinsic link between who the pastor *is* and what the pastor does: The spiritual director is also a pastoral administrator.

Churches tend to dichotomize administration from actual pastoral ministry, making them separate rather than synchronized. Pastoral administration is to be coupled with spiritual leadership.

KEY 2: We cannot separate the role of pastoral administrator and spiritual director.

In the Old Testament, we see administrators. Adam was in charge of naming animals. Noah was given the task of the floating zoo project. Moses became a supervisor of 600,000 people coming from Egypt to Canaan. Daniel became a Babylonian CEO over his jurisdiction, one-third of the kingdom. These are prototypical of pastoral administrators.

In the New Testament, Christ Himself is the administrator of 12 employees. In his second letter to the Corinthians, Paul identifies his daily stress; the care and administration of all the churches.

There are tension points connected with pastoral administration. Pastors wind up spending too much time doing it. They often lose sight of doing it as a ministry, thus losing sight of the ministry's purpose.

American pastors often occupy areas labeled *The Office*. In other parts of the world, those areas are usually identified as *The Study*. This difference in designations offers us a clue as to the administrative dilemma many US clergy face. Too often, the administration appears to be separated from giving spiritual direction.

KEY 3: The pastoral administrator can spend too much time administrating and too little time providing spiritual direction.

The pastoral administrator deals primarily with staff supervision, the mobilization of the congregation, and church leadership oversight.

Pastoral administration takes place in an environment that includes organization, direction, motivation, and support. These qualities are cultivated by both spiritual direction and pastoral administration. A balance needs to be maintained between the spiritual and organizational aspects of the task.

KEY 4: Pastoral administration can make the church more like a business than a spiritual organism.

An effective pastoral administrator focuses on three things:

- Using authority and power wisely, respecting the people they lead.
- Learning to delegate authority and responsibility for ministry to others.
- Equipping the congregation to be excited about, enlisted, and engaged in ministry.

The Definition and Place of Authority: The Prerequisite of Trust and Respect

The person who functions as an administrator is given the authority and power to perform it. Authority is a capacity given to us; power is defined as how we use it. Even in the church, absolute power corrupts absolutely. Leaders may forget where power and authority originate and how they are to be utilized. There is nothing intrinsically wrong with these twin capacities; they only become perverted when misused. Failure to use authority and power wisely inculcates mistrust and disrespect.

Christ gives unambiguous teaching about these things in the New Testament. In Matthew 28:18, He says. "All *authority* in heaven and on earth has been given to me." In John 19:11, He reminds Pilate, "You would have no *power* over me unless it were given you from above."

In Mark 10:43-45, Christ models how human leaders are to serve as administrators. An effective pastoral administrator recognizes that their capacity to lead and administer is given by God to be used to the glory of God. "Whoever wants to become great among you must be your servant. And whoever wants to be first must be slave to all. For even the Son of Man did not come to be served, but to serve and give His life a ransom for many."

History is rife with instances of men and women in church leadership, both clergy and laity, who have misunderstood this basic principle.

The result? People who think they have earned their position pride themselves in their status and misuse it by lording it over other people instead of serving them. (One only has to think of Jim Jones, David Koresh, and Jimmy Baker.)

The Psalmist in 75:6 reminds us that "Promotion does not come from the east or the west, but God puts down one and puts up another." No one from the President of the United States to the CEO of Starbucks would be in their position unless God allows it.

Peter reminds young leaders, "Be shepherds of God's flock that is under your care, serving as overseers, taking the oversight not because you must, but because you are willing, not greedy for money, but eager to serve, not lording it over those entrusted to you, being examples to the flock." (I Peter 5:2-3)

I have known pastors, staff, and church leaders who distorted how they viewed their authority. Resultantly, their leadership undermined the welfare of the congregation itself. (See 'The Supremacy of Shepherding')

KEY 5: Wise pastor-administrators must earn trust and respect from the people they lead, which results in effective spiritual leadership and administration of God's mission.

Learning to Delegate: Giving Up to Get Ahead

We live in a world where everyone wants to beat out the competition. We are trained to think competitively from our earliest years. We take the principles from T-ball and transfer them to the board room. But it is to be different in the parish. Giving up rather than getting ahead should be the norm in the life of the pastor and church leadership.

Christ demonstrates this principle as summarized in Philippians 2:7-10. "But He emptied Himself taking the form of a slave, being born in human likeness and being found in a human form, He humbled Himself and became obedient unto death, even the death on a cross. Therefore, God also highly exalted Him and gave Him the name that is above every name so that at the name of Jesus, every knee should bend in heaven and on earth and under the earth."

Note the elements of His example. Christ was secure enough to give up authority for people. He did not cling to it for security and fulfillment; He became fulfilled in sacrificing on behalf of the needs of others. His ultimate needs were met when He sacrificed His life to bring salvation. He understood delayed gratification. He gave up what He wanted, to provide what people needed; salvation through redemption.

In a conversation with my uncle, who was a pastor, he recounted, "Well, the church never really took off, but then I came here largely for the insurance benefits so I could retire here." As I reflect on that statement now, it impresses me that my uncle had misplaced priorities, which affected the church's growth. Thus, the pastor is called to get ahead by giving up, which occurs when the congregation's spiritual leader is willing to put the needs of those they serve ahead of their own.

Using authority rightfully by entrusting the work of ministry to others is both logical and practical. It relieves the pastor from having to do it all; it allows others to share in the task.

The do-it-yourself style of administration aligns with what a tourist visiting our country observed about professional football. "It looks like ninety thousand people desperately needing exercise are watching 22 people desperately needing rest." Too often, the pastor is trying to be the whole team while everyone else is watching in the stands.

The Scriptures teach us about administration being a shared responsibility. In Exodus 18:18, we learn from Jethro's advice to Moses, his son-in-law, the head judge of all hard cases. In his terms, "What you are doing is not good. You will surely wear yourself out, both you and these people with you. The task is too heavy for you; you cannot do it alone." Moses was playing all the team positions, and the people were waiting in long lines to be served. In our terms, "Man, you're going to stress out and burn out; give yourself some slack and let other people carry their weight." Moses was wise. He took the advice, changed his administrative style, and delegated the task. He allowed others to share in the task of the mission.

In the New Testament, the apostles learned about delegation the hard way. In Acts 6, there is a crisis in the congregation. The Word, the spiritual bread of life, was broken, but the physical bread was not distributed correctly. The natural tendency would have been for the apostles, the deacon board of their time, to take on more responsibility rather than delegating it. But they learned to live out the principle; work smarter, not harder. They made sure they didn't allow the primary task to be sacrificed for the secondary ones. In so doing, they protected their role as spiritual directors and pastoral administrators, teaching and preaching the Word of God while allowing others in the church to do the physical tasks of being a first-century Meals on Wheels.

They were natural leaders, goal-directed, and high-performance guys. They had a propensity for perfectionism and demanding their way. They could have been uncomfortable giving the task to someone else, risking the ministry not being done the right way, or not getting credit for it.

Christ again teaches us this lesson. He entrusts His work to 12 neophytes, fresh from such professions as fishing and tax-collecting, who failed their final exams after their three-year course of instruction. If anyone could have insisted on having things done His way, it would have been the perfect Son of God!

Partway through my first pastorate, one of the seasoned leaders took me aside and said, "Roland, God did not intend for you to do this job by yourself. You need to equip others to do it." My response: "That will take too long, and they won't do things the way I want them done!" I slowly realized a key concept: I needed people to help with pastoral administration in order to fulfill my primary role as a spiritual director. It was a lesson learned by my predecessors, Moses and the Disciples.

Here's the catch. It seems more manageable at the beginning to do it yourself rather than to delegate. But in the long run, it's harder. The leader winds up with too much work, and those they lead wind up with too little. It's like a coach trying to play all the team positions at once while the team watches! If you want to do it all yourself, people will let you.

KEY 6: Those in the role of pastoral administration unite the leadership and congregation to carry out the ministry.

Engaging the Volunteer:
Exciting, Enlisting and Equipping the Laity

The greatest natural resource in the local church is its people, often the most unused commodity. The concept of the volunteer is a biblical one.

I Chronicles 28:21, "The divisions of the priests and Levites are ready for all the work on the temple of God, and every willing man skilled in any craft will help you in all the work. The officials and all the people will obey your command."

The principle of using the people of God to do the work of God existed before the Church came into being.

I believe that every congregation has all the people it needs to accomplish its task. It doesn't always look that way. Sometimes, it seems like you have way too many music people and not enough teachers. Or, too many cooks (Is that even possible?) and not one mechanic or doctor in the whole bunch. In our different congregations, there appeared to be either a surplus or a deficit problem. But in time, God brought all that particular church needed.

Engaging volunteers implies the following:
- People knowing their spiritual and practical capacities.
- A clear vision of what the ministry is to accomplish and a plan to make it happen.
- Someone who believes in them enough to ask them to participate.
- Training along-side someone else with similar capacities.
- Term limits.
- Appreciation.

Spiritual Capacities:

Every believer in Christ is gifted. The portions of I Corinthians 12, Romans 12, Ephesians 4, and I Peter 4 substantiate this truth.

The four major areas of giftedness are:

Speaking Gifts   (Preaching, Teaching, Exhortation)

Serving Gifts   (Working the soundboard, Cooking)

Sign Gifts   (Prophesying, Speaking in tongues, Healing)

Special Gifts   (Celibacy, Martyrdom)

All gifts, though different, are equal; one is not more important than another. Since the first appearance of the tongue gift on the day of Pentecost, this gift has been made superior to the others. This distorted theology has caused misunderstanding, division, and competition in the church. God gives spiritual gifts to unify and edify the Body of Christ. "There are different kinds of gifts, but the same Spirit. Different kinds of service but the same Lord. Now to each one the manifestation of the Spirit is given for the common good." (I Corinthians 12:4,5,7)

Each believer has at least one and often several gifts. Each plays a role in completing the mission of the church.

This truth was underscored at a humorous moment in my pastoral life when the church was building an educational wing. I decided to check on the project to offer a word of encouragement to the crew. In the course of my inspection, I accidentally stepped through a piece of sheetrock. The project manager politely said, "Pastor, you work on the praying and preparing sermons, and we will take care of the building project!" (There is an actual piece of sheetrock that says: Pastor Rol stepped here!)

This incident also confirms that many ministry capacities are not listed in the Scriptural gift lists but are just as important. (Playing an instrument, woodworking, sign language, teaching aerobics, building an education wing.)

I catalog them as **T**(alents), **A**(bilities), and **G**(ifts). Each is given a divine endowment, a unique capacity for which they are held accountable.

For example, let somebody who loves to fix bikes join other bike lovers in a non-conventional ministry using a talent not included in the biblical gift list. This way, everyone gets a chance to use their capacity to service the whole church. (Talk about enjoying the cycles of life together!)

Paul uses the word picture of a hungry person to illustrate this concept. The mind tells the stomach they are hungry. The hand is then informed to pick up an apple and move it toward the mouth. However, upon arriving there, the mouth refuses to open, stating it is tired of talking and chewing all the time and being over-worked compared to the rest of the body. The dilemma causes the body to go without food and ultimately die, unable to reproduce itself.

Compare that to a spiritual body. People refuse to work with the other members in achieving what is best for the rest of the church, which is impaired by not fulfilling its potential, i.e., to reproduce itself through new believers.

A Vision: The congregation needs to know the overall outcome of the purpose and mission and how they can make it happen. When people see the vision, they will want to be a part of making it a reality. They are often eager to be used in something that excites them, allowing them to look beyond the immediate and make an eternal investment. (See 'The Pastor as Vision Caster')

148

Recruitment: People want to become participants in the mission, but they often lack confidence. They don't think they have what it takes to get the job done. This stems partly from not understanding what their spiritual gift and practical capacities are! One tool that is extremely helpful in identifying the gifts and capacities in a local church is called S.H.A.P.E. (Spiritual Gifts, Heart, Abilities, Personality, Experiences). This assessment can be completed as an individual or in a group setting in as little as 30 minutes.

In an ideal world, a bulletin or live announcement would elicit 20 people clamoring to teach the Jr High Sunday school class. (Imagine!) But it takes more than that.

Often people are just waiting to be asked. They haven't told you; they somehow expect you to know. And though they still may turn you down, they appreciate you considering them. Your confidence in them may constitute their call. And how do you know who you should recruit? (The S.H.A.P.E. inventory will help you.)

I have been amazed over the years when a Nominating Committee starts their assignment with few or no potential candidates. Then, lo and behold, some name floats to the top no one would have thought of; often, they say yes!

Recruitment could be through the venues of:

- Annual Ministry Fairs
- Testimonies in worship services
- On-site videos of ministry events

In short, we often have no idea as to what our congregation can actually do to make a difference!

Training: Sometimes, people don't know how to do the advertised job. Yes, I know. How many years does a person need to be edified before engaging in a ministry? (2,000 sermons, 41 Bible Studies, 25 church seminars, and still find no place of service?)

One of the best ways to prepare someone for this calling is to make them an under-study or trainee along-side a more experienced person.

People who have been gifted in a specific area are usually more inclined to do a particular task; it prevents putting a round peg in a square hole. Often a person's gift is confirmed by their using it. The best success is using a person in their gift area, doing something they love, and having it confirmed by others.

Term Limits: Every position should have a set period of service. The individual should not be in the role indefinitely. For the average Christian who volunteers in our churches today, the long-term is problematic. It is a sensible use of time and energy, and it allows the person to be a part of worship, Sunday school, and perhaps plug into other areas of the ministry. In a large church, it gives more people a chance to serve.

Appreciation: Find ways to let your people know that what they are doing is essential and that you are grateful for what they do. A word of thanks keeps volunteers from feeling taken for granted and incentivizes them to keep on doing a quality job in their ministry area.

A former associate made it clear that he disliked that I constantly thanked people in the church. He perceived it as unnecessary and artificial. I remember telling him, "You can't over-appreciate your people." And then, I thanked him for sharing his perspective!

I have always considered volunteers as free help with two jobs. These generous people give of themselves along-side their first vocation. We are indeed fortunate to have them; they are invaluable to the work of the ministry. That's why we need to use them carefully and thank them regularly.

There are several ways to thank your volunteers: Include a Worker of the Week under the bulletin praise section; host a Volunteer Recognition Sunday, annual Appreciation Banquet, or a Weekend Retreat. (With a Sunday off!)

KEY 7: Pastoral administrators help people discover and utilize their gifts and capacities by exciting, enlisting, and equipping them to assist in the work of the ministry.

The Concept of Co-Ministry: The Professional and the Pew

Historically, the church had made the clergy superior to the laity. In the scriptures, this is known as Nicolaitanism. The term literally translated: Victory over the laity. The clergy looked down on people and did not consider their gifts of value in the ministry of the church.

This position implies that people are a means to an end because they are of lesser value and importance. Thus, their capacities and contributions are minimized, underutilized, and unappreciated.

Scripture teaches that members of the Church, the Body of Christ, are called and equipped to serve the cause of Christ. It is a principle that is objectified in the annuls of the early Church.

Paul underscores this principle in his letter to the Ephesians. "Speaking the truth in love; we will in all things, grow up into Him who is the Head, that is, Christ. From Him, the whole Body joined and held together by every supporting ligament, grows and builds itself in love as each part does its work." (Ephesians 4:15-16)

Church leaders can view themselves as superior to the congregation; they believe that only professionals can carry out the work of the ministry.

Congregants can consider themselves Christian taxpayers who hire and pay professionals to do ministry. They are spectators who watch the pastoral team perform and rate their performance. (The Christian version of the Olympics?)

Our second church became one in which the great Co-mission was acted out through Co-ministry. It was the union of Pastor and people.

At our farewell, there was this huge sign that read: Love, from your Co-ministers. The people had come to understand the concept. It was one that worked. The concept of Co-ministry is biblical. As noted, the work of God throughout scripture implies cooperativeness.

In the Old Testament, it's evident that Moses didn't get the people out of Egypt without captains who rallied the people to occupy Canaan. Joshua didn't conquer it without uniting and assigning the troops to take possession of the land. Nehemiah didn't re-establish Jerusalem without delegating the former Babylonian captives to rebuild the walls and the temple.

The New Testament underscores the Co-ministering Church Body. The Book of Acts and the Epistles give numerous examples of the leaders and the followers carrying out the church mission cooperatively. The church did not function with an apostle or pastor running the whole show; many cast members were in the on-going production.

This idea has practical ramifications. The function of the church and the team is one of mutuality and cooperativeness. Pastors and people are meant to be team-mates in ministry and mission.

One of the immediate dividends of letting the laity loose is building their spiritual life as they work and minister together.

There was a group of young men we discipled during our campus ministry days. They were known as the Timothy Team. On one particular weekend, we built a building to be used for a summer camp later on that year. What I remember most were the bonds that were strengthened between us while building a latrine. Training and team-building were by-products of our being together, and laboring together was our common mission.

A mission becomes a residual of doing life while going into our daily world. It is living out the Great Commandment and fulfilling the Great Commission. I have a deep appreciation for the many fine men and women who have come alongside me in the common task. These leaders were ordained by God and confirmed by His people to give leadership to His Church. As volunteers, they rendered a significant service to the pastor and people.

One of the aspects of working together as pastoral professionals and those in the pew was congregational meetings and church governance. These are some of the things that were helpful to me.

- I let my leaders lead the Board and Congregational Meetings. (They were put in leadership positions, I utilized them!)
- I preferred shorter meetings. (They were long, but at least I didn't have to lead them!)
- I informed my leadership of where I stood on issues before meetings, thus reducing my contribution at the meetings. I led in prayer, of course, often before, during, and afterward. (I encouraged heads of committees and boards to have a season of prayer before every meeting.)
- I encouraged people to register complaints or criticisms before or after the meeting and resolve interpersonal issues privately. (To minimize unhealthy confrontation and detract from a productive meeting.)

- I learned I should always protect my staff and encourage leaders and congregations to do the same. (I failed at this several times by remaining silent!)
- I promoted a peaceful and conciliatory spirit within the congregation. (To prevent war between members, a form of a spiritual autoimmune disease!)
- I re-enforced the concept of the church being informed of and involved in the decision-making process. (This is fundamental to exciting, enlisting, and equipping them in ministry!)

A large church in Fresno, California, had a ten-minute Annual Meeting, at which time the pastors and the leadership simply announced what the plan and the budget were for the next year; the people voted, the meeting was over. (Sounds good if you can get away with it!) There was no doubt a great deal of congregational information and trust-building which preceded that meeting. It indeed reduced tension and potential discord, but it also risked detachment and the loss of congregational involvement in the process.

Another church I attended had no congregational meetings; the pastor and the elders made all the decisions; the information was published in the annual report. Ideally, it should be a both/and; not an either/or proposition when it comes to decision-making in the church.

With a few exceptions, I have survived church board meetings and had peaceful congregational business meetings. I have two remembrances, however.

In a one-hundred-year-old church, the board was pretty much a dynasty; people simply went off and came back on the board. The elder board was restricted to six leaders, all men, and the pastor. The board members were more often than not governed by traditions that tended to make them reticent to change and

154

resistant to risk-taking. I dreaded and endured those meetings. Their attitudes were reflected in congregational meetings that were often combative and promoted disunity.

In another assignment, I looked forward to and enjoyed these meetings. The council was fluid and made up of new people, some of whom had not had a position before the election; they were young but fresh, as was the 15-year-old church. It included women who brought intuition and perceptiveness to the system but also lightened things up! The leadership was single-minded; they remembered the real reason they were there and were willing to allow God to do things differently than in the past. These meetings were fun but no less productive. They were marked by laughter and decisions facilitated by unity of purpose and direction. (I actually grew to like them!)

Co-ministry then includes those we are called to lead; the staff, the church leadership, and the congregation. It is a pattern given to us by the Master Pastor-Administrator, Christ Himself. He recruited and equipped others to carry out the great Co-mission, each being called and endowed with gifts to make it succeed. He energized them with a vision for the ministry and created an excitement that motivated their involvement, which will be the focus of the next chapter.

I learned this truth in real life from a dairy farmer before entering the pastorate. During my years as a campus ministry coordinator in Portland, Oregon, I was assigned to direct the July Fourth Pageant.

In my first week on the set, I observed the arena filled with antique cars, animals of all varieties; livestock, pigs, and all the things that go with them. The staff uniform bore the Alpenrose Dairy name, neatly monogrammed on them. But one of the staff stood out. He tackled his tasks with unusual vigor and energy. He worked harder and moved faster than anyone in the sawdust arena.

Finally, I asked someone who is THAT guy? I was amazed at the answer: The owner of the dairy!

Carl Cadanou taught me a lesson that day that would permanently impact my ministry. Use your authority wisely. Never ask anyone to do anything you aren't willing to do. Never forget the power of example or minimize the importance of uniting your people with a common cause.

This humble dairy owner excited, enlisted, and equipped his people to walk through manure and wrangle wayward cattle to pull off the production that ministered to an entire community of people for many years. Christ was a first-century Carl Cadanou. Christ became one of us and came alongside us as a servant-leader to share in the Co-mission of reaching a wayward world.

Summary: Many people think that the church should be run like a business; others believe it should be nothing like a business, but only a spiritual organism. The church can become too much like a business and less of a spiritual entity. The administrative pastor supervises the staff, mobilizes the congregation, and coordinates the church leadership. Lead pastors will often be involved in some administrative tasks, especially in a smaller church with less staff. The pastoral administer is challenged first to be a spiritual director who uses their authority and power wisely and builds trust and respect with those they administer. This encourages the people in the pew to come along-side the professionals in the varied dimensions of church life to carry out the Great Co-mission through the Co-ministering Church Body.

Peril: Substituting organizational leadership for spiritual direction, misusing authority, and failing to excite, equip, and engage the congregation to make Co-ministry a reality.

Privilege: Motivating and equipping the congregation to be a part of and celebrate the actualization of the Co-mission.

Questions for personal reflection: Chapter 10 The Pastor as Administrator

1. What is the link between ministry and administration?
2. Why is the proper use of authority and power essential in these roles?
3. Identify creative ways to develop and carry out the concept of Co-ministry.
4. What are the benefits of enlisting volunteers in the work of the Co-mission?

11 The Pastor as Vision Caster

The Vitalness of the Vision:
The Coach and the Game Plan

Let's start with Proverbs 29:18, "Without a vision, the people run wild, but one who follows instruction will be happy." (The Spurgeon Study Bible) The original Old Testament text declared the vision to be God's law, without which the people of God would lack direction in living successfully. But the principle also applies to the church today. When there is no vision and plan for His ministry, the congregation is directionless. When people don't know where they are going, it will eventually deplete their energies and render them unproductive. They are not directed but diffused and confused.

Most church leaders assume that everyone knows what the vision of the church is. When we rattle off the great commandment and the great commission, we think we have it covered. In reality, everyone has their own idea of what the vision should be and how it should be realized. God calls the pastor to *discern* and *declare* God's vision for that church.

One of the fundamental realities in the vision casting process is knowing that the sovereign God has a unique plan for each church. He has a *general design* and strategy for the Church to fulfill the Great Commandment and the Great Commission, but He also has a *specific plan* for the local church. Catch the key

158

concept. God didn't make a one-size-fits-all when it comes to the church and its ministry.

However, the tendency is to listen to and follow what other people are trying to tell us and sell us instead of discovering God's direction for our congregation. In modern-day Christendom, we want quick, slick answers. So, we attend the latest workshop or sign up online for the next church webinar, always searching for the next and newest idea. It is one we're sure will work at our church because it has been used somewhere else. (Usually a big, successful church!)

To cast a vision is to dream with God and know what design He has in mind for your congregation. If you can't cast it, you can't plan it!

Looking to Him instead of to others takes off a lot of the pressure. We can determine what His vision-plan is for our ministry without competing with or duplicating someone else's success. In reality, the only thing we have to compete with is God's standard of expectation. Each of us is unique. His ideal for us is not to become just like someone else.

We can learn from each other, adapt different ways of doing things or improve the way we operate. Yet, seeking resources by which to implement the plan is not intended to replace the plan itself.

Martin Luther didn't have the Better Book and Bible Center or Andy Stanley's latest book or online resources, and he turned out pretty well. Would he have used them? Probably. But remember, no one came up with the *95 Theses*; they were his vision and strategic plan for the church. He didn't borrow that idea from the Catholic Church; after all, it was one he didn't even like, much less, want to duplicate!

It's safe to assume that God's vision and strategic plan are unique to the church you lead. He is willing to let you in on it if you're interested enough to ask Him. And by the way, you don't determine the vision-plan only one time. I reviewed it with my leadership annually.

A pastor friend of mine related his personal story about casting vision. He took the call to a small country church in Washington State. He proceeded with a vision he felt was from the Lord. The church grew. But after the first year, he was presented with a letter from the church informing him that one-third of the church wanted him to resign. Instead, he went to each of the members, said he wouldn't resign, and prayed with them for God's vision. 100% of the congregation approved of his leadership. He said, "*Listening and prayer* were the keys!"

The Environment of Enthusiasm:
Helping People Catch the Vision

Many pastors do not realize that their primary arena for casting vision is the pulpit. Casting vision from the pulpit has to do with the pastor's attitude and mindset. More is caught than taught when it comes to declaring direction. People can tell if a leader is excited about the church's mission. Most people in the congregation are there to sense the Spirit's direction not only on Sundays, but beyond.

The leader of the church is the point person for dreaming. Their communication with God is the basis for the vision *cast* by the leadership and *caught* by the congregation. When there is a vision, the people are inspired to commit to a direction they are excited to pursue. Too often in a church, there is no vision or plan to carry it out.

I am currently part of a church fellowship where two things happen every week. Our pastor highlights reaching the lost and invites those without Christ to come to the altar after every service.

The deacons of the church assist in helping those who inquire.

The first item in the weekly prayer guide is salvation for the lost. The pastor and the congregation expect lost people to be found, to find salvation through Christ!

Each church needs a large banner behind the pulpit that reads:

KEEP THE MAIN THING THE MAIN THING!

The main thing is the mission of the church, as visualized by the vision statement.

Church activities, visiting in parishioner's homes, and special events also provide the arenas for vision casting. Pastors and Church leaders initiate, and people pick up on the vision in regular conversations and interchanges.

As the gatekeeper, the pastor is the vision caster who continuously creates an aura of expectation and excitement for the ministry. They provide holy contagion; I like to call it Christian chickenpox. The pastor makes sure everybody catches it.

A biblical example serves us well here. Caleb and Joshua headed up a search party to spy out the promised land. Three things characterized their report, which highlighted the vision and the plan to carry it out!

- They were excited about taking the land.
- They had confidence they could overcome the obstacles that they faced in taking it.
- They believed the God who had revealed the plan to them could help them carry it out.

It is essential to have a vision, cast a vision, and engage people in working it out practically.

The Place of Strategic Planning: Blending of Faith and Sight

After listening as a collective leadership in our churches, we attempted to externalize what God had conveyed to us. The ideas of vision must be translated into the reality of a plan. Planning provides the context and strategy for working it out.

Pastoral leadership is called to cast vision and create an implementation plan. A vision must be both a concept and a project. The God who gives the vision is the very one who ultimately helps us carry it out through a plan. He works through a divine cooperative of His power and our participation. Vision + priority + passion + participation = plan fulfilled.

Yet, many church leaders and church members have grown up being told to walk by faith, not by sight. But when it comes to working out the vision, it can translate to we don't need to plan. Why? They believe planning is of the flesh; it preempts the Lord from having His way. More often than not, that may also translate we want it done the old way. This mindset can simply be an excuse for not changing, risking, or stretching beyond ourselves and our comfort zones. Resultantly, we miss the promise of all the Lord has for us.

After all, the same people who are affronted by planning as an act of non-faith are the same people who save for their kid's college education, put money aside for a tropical cruise, and plan for their retirement.

Planning does not pre-empt faith. To plan is to act on our faith. (Our Part). We place our faith and trust in a God who enables us to make it a reality. (His Part). When we don't plan because we lack faith, we limit what He can do. We plan by faith; He rewards by sight. Contrary to our culture, believing is seeing.

Isn't it funny that people who claim to follow Christ to have victory over all obstacles on Sunday can't remember the hymn *Faith is the Victory* at the budget meeting on Monday?

We exercise faith every day. We drive over a bridge and don't know the architect; we travel on a plane and don't see the pilot; we eat in a restaurant and don't meet the cook. Yet we don't believe in a God we do know who has proven Himself to us.

A strategic plan can be defined metaphorically as a blueprint, a road map, and a game strategy. It helps us get where we need to be going and succeed in our undertaking. Such a plan is strategic.

I would like to suggest a paradigm for such a plan, inclusive of the following components.

Purpose: This answers the question, **Why?** What is the reason this organization exists?

Samples: "To care for each other so we can reach the world." "A Heart for God, each other, and the world." Another example is Willow Creek's now-famous purpose statement: "To turn irreligious people into entirely devoted followers of Jesus Christ."

Years ago, I spotted the T.C.B.Y. purpose statement. (This Country's Best Yogurt) I thought to myself, that does it; if the yogurt store has a purpose statement, our church can. And it did soon after. In the churches we've served, we had the vision/mission/purpose statement made visible in several ways. We printed it on small signs around the church, and cards people could hand out in the community, and banners behind the pulpit. It often stimulated conversation with people in the broader community.

Objective: This answers the question, **What?** What are the main things this organization desires to achieve? These can also be called Core Values, the central beliefs that direct the course of the mission. They are general statements that identify what is vital to realizing the purpose.

Sample: To provide lifelong educational opportunities for adults and children.

Goal: This answers the question, **How/Who/When?** What are the means by which the objectives will be realized? Who will be responsible for them? What is the timeline for completion?

The difference between an objective and a goal is this: An objective is general without specifics. The goal is specific and includes the essentials of the method, people, and timeline. More importantly, the goals can be assessed and measured.

Let's put the three elements of the strategic plan together:

Purpose: To care for each other so that we can reach the world. **(Why)**

Objective: To Provide life-long Christian education opportunities for adults and children. **(What)**

Goals: To begin a Home School Training Program. **(How)** Under the Children's Commission. **(Who)** Completed by the Spring of 2020. **(When)**

This is planning on purpose. Often, the objectives and goals are assigned to specific boards, committees, or other individuals in the church. They collaborate to share personnel, resources, and finances necessary to complete the projects. The goals should be prioritized within a given year; this enables leadership to be accountable for working out the plan.

The strategic plan makes several significant contributions to the life of the congregation.

It helps people keep the main thing the main thing. It is too easy for churches to be distracted by lesser things.

It helps people become engaged in the ministry. If people know the plan, they can get excited about it and are more likely to get involved using their gift, talent, and ability to help! People need to be challenged and utilized to invest in something bigger than themselves.

It helps leadership stay accountable for working out objectives and goals. At the annual meeting, leaders can review the things they have accomplished and the things yet projected to be completed.

It helps the congregation get excited about what is happening, and they tell other people about it. "Hey, we built a playground for an apartment community that had no outdoor play area!" This is a church that people in the community want to plug into.

Scriptures illustrate how a vision and strategic plan help a congregation fulfill God's mission for the Church.

One of my favorite biblical examples of this principle is found in Acts 1:14. "They all joined together constantly in prayer." This prayer meeting took place shortly after Jesus left the earth on the Eve of Pentecost, the birthday of the Church. One hundred and twenty people were focused on one thing: birthing the Church. Prayer gave birth to the vision.

I have tried viewing this event through a contemporary parishioner's eyes. "Oh, the old tired few are here for the prayer meeting. It's the same ol', same 'ol. I wonder if Mary M. is going to dominate the whole time talking about her past...again, or if Thomas will go off on his weekly critique of Peter's sermon. And you know we need to paint this room; I hate the color; it's been this way since before Jesus came. And those silk plants; They've even wilted. And let's hope Andrew and John don't bring the same

Pizza with that flat Matzah crust like they did last week!" This is often the picture of the modern church lacking purpose and thus distracted from its central mission.

Although the church needs a vision and a strategic plan to carry it out, not everyone will agree on how that is to be accomplished. It is the fiery darts of distraction and dissension that keep people from being united. The devil knows how to divide and conquer to get us fighting each other rather than reaching the world. The gates of hell may not destroy the church, but distraction can come pretty darn near! The enemy will use anything to keep us from doing what we're supposed to be doing. And we let him do it! (See 'The Pastor as Warrior')

Something else about a strategic plan is essential: The same God who gives us a vision-plan for His work is the same God who has a right to change it. We always need to allow God, the Holy Spirit, to change the plan; the blueprint is only a guide, not the Decalogue. The only thing God carved into stone is the Ten Commandments. Everything else is subject to change.

The year was 1999. Our church and leadership had waited on the Lord, surveyed the congregation, and formulated a new strategic plan. God gave us one more part of the vision to add to the plan. Two families in our church had contacted a ministry in Mexico. We sent out a team to Reynosa for the first time. The first project was to renovate an old deserted hotel into a convalescent center. God wanted our church to do something we had never done before. This changed the focus and the ministry of the church permanently.

The Right to Risk: Adventures in Possibilities

Perhaps, you've heard the seven last words of the church, "We've never done it that way before!"

A failure to keep the *main thing the main thing* or formulate a plan is a deterrent to completing the vision in the local church.

You can have those things in place and stifle your mission by failing to think outside the box. The failure to risk can keep a church from moving past fixed parameters. We can't put new wine into old wineskins. Many ministries are plagued by paralysis, the inability to move beyond maintenance. It seems easier to stay in place than to move forward. But this distorted thinking is another product of deception.

Think for a minute how Moses and the children of Israel felt about leaving Egypt. Even though life there wasn't Nirvana, it was familiar, and the promised land wasn't. The people of God needed to leave the past behind and move into a new present. It was a faith risk.

It was risky for the leaders, too. These men, Moses, Aaron, and the Board of Elders, had to sell the people on the vision and mobilize them to follow the action plan and make it a reality. They kept in mind the main thing: to get out of Egypt and into the Promised Land. If leaders and people hadn't risked, they would never have made it there, even though failure to risk initially made them arrive 40 years late! Someone asked, what if Moses had used a GPS to make the trip? It would have recalibrated over and over. "Continue on Wilderness Avenue for 40 years and then turn left!" So they departed, but it wasn't long before the old looked good. The discontented Israelites longed for leeks, and they cursed their leaders for leading them to this new place.

The willingness to risk and change isn't for cowards, weak-hearted Christians, and modern-day Israelites. Besides not wanting to change, we fear failing in going where we haven't gone before; Egypt is comfy, Canaan is challenging.

Faith and courage are prerequisites in fulfilling the plan for the mission. Thomas Edison knew a bit about a vision and a plan to make electricity a reality. Edison knew about working hard while waiting for an idea he believed would happen. It took him over 1,000 tries to produce the electric light bulb. (To which Mrs. Edison retorted, "Tom, turn the light off and come to bed!")

Suppose your purpose/objective statement embodies the idea of reaching the community. It might mean that we open our doors to afterschool latchkey kids or get involved with a group of developmentally challenged residents in a care facility who might start coming to our church. Well, of course, we're committed to outreach, but not if it involves what inconveniences us, disrupts our comfort zones, or rearranges our familiar peer networks. Helping people clean up their lives may involve getting dirty; the ministry is messy! It's not hard if you keep the church's real purpose in mind.

When people keep the main thing, the main thing, they see the bigger picture of what the church is striving to do to realize its purpose. We may need to learn to adapt to people who would rather come to a concert in the park than come to a service in a church building. We need to accept that people needing to be reached may dress and act differently.

Let's look at another portrait of the Pentecost Church in Acts 2:46-47. "Everyday they continued to meet together in the Temple courts. They broke bread in their homes and ate together with glad and sincere hearts, praising God and enjoying the favor of all people. And the Lord added to their number daily those who were being saved." Here we can see the church's dual function: to care for its own, within, and to extend care to those who are outside.

Often we focus on the needs of the church. We build bigger buildings, have a larger staff, and increase our programs. We can wind up building up *our* kingdom rather than expanding *His* kingdom. Our building, staff, and programs can become an end rather than a means; we spend budgets on ourselves. Statistics on church budgeting would bear that out!

Truth: God does not want us to be focused on ourselves only. He wants us to focus on the people in our lives who yet need to know Him as Savior. This is why a strategic plan is so crucial to the operation of the church.

God does not want us to focus on what we think we can do but to believe Him for what He can do. He wants us to venture into miracle territory, to put our faith deep into His ability to do the impossible.

When we do this, we are reckoning on His resources. We are putting them to use for the work of the ministry. The term reckoning in the scriptures is an accounting term. It means to draw from the reserve you have in your bank account. As long as you have funds in your account, you can write checks. The reality is that our spiritual accounts can never be overdrawn. The reserves are inexhaustible. Think about it! We trust the invisible God to do the impossible through His pastors and people as we reckon and risk on His resources, who He is, and what He can do.

His past track record of doing the impossible is impressive! He is the impossibility specialist. (Mark 10:27) I have a plaque on my wall that reads: "When God wants to do something great, He starts with a problem. When God wants to do something spectacular, He starts with the impossible." (And we sure have a lot of impossibilities for Him to work with!)

Pastor, church leaders, and congregations are pivotal to this process. They are called to make it happen, combining faith and sight in believing Him for the plan and then uniting to carry it out.

I believe we need to cultivate a new spirit of adventure in our churches today. We do what is safe. We need more opportunities in a common mission, inside and outside the church walls. In an age where we have seemingly conquered all frontiers, we need new ways to Go West. The mission of today's church still provides the possibility for that kind of adventure!

The Challenges of Casting Vision and Strategic Planning: Facing Opposition

The ministry has been compared to walking through a landmine field. You need to watch where you step for a whole host of reasons. The metaphor describes what a pastor with a mission plan encounters when attempting to move the mission forward with the people's consensus and cooperation. Yet, no matter how hard a pastor may try to cast a vision for the church, the church itself may restrict its leadership from forging a vision into a plan to be carried out.

When dealing with the vision, pastors learn that trouble is something you'll never know until you try to change the status quo.

But, it is hard for a pastor or church leader to do this when the finance committee or the women's ministry board is sitting across from you, arms folded with the look of defiance on their faces. They are not exactly excited by your vision that will require a change! (Remember, not all the children of Israel were happy with Joshua and Caleb's vision!)

One of our church's strategic plans called for two things, among others. One was to integrate more praise songs in the services; another was to discontinue Sunday night services for various reasons. People heard and voted "yes" on the plan.

However, when it was time to implement the plan and make the change, a few vocal people declared with their age and authority that God's vision was to sing only hymns and to do less was irreverent! They also resisted discontinuing Sunday night services based on an old tradition when people came to evening revival meetings after their chores were done.

It is possible to formulate a church's vision and strategic plan and yet have differences of opinion and alternate ways of doing things. Variance is vital to the health of the planning process. It's unhealthy to have people simply rubberstamp the leader's ideas like a sea of yes men. It's equally unhealthy for people to insist on doing things their way.

This is often a ruse for not being willing to change. It is symptomatic of people who do not attempt to listen to or be obedient to God speaking to them through their leaders!

Avoiding the landmines often means not stepping on anyone's toes, hurting anyone's feelings, alienating them, losing them as friends, or being the brunt of their anger. Sometimes it means doing nothing because pastors find the price too high to make the vision for mission a reality. Thus, the enemy thwarts the work of the kingdom. But congregations also pay a high price for failing to take the faith risk.

Their reaction may mean one of several things: Don't lead us, let us lead you; don't make a change; it's uncomfortable. These statements could also be translated, "We were here first, and we'll be here after you go!" Too, a lot of parishioners don't care about a vision or a strategic plan. They are more than happy to let the leaders do it all for them and simply enjoy the benefits of the process.

If the pastor and leadership listen to the Lord, determine His course, and motivate the congregation to move in the right direction, the control of a small opposing group can be diminished.

But people who may oppose leaders are often not in leadership, at least not in formal leadership positions. But, they are still leading, albeit indirectly, because they have a long history with the church. They wield a certain influence over others. They run things by remote control. (See 'The Supremacy of Shepherding')

The fundamental problem here is that they have their own version of the vision. These folks are stubbornly sure that their way is God's way; thus, the right way, and no one is going to stand in their way!

In our second pastorate, we had a cadre of people trying to control where the church and leadership were attempting to move. From secret meetings in their homes to withholding their money, they attempted to exert pressure to keep things the way they were. They ultimately lost the battle and left. One senior missionary called it a backdoor revival!

The potential for conflict is never greater than when the pastor attempts to put the principles of vision casting into practice. Thus, there were many times of discouragement and despair for this leader; there will be times when we try to lead people in the direction we believe the Lord has given us and have to deal with those who oppose our leadership.

And remember, although people may be resistant to a leader's dreams for the church, the leader is yet responsible for casting the vision.

The dream is essential to vision and, thus, critical to planning. Let God plant a dream in your mind and then plant it in the heart and mind of your people whose hands and feet can make it happen.

Leaders who cast a vision are those who take risks. They walk through the Red Sea and overcome their fear of changing the status quo as they strive to follow the vision of the God who leads them into the promised land.

Once upon a time in Gooseville, there was a goose church pastored by a little goose pastor. One week, in his sermon preparation from the goose bible, he made an astounding discovery: That geese had wings on both sides of their feathered bodies, which would allow them to fly. He could hardly wait for the next Sunday to come when he could share this good news with his fellow geese. He concluded his sermon with the words. "We can Fly, We can Fly. We can Fly!" The geese were stirred by the unbelievable message. Then they stood, sang a triumphal hymn, *I'll Fly Away*, and they all *waddled* home!

The modern church will always need to be challenged and responsive to the vision of God and what He can do through His people in every generation.

Summary: People in any enterprise need a dream, a vision for what might be, and how they can be a part of it. In order for them to win, they need a game plan. The pastor is a vision caster who motivates the church to make it a reality. This requires strategic planning, formulating a game plan based on Purpose, (Why) Objectives, (What) Goals, (How, Who, and When). The pastor is the gatekeeper who opens the door and promotes the faith, risk, and the effort needed to realize the possibilities through the help of Christ, who can do the impossible.

When people believe in, commit themselves and their resources to make the vision happen, enthusiasm and a united effort combine to do the incredible things that God is prepared to do through His Church. The church needs to keep the main thing the main thing, fulfilling its mission even though people may not always agree on how it is to be carried out. The congregation needs to support their pastors and church leadership, not circumvent obedience to God and His plan, which He intends them to envision and implement together.

Peril: Not waiting on the Lord for His vision for your unique ministry or not implementing it for fear of upsetting people who need to be a part of working it out.

Privilege: To see the God of the impossible actualize the plan that creates excitement and success as it comes to fruition through the united effort of leaders and the congregation.

Question for personal reflection: Chapter 11 The Pastor as Vision Caster

1. How is vision transmitted to the leadership and congregation?
2. How can the pastor blend faith and sight in the planning process?
3. What keeps churches from risking to realize new possibilities?
4. How does a pastor deal with those who oppose a vision-plan?

12   The Pastor as Worship Leader

Genuine Worship:
How to give God What is Rightfully His

The term worship is taken from an Old English word, meaning ascribe worth, pay homage, reverence, and venerate.

One of the most explicit definitions of worship is in Romans 12:1-2, where Pastor Paul defines it as presenting ourselves to God, which is our *reasonable* act of worship. Ultimately we give what is of greatest worth to God; ourselves.

Worship is first an *attitude* of knowing, respecting, and honoring God, which externalizes itself in offering praise to God for who He is and what He does.

True worship is a *response* to God's initiative. When we accept the invitation to come before Him, we must be willing to change. We cannot have a true encounter with God and remain the same; we become different.

This encounter is not confined to the sanctuary on Sunday morning. God comes to indwell His people every day of the week. More than an event, genuine worship is an environment in which we are continuously giving ourselves to God. Sunday can impact every day.

I am moved by Paul's description of worship in I Corinthians 7, a chapter devoted to explaining the importance of worship. "That you may live in the right way in *undivided* devotion to the Lord." (I Corinthians 7:35b)

Think about that in the context of a worship service. Do we ever really come to the point of being undistracted in our worship and our devotion to the Lord?

Today's churches are often more impressed with the number of worshippers or the number of services rather than authentic worship. God is more impressed with the quality of worshippers and the impact of worship on their lives.

Israel got the quantity/quality issue confused, too. Hear what God has to say through the prophet Isaiah to the worshippers of his day. "For day after day they seek me out; they seem eager to know my ways, a nation that does what is right and has not forsaken the commands of God, they ask me for just decisions and seem eager for God to come near them. Why have we fasted, they say, and have you not seen it? Why have we humbled ourselves, and you have not noticed? Yet on your day of fasting, you do as you please." (Isaiah 58:2-3)

Isaiah gives us a picture that characterizes church worship throughout the centuries. Outwardly, people are attempting to impress God without giving Him what He required on the inside. In the Old Testament, Samuel warned Saul, in I Samuel 15:22, "To obey is better than sacrifice and to heed than the fat of lambs."

Christ put it yet another way in the writing of the New Testament. "These people honor me with their lips, but their hearts are far from me." (Matthew 15:8)

The worship leader must come as a useable vessel unto the Lord. To quote the Psalmist, "Who can ascend the hill of the Lord? Who may stand in His holy place? He who has clean hands and a pure heart, who does not lift up his soul to an idol." (Psalm 24:4 KJV)

Christ presented Himself as a living sacrifice so we can present our sacrifices and offerings back to Him. It was David in Psalm 51:10-12 who prayed, "Purify me, and I shall be clean, wash me, and I shall be whiter than snow. Hide thy face from my sins, and blot out all my iniquities. Create in me a clean heart, O God, and renew a right spirit within me. Cast me not away from thy presence and take not thy Holy Spirit from me. Restore to me the joy of my salvation, and uphold me with thy free spirit." The preparation of the leader always precedes the presentation of the service.

The pastor-worship leader who comes to the altar to lead the people of God in worship needs to be reconciled first to God and with others. This is underscored by this principle in Matthew 5:23, "Therefore if you are offering your gift at the altar and there remember that your brother has something against you, go and be reconciled to your brother and then come and offer your gift."

God has chosen to do His divine work through fallen and disobedient people, but He makes the conditions for our worship and leading worship quite clear.

Here it is: We can't be viewing pornography after the kids go to bed or be at war with our staff, or flirting with a staff member, or fail to reconcile with an offended brother or sister and lead our congregations in authentic worship. It is only when these admonitions are heeded can our sacrifice be holy and acceptable unto God.

Remember Samuel's encounter with Jesse in selecting a king for Israel. After reviewing all the other sons, God reminded Samuel of a fundamental principle when seeking godly leadership. "The Lord does not look at the things man looks at. Man looks at the outward appearance, but the Lord looks at the heart." (1 Samuel 16:7) (See 'The Life of Devotion')

Then as now, it is too easy to substitute charisma for character. How often do modern-day churches look for a professional who can wow crowds and swell attendance? It is easy to adapt to the way of the world. It's easy to be caught up in the star mentality.

There are many religious professionals who are true men and women of God, sincere in bringing His people into true worship and a deeper walk with Christ. However, many big names in Christian ranks have fallen by the wayside, taking many others down in the fall. In the preventative words of the Apostle Paul, "Therefore I do not run like a man running aimlessly; I do not fight like a man beating the air. No, I beat my body and make it my slave so that after I have preached to others, I will not be disqualified for the prize." (I Corinthians 9:26-27)

I served a parish where the pastor before me was a former pro-ball player, gregarious, and dynamic. The packed-out church grew to over 1,000 until he was discovered having committed adultery with several women in the church, as disclosed by a disgruntled husband. The pastor was confronted by the church leadership on a Sunday morning and asked to leave immediately without preaching. He left the pastoral ministry, and many people lost complete confidence in ministers because of his lack of moral integrity. (See 'The Imperative of Integrity')

How many Sundays did this playboy pastor come before God and call His people to worship while knowingly involved in sin?

We have a biblical star who illustrates this modern-day dilemma. His name was Saul. The people of Israel demanded a king, although warned about the consequences of a poor choice. One of the main characteristics of this first ruler was that he was the most handsome man in Israel. His exterior was impressive. Yet internally, he began to change; his heart towards God became cold and distant. Even though he started well, he gradually ceased to walk with his God, made ungodly choices, and was dethroned by a shepherd boy he tried to kill!

What also accompanies the star mentality is the show mentality. The centrality of the personality and performance has created a generation of spectators who watch someone perform for them rather than become participants in true worship.

The Old Testament gives us a portrait of modern worship in Ezekiel 33:30-32, "As for you, son of man, your countrymen are talking together about you by the walls and at the doors of the houses, saying to each other, Come and hear the message that has come from the Lord. My people come to you as they usually do and sit before you and listen to your words, but they do not put them into practice. With their mouths, they express devotion, but their hearts are greedy for unjust gain. Indeed to them, you are nothing more than one who sings love songs with a beautiful voice and plays an instrument well, for they hear your words but do not put them into practice."

Could there be a better description of much of modern-day worship? There are well-intentioned and self-effacing pastors whose congregants nonetheless expect them to be stars who perform for and entertain them. The condition is enhanced by pastors seen on large movie-type screens on-site or live-streaming on location. Some pastors want to be stars; they enjoy the admiration of others. And like their Old Testament counterparts, many parishioners simply walk in and out of the revolving door of religious ritual, not intending to be different, thus leaving the same way they came in. A contemporary phenomenon? It has been a characteristic of God's people for centuries.

There are two issues here. Pastors and worship leaders can indeed be actors and stars, and congregants can treat worship like a performance. When the show is over, they simply go back to the way of life they were pursuing before it started.

I often find myself musing at the Sunday morning folks who come to service with their cup of coffee but without their Bible. They stroll in after the service has started as if coming to a movie, to be entertained, not edified. They expect nothing but to be part of a social gathering and a religious ritual. Sadly, their expectations have been realized.

In one of the cities where I lived, I auditioned for a community theatre production. After I read the script, the next person to read asked me if I had done much acting. I replied that I was a minister, to which she responded, "Well, I figured all pastors were actors anyway." A bit startled by her candidness, I had to agree that sometimes that would be true.

You may find yourself asking, despite the attitudes of modern-day worshippers, doesn't the Holy Spirit still work in people's lives? The answer: Yes. Yet, the mindset of many believers impacts their worship and their Christian walk. God never retracts His promise to meet His people in authentic worship if they genuinely seek Him.

Like Isaiah, leaders helped their people come into the presence of and become intimate with the Triune God. (Isaiah 6) Who they were before God was more important than where they worshipped.

The Lord reminded the Samaritan woman at the well in John 4 of this principle. It was *not where* she worshipped; it was *who she worshipped* and *who she was* in presenting herself to the true God in worship. "God is spirit, and those who worship Him must worship in spirit and truth." (John 4:24) It didn't depend on where she worshiped; it depended on the encounter changing her. It meant not living in an adulterous relationship.

Ultimately true worship is that which turns us toward God and allows us to take on His likeness. The pastor-worship leader guides us through this continual pilgrimage.

Setting the Spiritual Tone: The Absolute of Authenticity

The qualities of godliness, transparency, love, and zeal should characterize those who lead in worship. These are the elements of *authenticity.*

We can look at Moses as the prototype of a worship leader. Exodus 34 and II Corinthians 3 record that Moses had spent time on top of the mountain with his God. The two of them entered into divine dialogue. Scripture records that the face of Moses shone because he had talked with God. Moses was the real deal; he was authentic. (See 'The Primacy of Prayer')

The pastor comes from the presence of God into the presence of God's people. The presence of God must be clearly evident in worship.

I am reminded of the winsome story of a young boy saying his bedtime prayers on a Sunday evening when he prayed, "Lord, church was pretty good today, but it would have been a whole lot better if you had showed up!"

We can only wonder how many services would be better if the Lord had indeed shown up. Of course, He is there; but how much freedom does He have to manifest Himself?

The quality of presence is exuded both by Moses, Christ, and His followers. The glow of God's presence was within them. When these people showed up, it was instantly discernable that the Spirit of the Lord came upon and resided in them.

Worship is also enhanced when we are able to focus, free of distractions. Those of us in pastoral ministry are vividly familiar with the potential distractions of a Sunday morning. It would appear that an announcement-free worship service is hardly possible. No amount of planning can pre-empt the possibility of last-minute surprises. Several alternate venues are possible. Announcements could be shown on the screens before service begins or given live after the service, or printed copies could be available for pick up in the foyer.

On occasion, my music minister might decide to do some extemporaneous preaching as part of leading the singing segment. These factors can all cause the pastor to shorten his message in order to end on time.

Collecting the offering at a receptacle in the back of the church could also prevent distraction. It focuses less on finances, one of which many people outside the church are often critical.

Preparation and planning helped me extend more *sensitivity* to the people of the congregation; it freed me to move amongst them without being rushed or preoccupied. It also allowed for meeting and welcoming new visitors.

A pastor in another denomination was escorted to and from the pulpit by security guards so he would not be distracted from preaching by having to talk to people. I was tempted to ask this guy, "Where do you get off not talking to people on Sunday because you're preaching? The rest of us do both all the time." The truth is, we probably preach better because we have interacted with the people to whom we are preaching.

Authenticity is made possible by the leader being empowered and giving the Lord freedom to work in all elements of the worship service.

Empowerment is enhanced by praying for the congregation and practice preaching before the service starts. I usually combined praying and practicing in the sanctuary. (In one pastorate, I prepared in the boiler room, which Charles Wesley appropriately called the Prayer Room.)

When the congregation is enabled to do the following, the worship experience is enhanced and becomes more authentic.

- To be themselves without having to perform.
- To be able to express their worship toward God in whatever way they choose.
- To have both quiet and robust moments to seek and find God.
- To share in genuine and effectual prayer led by pastors, individually or in clusters of people.
- To experience the love of God through others and safely share their needs.
- To interact with empowered biblical, expository, and practical teaching.
- To counsel or pray with someone after the service.
- To feel challenged to put the truths into action.

Cultivating the Spirit of Celebration: Overcoming the Fear of Irreverence

In a party hardy culture, people need a reason to let loose, which they often do in every other arena except worship. Enthusiasm accompanies other realms of activity, certainly in the world of sports, theater, and social happenings. This is true in other aspects of celebration. For those who are into football, there is the exhilaration of winning. For the shopper, there is the elixir of having found the sale of the century. The celebration involves adrenalin; it's a rush!

We cannot read the Old Testament without realizing that worship was not rigid, regulated, or ritualistic. It was meant to be robust and resounding! People had a good time coming to God. Read about it: (Exodus 14 and 15; II Chronicles 16; Psalm 149/150; Nehemiah 8 and Esther 9) The people of God met in a celebrative spirit, enthusiastically!

Israel celebrated what their God had done. They brought out the band; they sang, danced, cried, sent gifts, and expressed joy. Here is real worship, much of which we have neutralized in the modern church today.

After all, why should the secular world have all the reasons to celebrate? If any people should have reason to celebrate, it should be the people of God.

The Jewish national days of observance were called holy-days. People were called to celebrate these special days several times a year. These days are described by the Hebrew word, Modem, which means a divine appointment; preset times when God met His people. God commanded them to remember and rejoice in what He had done for them in their lives and their land. They marched in parades and had plenty of party spirit. Their neighbors usually knew when Israel was having a national day/season of celebration because of the volume! Their spirit of celebration was contagious; it was a living advertisement of God's performance.

Unfortunately, the world has taken the **y** and replaced it with an **i,** changing a holy-day to a holiday. Unlike the children of God who celebrated Him, the contemporary culture has taken God out of their celebration. Santa Claus has replaced the gift of God's Son at the birth of Jesus with gift-giving. Easter centers on finding eggs rather than celebrating the Christ already found alive after death!

The reason for their celebration was God's work amongst them: His continuous acts of provision, protection, and His intervention against their enemies. Major milestones of God's deliverance gave cause for celebrations. (Joshua 4:18-23)

Although there is something to be said for quietness and solitude in preparation for worship, there is undoubtedly a place for feeling joy and excitement in meeting God. It is possible to be reverent and rollicking at the same time!

Contrary to the opinion in many quarters of Christendom, having a good time in church is not secular or irreverent. (Contraire!) Celebration is fundamental to authentic worship. (Note that the first three letters of fundamental are F-U-N, something the worship experience should be!)

However, as a worship leader, I struggled to balance greeting each other with a holy kiss, (A sequel to pre-service chatting) and being still and knowing that He is God. (Quiet preparation and meditation). Herein is a need for balance in our worship experience.

Yet, every aspect of the gathering of God's people should be characterized by preparation and celebration. Let's consider them.

Coming to the house of God   Psalm 113-118   A holy procession marked by anticipatory joy and shouting prior to worship.

Singing   Psalms 96 and 98   A new song is to be sung unto the Lord. It was not necessarily a brand new song but an old song sung in a new way with excitement for what God had done.

Testifying   In both Hebrews 2 and III John, there is an indication that people bore witness of the acts of God in front of everyone with vigor and cheering.

Giving   In Exodus 35 and II Corinthians 9, there is strong evidence and incentive for bringing the tithes and offerings into the storehouse with great joy!

Receiving the Word of the Lord   In Nehemiah 8, the people's response to hearing the reading of the Law was sorrow, yes, but also a celebration. Governor Nehemiah combines both the silence and celebration components. "Be quiet, for this day is holy." "Do not mourn or weep." (Preparation). "Go your way, eat the fat and send gifts." (Celebration), a combination of Thanksgiving and Christmas!

Going forth to declare the Lord The response of God's people reverberated throughout the land. (Esther 8:17)

When we look at the church worldwide, our celebration of worship may look a bit anemic. For many people in countries where religious persecution is present, worship is dangerous; they do it with the risk of being imprisoned or even killed. Despite that, they are fully engaged in authentic worship because their God is the only true God; He is all they have.

I presented a School of Prayer in a small town in Iowa. The people were mostly placid. Their demeanor, their spirit, their worship, all were listless. During my message, I asked a question I have never asked before or since that morning. "If we were to videotape this service and distribute it to the neighborhood, I wonder how many of your neighbors would be motivated to come and worship with us?" (Of course, that's the kind of a question a visiting speaker can ask!) And judging from the reaction to the question, I won't be going back to preach there any time soon.

Let's listen to the words of Psalms 149 and 150 to hear and feel the celebration. "Sing to the Lord a new song, His praise in the assembly of the saints. Let Israel rejoice in their maker. Let the people of Zion be glad in their king. Let them praise His name with dancing and make music to Him with tambourine and harp." "Praise Him with the sounding of the trumpet, praise Him with harp and lyre, praise Him with tambourine and dancing, praise Him with strings and flute, praise Him with the clash of cymbals, praise Him with the resounding cymbals."

A pretty convincing case for a party at church, isn't it? It is not a symbol of irreverence; it's just the opposite. We are to be enthusiastic. The word enthusiasm translates (en Theos - into God). When we are into God, all He is and all He does, we truly worship. And that is worth cheering about!

Making God the Audience: Participants not Spectators

The real question is: What does God expect, want, and like? How does He want us to perform for Him? Much of today's worship is a show put on by star performers for the benefit of the audience. In reality, God is the audience of one, and worshippers are the performers, not merely spectators.

In an age of media, from playing games on our phones to streaming Netflix movies, it's easy to get into the remote control mindset when we attend church. We worship like we watch media; we sit, expecting to be entertained, uninvolved, and changing channels when we don't like what we are watching.

We tend to judge the church by its ability to entertain us, satisfy our needs, and give us what we like. Ours is a convoluted perspective. Often the modern-day parishioner comes to a church, checks out the worship, music, preaching, productions, and special effects, and makes their church choice based on how well the show stacks up against the competition!

This puts immense pressure on those of us called to lead worship. We need to be trained professionals and be the best in our field. After all, you're being compared to the pastor at a well-known mega-church, who people probably heard on the way to your service!

Besides, if they don't like you or your show, they can go down the street to find one they do like for a while. It's called sheep swapping; it is an exchange of church members looking for the best show in town, at least for now. (It's a little like how they pick restaurants! Primo Pizza, WOW, that is until the Pizza Palace opens!)

This basis of selecting a church is pretty much about what's right for me and what I like. If I don't like it, I go somewhere else to find it. It's a subtle form of consumerism, rampant in the culture and invading the church.

Bottom line: if the Lord shows up and we meet Him, the modality and format will be secondary.

I contend that anyone wanting to meet God and prepares to do so in authentic worship honestly will not be disappointed. With sincerity, I have said that I could meet God sitting on a piece of cardboard in a tent singing with bagpipe accompaniment! But for many people in our churches today, the method of worship is more important than meeting with God Himself.

Worship has devolved into a one-way communication event. One simply goes to church to be appeased and pleased. The demand for customized services continues to force churches to outdo each other in vying for attendees. It primarily centers on styles and methodologies.

This mindset is often reflected in the area of music. Many traditionalists reared on standard hymnology have great difficulty with much of contemporary music. They feel it's too loud, secularized, and lyrically redundant. Lovers of the modern music idiom contend that hymns are old-fashioned, use archaic language, and the tempo and style are foreign to contemporary ears.

Many churches have attempted to resolve this dilemma by creating blended services and utilizing re-styled hymns integrated into modern praise songs. A balance is challenging to achieve, and often both groups with divergent preferences are not satisfied. Many use this as the basis for leaving a church fellowship. Another tightrope!

As a pastor-worship leader, I understand the traditionalist's comfort with hymns and commend them for accommodating contemporary music geared to reach the seeker. But the contemporary fans need to be sensitive to volume and the use of secular songs to reach people outside the church. Not every traditionalist who supports the modern music ministry is comfortable when their chairs vibrate or their ears hurt or with a Led Zeplin or Katy Perry number to illustrate the sermon on non-conformity!

Again, we ask the question, were God's needs met? It sounds like a strange question. Our God is entirely self-sufficient and lacks nothing, but He desires our fellowship, devotion, and worship. The Great Commandment to love Him with all our heart, soul, and mind should characterize our worship.

Within the paradigm of a celebrative worship service, we can identify ways to be involved in the service as a participant, focusing on God's needs rather than our own needs.

In his song, *The Heart of Worship*, Matt Redman speaks to this modern worship dilemma, where he confesses that worship is all about God, not all about us.

Church leaders today can re-educate their people by precept and example.

The Service: A Means or an End?

The purpose of worship is to glorify God, edify the believers to evangelize and bear witness. Worship is not an end in itself; it is a means to a greater end.

Ours is the tendency to become myopic and ingrown. We tend to forget that the mission of the church is not only for us but for those yet to be reached with the gospel message. This is a sequel to the Old Testament people of God, whose perverted worship caused them to fail in carrying out His mission to the world.

Christ gives us several purpose statements concerning His Church in the writings of the New Testament. In Mark 1, He heralds the coming of the Church as a kingdom, one entered by repentance and belief. In the Gospel of Matthew, Christ affirms that the church's purpose is to make disciples of all nations based on His power, authority, and presence in them. In Matthew 13, the church kingdom is compared to a tree, one in which the birds of the air would come to nest in its branches, a place of safety and fruitfulness.

When biblical truth is well presented and true worship takes place, it engages the church member to both hear and do the truth.

The Church Gathered to Be Scattered:
Does Sunday Make Any difference?

We must be continuously reminded of two central questions; What is the church, and what is its purpose?

The church is not a building. It is the Body of Christ coming together to worship and then go out to bear witness of the works of God. We need to remember that our gathering is a means to a greater end. We go forth from meeting God to meet our world. We are God's traveling tabernacles, which He inhabits.

The church gathers to fulfill the *Great Commandment,* "To love the Lord your God with all your heart, soul and mind and your neighbor as yourself." Then the church goes forth to fulfill the *Great Commission,* which is to make disciples of all men. Again, edification within becomes the basis of evangelization without. The first is the means; the second is the end.

In evaluating our worship, the following questions should be considered:

- Was the environment of the service one of authenticity and transparency?
- Was it a genuine celebration or just going thru the religious motions?
- Was the worshipper a spectator or a participant?
- Did our worship bear witness to the world of our encounter with God?

In Mark 1:40-44, we have a biblical event that illustrates a reaction to authentic worship; meeting God. It is the account of Jesus healing a leper. The man was overjoyed, but Christ warned him not to tell anyone what happened. But instead, the once leprous outcast began to talk freely and spread the news about the miracle.

There is a correlation between his encounter with Christ and our worship experience. The worshipper is diseased by sin and in need of cleansing and healing. They have a divine encounter with God. But *unlike* the leper who was instructed not to share it with others, we are compelled to share our worship experience. The leper was so excited about how he met and was touched by Jesus that he couldn't help but tell everyone. And one more thing; it was obvious to anyone who had known him in his former condition that he was made new; he had met Jesus, and it changed him!

Our worship should reflect the leper's grateful response, that we have met God, been touched and changed by Him, and it should be evident to others.

Summary: Worship is giving something to God that is worthy of Him; that is rightfully His. Primary to the task of leading worship is the authenticity of the person orchestrating it. True worship comes from a prepared heart and emanates from a cleansed life; it places a premium on obedience over sacrifice and realness over ritual. It is a celebration which exceeds people's enthusiasm for all other life celebrations. Authentic worship meets God's needs, not only those of His people. Worship is not a performance by professionals to be watched by spectators, but one where participants perform for God. It is not an end in itself but a means by which God's people can advertise Him through how they live. Those gathered for worship are scattered to proclaim the gospel in common mission to a waiting world.

Peril: Treating worship as a performance for people rather than for God and focusing on the needs of the congregation who consider worship as an end rather than a means of reaching people outside the church.

Privilege: Celebrating authentic and enthusiastic worship services where people truly meet God and live changed lives before the world.

Questions for personal reflection: Chapter 12 The Pastor as Worship Leader

1. How does the pastor prepare to lead worship?
2. What are the elements of an effective worship service?
3. Why is it appropriate to make worship a true celebration?
4. Why are congregants to be participants and not just spectators?
5. What is the difference between a service being a means or an end?

13   The Pastor as Preacher/Teacher

Two Essential Elements:
The Messenger and the Message

One of the most daunting tasks in the pastoral calling is declaring God's eternal and life-changing Word nearly every week! Even Martin Luther, when asked to preach for the first time, excused himself.

The Messenger

The preparation of the messenger is a priority. The basis of declaring the truth to others is hearing and practicing the truth. The one who presents it must desire to seek, know, hear, and draw close to God who authored the written Word and Christ, the living Word. (See 'The Life of Devotion')

The New Testament emphasizes the one who presents the truth must first practice it. I Timothy 4:15, "Put these things into practice, devote yourself to them so that all may see your progress. Pay close attention to yourself and your teaching; continue in these things, for in doing this, you will save both yourself and your hearers."

To put it another way: Put into practice what you preach before and after you preach it!

We may revere the one who delivers the message more than the message itself. In many political circles today, what is said goes unquestioned if the person who purports it belongs to a particular party or group or is our favorite anchorperson on one of the leading networks.

During the Clinton Administration, Yassar Arafat, the Arab potentate, was wined and dined at the White House. He was prompted what to say, so it appeared that he was for peace.

Let's try our messenger formula on good ol' Yassar. The messenger was an enemy of peace, a wolf in sheep's clothing, and a false prophet. His content was born out of a deceitful heart. (Character) His message was not valid. (Content) The messenger and his message lacked legitimacy; his character and content were both corrupted. Yet many were taken with his charisma and placed great confidence in what he said.

When we examine the scriptures, it is easy to see the difference between messengers who were reliable and told the truth and those who were the opposite. In Jeremiah 23:16 for example, the narrative is about false shepherds who destroy and scatter the sheep. "Do not listen to what the prophets are prophesying to you; they fill you with false hopes. They speak visions of their own mind, and not from the mouth of the Lord."

Sadly, this is a portrait of some modern-day pastoral messengers. There are those in our churches today who give no allegiance to the Living Christ or His Gospel. They substitute their own words that mislead. They rely more on the power of their personality and position than the inertia of the Spirit, which should be the fundamental basis of their preaching ministries.

According to James, God holds teachers of truth to a higher standard than those in other fields. It is a fearful thing for a false messenger with a false message to ultimately stand before God. (James 3:1)

The Message

The second factor is the preparation of the message. This was the most crucial component in my weekly schedule. I set aside early morning hours for study, leaving the afternoon and evening hours for other responsibilities. It is tempting to download the work of others or preach old sermons. Though I referenced the work of others, I never plagiarized a sermon or served leftovers; it was scratch cooking. This allowed me to discern God's current word for each church. A leftover sermon though biblical, was for a different congregation at a different time.

My goal was to always leave the study on Friday afternoon with the preparation completed, then let the sermon simmer in my spiritual crockpot. It was in the melding of the message that the real flavors of the truth come together. I never deviated from this regimen.

It reminds me of the old story of the pastor who put off preparing all week. Finally, at the urging of his concerned wife, he came up with an answer. "I don't have to prepare," he contested; "the Lord will give me a message." So, Sunday morning came, and with it came the ill-prepared but very confident pastor to whom the Lord said, "Delbert, you should have prepared!"

Sitting under modern-day messengers is somewhat akin to watching television. (The Big Screen Syndrome) We are taken with the flash and attraction of media-driven messages. And the more advanced media becomes, the more we expect to be wowed by the technology and the more it takes to wow us! However, the appropriate use of media can make messages relevant and understandable. (See 'The Pastor as Worship Leader')

The preacher who takes the podium takes on the challenge of presenting eternal truth to contemporary people. Yet, their desire to be relevant and sensational can undermine biblical truth. The ideal is to present the truth impactfully and without compromise.

Paul addresses this issue in II Timothy when he forecasts, "For the time will come when men do not put up with sound doctrine. Instead, to suit their desires, they will gather around them a great number of teachers to say what their itching ears want to hear." In other words, people want their pastors to tell them what they *want* to hear rather than what they *ought* to hear. (II Timothy 4:4-5)

Seeker-sensitive churches defend themselves by asserting that you need to appeal to someone before revealing the gospel's full message. The truth is we need to assess the substance of the appeal carefully.

Pastors need to be careful that the audience is not calling the shots when it comes to declaring the ultimate authority of the Word of God. God asks us to accommodate His truth, not the other way around. The presentation needs to be distinctly contrasted from secular communication in content and style.

Paul reflects this dilemma in writing to the Corinthian Church in his second letter. "But I do not think that I am in the least inferior to those super-apostles. I may not be a trained speaker, but I do have knowledge." (II Corinthians 11:5-6a)

If we're not careful, we can easily come to rely on special effects more than the impact of the Holy Spirit. He desires to use the humble, simple, empowered declarer of the Word to convey the eternal truths. The anointing of the Spirit of God can ultimately work even without modern media dynamics to communicate this life-changing message. Creativity may help engage the hearer but it is never to substitute for the substance of what we present. The message's impact does not depend only on the presenter's personality and performance but on the innate power of the Word's authority. The super-apostles of Paul's day relied on their performance more than the power of the Lord.

Allow me to visualize this concept for you. In a church we attended, the lead pastor wore a casual sports coat, no tie, and preached from notes behind a music stand with a single PowerPoint slide, which gave the sermon series, title, and scripture portion. The expository message was thoroughly prepared and made relevant by key illustrations and personal examples; it was powerfully presented and effective. He was not a star on a screen, and the congregants were not mere spectators at a show; they came to a service to be enlightened and not entertained. There's no fog machine, no spinning glitter ball, or flashing colored lights. They came to hear the simple Word, taught in a simple way that could transform their life.

The Word of God must remain non-conformist and unchanged in a contemporary world which often wants to change the Word rather than being changed by it!

These are what I consider the central truths of preaching and teaching.

The basis of our belief. The Bible is the true Word of God. II Timothy 3:16-17, II Peter 1:19-21, Matthew 24:35

The attributes of God. Genesis 1, Isaiah 6, Psalm 103, Psalm 139, John 17:1-3, 1 Timothy 6:13-16

The person of Christ. The Son of God and Son of Man, Virgin Born, perfect, and the only way to God. Isaiah 7:14, Luke 1:34-37, Luke 2:52, John 1:14,18, John 14:6

The elements of personal salvation. His work, not human works. Acts 4:12, Ephesians 2:8-9, Titus 3:4-7

The centrality of the personal commitment to Christ as Savior. John 1:11-13, John 3:16-18, Romans 10:8-10

The Christian belief as the basis of our value system and lifestyle. I Corinthians 3:16-18, Colossians 2:8, Matthew 6:19-21,33, II Corinthians 6:17-18, II Corinthians 4:18, Romans 13:11-14

The importance of being a Christ-follower, not simply a convert. Luke 9:23, Matthew 10:38-39, Mark 10:28-30, John 6:66-69, John 15:20-25

The role of the Holy Spirit. I Corinthians 12:13, John 16:7-11, 13-15, Romans 8:11, 27-28, I Corinthians 12:4-11, Acts 1:8

The reality of Satan and the need to overcome him. I Peter 5:8-9, James 3:7-10, Ephesians 6:10-18

The necessity of bearing witness to the world of our ultimate hope. Acts 1:8, Philippians 2:12-15, Titus 2:11-14, I Peter 3:15, II Corinthians 4:17

The confidence in Christ's return to rule the world. Acts 1:10-11, I Thessalonians 4:13-18, Revelation 1:7, Revelation 20:4-6

The final judgment of all believers and non-believers. Ecclesiastes 12:13-14, II Corinthians 5:10, Revelation 20:11-15, Acts 17:31

The Place of Authenticity and Authority: Not as the Scribes

Christ was proof of this principle. For starters, the Old Testament doesn't describe the Messiah as the John Kennedy of his day. "He had no beauty or majesty to attract us to Him. He was despised and rejected by men, a man of sorrow familiar with suffering." (Isaiah 53:2-3a) Consider the Apostle Paul, who was no oratorical standout, no competition for Sean Hannity. (I Corinthians 2:1-5)

In the New Testament, Christ was perceived as a common laborer, one certainly incapable of having any notoriety or celebrity status. John 1:46 corresponds with this when Nathaniel asks, "Nazareth, can anything good come from there?" Or in Matthew 13, "Where did this man get this wisdom and these miraculous powers?" "Isn't this the carpenter's son?" Jesus had a different appeal from Benny Hinn, who had the charisma but lacked the character as reflected in fraudulent business practices. (See 'The Imperative of Integrity')

The texts of the Gospels support the real authority of Jesus as demonstrated in His earthly ministry. Matthew 9:6 records that God gave Christ authority, which was linked to His ability to heal people and forgive their sins.

Although there are presumably many faith healers today, none would have the audacity to suggest they could also forgive sin. But, it is the very union of working miracles and forgiving sin that confirmed Christ's unique authority.

In Mark 11:37,53, Jesus is questioned by the chief priests, scribes, and elders as to His authority. In John 7:15, the religious leaders ask how He knew the scriptures so well, not having been educated by them. His very presence makes the origin of His knowledge evident. By contrast, they confirmed where theirs originated.

In Matthew 7:28-29, the text correlates His authority with His preaching and teaching ministry. When He had finished the sermon on the Mount, one of the greatest sermons of all time, there was a significant reaction. "Now, when Jesus had finished saying these things, the crowds were amazed at His teaching because He taught them as one who had authority and *not* as their teachers of the Law." It was no wonder the scribes were so interested and intimidated by the source of their competition's power.

The connection between character and content could not be more defined. Who Christ *was* preceded what He *said* and *did*. The crowds noticed the power behind the preacher. He spoke differently; He both believed it and lived it. His appeal was distinctly different.

The charisma that attracted people was the power of the Father upon Him. The word charisma comes from the Greek word, charis, translated grace, or grace gift. In other words, it was the grace of God, given Him by His Father, that drew people to Him. Christ was not a star to be worshipped but rather a servant who was to be followed. His objective was to draw people to His Father. He was not interested in attracting people to Himself, but to the truth He embodied. It was hardly the persona of most Hollywood personalities who don't want anyone else to upstage them! (We would not find Jesus on the Red Carpet with Brad Pitt.)

It is this authority that is absent in some pastors and their preaching and teaching today. Modern-day spokespersons for God forget that the message's impact depends first upon the genuine power, authority, and model of the presenter; someone with authority given by God, not driven by ego.

People today are less discerning as to what is true and what is false. There is a tendency to water down historical biblical truth to make it more palatable and less offensive in modern times.

The Emerging Church seeks to live their faith in what they believe is a postmodern society. It is one which supports the deconstruction of modern Christian worship, modern evangelism, and the nature of the modern Christian community. Most of all, they seem to agree on their disillusionment with historic Christianity.

The Progressive Christianity Movement purports Christ's death is non-redemptive, He was only a martyr, that the miracles of Christ are merely symbolic, and the concept of hell is only figurative. Peter references these movements in Paul's writing, "His letters contain some things that are hard to understand, which ignorant and unstable people distort, as they do other scriptures, to their destruction. Therefore my dear friends, since you already know this, be on your guard that you may not be carried away by the error of lawless men and fall from your secure position." (II Peter 3:16-17)

I recall a conversation with a pastor in a mainline Protestant denomination. I asked him if he preached on sin. The answer was no! The reason? That might offend someone. Remember what Paul said, "For I am not ashamed of the Gospel of Christ for it is the power of God unto the salvation of everyone who believes." (Romans 1:16)

Let's face it. People often prefer what doesn't confront the real issues in their lives. The self-gratification and non-accountability mentality of modern times directly affect the presentation and reception of the truth.

Though not always a pleasant task for present-day presenters, preaching the truth is imperative for congregational health.

There is a growing tendency to avoid truth-telling from the pulpit and a failure to deal with and confront sin, which compromises the Christian witness. It also reduces the redemptive force in our secularised society.

This very condition was present in British churches surveyed in 2017. Approximately 2,000 church members indicated they were not given the basics of the Christian faith but rather a watered-down version of those beliefs. The most prominent concern was believing the accuracy of Christ's resurrection as an adult.

Foundational beliefs were disassociated from social concerns;

often, the discourse was politically motivated. Most significantly, they lamented the absence of being challenged to live their lives according to those beliefs. There was a cry for the clergy to stand for, present, and apply the biblical truths to life in a post-modern age.

Christ provides the model for the modern-day messenger. Christ relied upon God, the Father, for His authority. Yet His message was out of sync with popularized religion. It was peculiar to the ears of those who had been fed a steady diet of deception.

His message was nonetheless alive. It was life-producing. Why else would Jesus be called the Living Word? He was the very embodiment of what the Father had taught Him. He was the Word incarnate. People could see, hear, touch, and be changed by Him. Pastors would do well to assess themselves and their ministries by the standard of the person and presentation of Christ and His message.

To Preach is to Teach:
The Interaction Between the Pastoral Art Forms

Over the years, I have had parishioners say to me, "Preacher, you really are a teacher, you know." Their reasons intrigued me. "You make the truth easy to grasp; you don't use big words we don't understand; your illustrations are relevant and practical. You use printed outlines." (I call this putting the cookies on the bottom shelf.)

Interestingly, I always believed myself to be more of a teacher than a preacher. My wife saw me as more of a preacher. She sat under both art forms for over 40 years, for which she is to be indeed commended!

"Now a man came to Jesus, Rabbi what good thing must I do to get eternal life?" (Matthew 19:16) In addition to being called Lord,

Son of God, and Son of Man, Jesus was also called Rabbi, which meant a teacher of the law. "After Jesus had finished instructing His 12 disciples, He went on from there to teach and preach in the towns of Galilee." (Mathew 11:1)

I've come to understand that a preacher is also a teacher. The artforms of preaching and teaching are interchangeable; the two become one. Let's examine that assumption.

- Preacher/Teacher is a noun. Preach/teach is a verb. The effective communicator is *and* does both. Temperament, personality, and gifting are all factors in the way these functions are implemented.
- They share common qualities and capacities. They are an academician, instructor, story-teller, and exhorter. They are thinkers and practitioners. They have the speaking gifts.
- They share standard components. They let the Word in and then let it out; it becomes part of the one who preaches and teaches it; it impacts them in order to impact others. (See 'The Life of Devotion')
- They share a common objective. They declare the Word of God accurately and passionately.
- They seek to be conduits. They allow themselves to be used of God to transmit the Word of God with authority, power, relevance, and practical application.
- They face a common challenge. To know, understand, and communicate biblical truth effectively in the context of modern culture.

I believe that preaching and teaching also communicate meaningfully to people who are tired of being in a world of superficiality, consumption, and eroding moral values. To relate the truth contextually allows people to apply the truth and connect it to Monday through Saturday, not just Sunday only.

Issues and Answers, an online eBook I have written, presents a biblical background on contemporary issues in a handbook designed for Christian parents and children. The objective is to help relate the scriptures to over 40 different topics such as: Eating Disorders, Euthanasia, Abortion, Marriage and Divorce, Homosexuality, Pre-Marital Sex. This eBook is an example of how the ivory tower truth can be brought down to the trenches of modern life.

(This eBook is available free of charge. Contact me at rolboyce@theultimatecalling.com)

The Place of Christian Education:
Five Contemporary Objectives

Objective 1: Combatting Illiteracy. A significant factor in the Christian Education ministry is the glaring lack of biblical literacy. Congregations, for the most part, are not skilled in the scriptures. They hear sermons, attend Sunday School classes and seminars, become part of a Bible study, and involve themselves in small groups. Yet, the level of biblical comprehension is often seriously deficient.

Throughout history, the church has been labeled as dull of hearing and spiritually obese for lack of exercise. Our response to these conditions can stimulate active listening, critical thinking, and creating forums to allow messages and teaching to be questioned, explored, and discussed.

Objective 2: Involving parents in their children's spiritual education. A prime factor in religious education is parental involvement. If the parent is a spectator, not a participant, why would they expect their child to be any different?

The scriptures underscore the role of the parent in the life of the child. In Deuteronomy 6:6-7, Moses instructs families, "These commandments that I give you today are to be upon your hearts. Impress them on your children. Talk about them when you sit at home and when you walk along the road, when you lie down and when you get up."

In Ephesians 6:4, the pragmatic Paul reminds parents, "Fathers do not exasperate your children; instead bring them up in the training and instruction of the Lord." The Jewish education model was for the father to be the instructor of truth and the mother to help the child live it out practically.

Ours is an age where parents are prone to abdicate the responsibility for raising children to everyone else; the public school, Sunday School, the scout troop, and the local youth group. In a sense, these agencies become surrogate parents and are expected to do the parent's job. This job includes religious education and values clarification, both things for which other people should not be primarily responsible.

What happens outside the home should be a *supplement*, not a *substitute* for what happens inside the home. Ecclesiastes 12:1, "Remember your Creator in the days of your youth." We need to teach our children when they are still moldable when the cement is still wet.

Objective 3: Helping people to feed themselves spiritually. People are to be fed on the Sabbath. More importantly, they are to learn to feed themselves during the week to be spiritually nourished. This is expressed in the old proverb: "Give a man a fish and feed him for a day. Teach a man to fish, and he is fed for a lifetime."

The writer of Hebrews put it this way. "You are babies on milk rather than grown up on meat; by now you ought to be teachers not still being taught." (Hebrews 5:12)

What parent would expect a newborn child to come home from the hospital and tackle a T-Bone steak, complete with knife and fork? On the other hand, what parent would expect the child to still be on strained meat at age 15?

If we become dependent on someone else to feed us rather than learning to feed ourselves, we grow up with imbalanced spiritual diets and stunted spiritual growth. God expects His spiritual kids to grow up into mature adults in Christ.

Objective 4: Integrating biblical truth into the believer's life. Professing Christians have a personal responsibility to obey and apply biblical truths to their lives. Hearing is simply not enough. The truth must be integrated into daily life, directly impacting themselves and others. "Do not merely listen to the Word and so deceive yourself. Do what it says. Anyone who listens to the Word but does not do what it says is like a man who looks at his face in a mirror and, after looking at himself, goes away and immediately forgets what he looks like." (James 1:23-24)

The church has become a media room where people watch instead of a gymnasium where they work out. When you watch, you sit passively; when you work out, you get actively involved. Learning can also be stimulated by opportunities to do the truth.

For instance, on one Sunday morning, I gave my parishioners something to do with the message, a homework assignment. Personal involvement in applying the truth is always the highest form of learning. For example, after a message on stewardship, I called up seven people from the congregation, gave them $15.00 each, and asked them to find a way to use the money to serve someone in the community. The testimonies and reports of the investment adventure made a profound and lasting impact on the congregation. We need to think more creatively about getting hearers to heed the word by applying it in action.

206

A critical element in Christian education today is the growing dichotomy between what we believe and how we behave. There is a serious division between Sunday and the rest of the week, the person at worship and the one at work. A synonym for dichotomy is a divorce, two entities are separated that belonged together. Knowing and living out God's truth are not to be separated.

We often hear about surveys indicating that a preponderance of Americans believe in God, read the Bible or at least own one, go to church, and even believe in the second coming of Christ. But they also think there's nothing wrong with lying, cheating on their income tax, or watching TV with questionable content.

Many modern churchgoers have a foundation of faith based on the *work* of Christ but have built poorly; they have little to show for the living out of their faith, as demonstrated by their *works* through a distinctive lifestyle.

"By the grace God has given me, I laid a foundation as an expert builder, and someone else is building on it. But each one should be careful how he builds. If any man builds on this foundation using gold, silver, costly stones, wood, hay, or straw, his work will be shown for what it is because the Day will bring it to light. It will be revealed with fire, and the fire will test the quality of each man's work." (I Corinthians 3:10-13)

Objective 5: Recapturing the culture for Christ. We live in a world increasingly hostile to Christianity, one in which the Christian witness has often been rendered virtually ineffective.

Recent studies indicate only a small percentage of church youth hold a biblical worldview, can answer basic questions about the Christian faith and have values that contrast those of secular culture. This percentage is only slightly lower than that of adults who also reject a biblical worldview or believe that the principles of the Christian faith are relevant to their lives. This has been a significant factor in losing past generations of our youth regarding belief systems, moral choices, and conduct. It has had a direct impact on the spiritual decline and direction of our country. Every pastor, church member, and parent is called to renew their role as educators.

The Psalmist reminds us of the importance of transmitting biblical truth to each generation. "Great is the Lord and worthy of praise; His greatness no one can fathom. One generation will commend your works to another; they will tell of your mighty acts. They will speak of the glorious splendor of your majesty and meditate on your wonderful works." (Psalm 145:3-5)

Declaring the Divine Truth:
The Elements of Effective Presentation

Like a good recipe, declaring the Word of God requires the right ingredients: Study, prayer, power, passion, impact, and fruitfulness. These are the elements that Christ, the consummate preacher-teacher, integrated into His ministry.

- Study: The academic component of preaching and teaching requires useful tools such as familiarity with biblical languages and adequate aids to research.
- Prayer: Communicating with the author of the Word to hear the message He wants you to declare and for its impact on the hearers.
- Power: The authority and the anointing of the Holy Spirit on the messenger and the message.
- Passion: Having excitement about what you are declaring. If it doesn't excite us, it probably won't excite the congregation. The delivery can be enhanced by humor, emotion, and personal example.
- Impact: The certification of authority and anointing means

that the message has made a difference in their walk and witness.

- Fruitfulness: The long-term outcome of the preaching and teaching process cultivates an understanding and integration of the truth. This is evident in the individual's worldview, principles, values, lifestyle, and daily choices.

People in our society learn differently than they did a generation ago. Media sources continue to proliferate and bombard us: Television, sensational tabloids, the internet, email, Twitter, Facebook, Instagram, iPods, smartphones, computer games, Netflix, and LCD screens on the seatbacks of airplanes and cars.

Additionally, the post-modern mind is less interested in Christianity's historical and theological tenants and is much more interested in the relational and practical dimensions. The surge of YouTube trumping traditional book learning is a cultural mindset also reflected in the audience's reception. Whoever is communicating must be sensitive to the context in which the truths are presented. (See 'The Pastor as Evangelist')

Christ had a variety of methods He used during His preaching and teaching ministry, which He adapted to the culture of His day.

He taught the Word by coming alongside His hearers, translating the divine truth so people of that time could apply it to their daily lives.

During His presentation, Christ used synonyms and figures of speech to make His message clear, relevant, and practical. Example: "He shall cover thee with His feathers, and under His wings, you will find refuge." He is speaking of God's protection in Psalm 91:4a.

In the New Testament, this was done by Jesus teaching in parables. A parable is defined as an earthly story with a heavenly meaning. He used the idioms and the figures of speech in His day, often agricultural terms, to relate the truth to His congregations. Example; "I am the Vine; you are the branches." Speaking of our relationship with Himself in John 15:5.

He certified comprehension with questions. Example: "Therefore, when the owner of the vineyard comes, what will he do with those tenants?" Matthew 21:40. Christ was explaining how His people would reject Him. Jesus was a proponent of active listening. He wanted His listeners to interact with the truths He was teaching them. He desired that they question, think through, and make the truth their own.

What is vital in the educational process is to create an environment for maximum receptivity on the part of the hearers.

I used visuals to communicate in my presentations, which appealed to both seeing and hearing the truth. (PowerPoints, movie excerpts, song lyrics). Additionally, I've used compelling stories, life illustrations, humor, and object lessons. Example: When preaching on Romans 12:1-2, I obtained a 'YIELD' sign from the local traffic department and placed it in front of the pulpit. (And yes, I did return it!)

I also found the children's sermon was also as a means of communicating truth. I figured that if the kids understood it, the adults would. The adults sometimes told me they got more out of that than the adult sermon. (Oh great, maybe I should have just prepared one message!)

This evaluation form helped determine the effectiveness of my preaching-teaching ministry.

- Was I personally prepared? Was it evident that the presenter had prepared spiritually and academically?
- Was my message delivered with real power and authority?

- Was it evident that the Spirit of God was residing and released through me and my preaching-teaching?
- Was my message understandable, relevant, practically applicable, and transferable to life and witness?

Wouldn't it be interesting to have Christ sit in on one of our presentations? I mean, can you imagine preaching with Jesus in the congregation. It reminds me of the man who lost his life in a huge flood and, upon arriving in heaven, made mention of the fact that he would like to share his story, to which the royal gatekeeper replied, "That's perfectly fine, but remember, Noah will be in the audience."

I spoke at a High School Baccalaureate Service. I had forgotten that the daughter of my seminary president was one of the graduates. And there he was in the second row looking up at me; I wasn't too sure I wanted to go through with the presentation, but I did survive! (He even complimented me on my use of the Greek language.)

Realistic Expectations: The Fear of the Weekly Assignment

This chapter would have been incomplete without a postscript.

One of the first realities of the pastorate is that you're up, and you're on stage pretty much every week. (Unless you have a choir cantata at Christmas or an annual visit from the Gideons, or you have a large staff!)

I've often wondered why God didn't set up the church calendar to have Sunday once a month? Wow, that would make it so much easier.

And think about all that extra time you would have to prepare, although some people would still put it off until the last minute; remember Delbert? (A word of encouragement: if you had a bad

Sunday, you've got three or four more in a month to make up for it!)

People have asked me if I had any fears coming into the ministry. They asked me that same question about coming into the marriage, to which I said, "If something broke, I wouldn't know how to fix it." As for ministry, I feared two things: One, that what I said wouldn't make any difference. Two, I wouldn't be able to come up with illustrations every week.

As to my fear in ministry, I have never stopped wondering about making a difference. But I learned that I was never supposed to answer the question. It is His to know the outcomes, not us. Our task is to be faithful; it's up to Him to do the rest and render the results.

And coming up with illustrations every week? The Lord never ceased to supply me with quotes, illustrations, or real-life events. Most of those elements came from daily life! (Example: talking about how wonderfully we are made while taking a kid with a broken arm to the hospital.)

I remained true to my commitment to prepare for preaching; the assignment was given priority. The Lord consistently readied me for Sunday, no matter how many interruptions came my way during the week, even those weeks when I couldn't imagine how I would have enough time to prepare.

I usually experienced the same things when I presented. *Before:* Nervousness, struggling to remember my outline, anxiety over people caring about or understanding the message. *After:* I became self-critical of my presentation, and I realized that I needed to start the process all over again for the next Sunday.

One thing was helpful for me to remember; my people knew I loved and truly cared for them. They received the word more readily because they knew my heart and motive.

I am convinced that when the heart of the pastor is diligent in both intent and preparation for the sacred assignment of preaching-teaching, God will multiply the time to prepare for the presentation. The same God who issues the **ultimate calling** will provide everything by which to fulfill it!

Remember that the Word of God never returns void. This is His promise through the Prophet Isaiah. "As the rain and the snow come down from heaven, and do not return to it without watering the earth and making it bud and flourish so that it yields seed for the sower and bread for the eater, so is my word that goes out from my mouth: It will not return to me empty, but will accomplish what I desire and achieve the purpose for which I sent it." (Isaiah 55:10-11)

This truth came home to me in a powerful way recently. I received an email from a couple I had married in Stockton, California, in the '80s. I had also baptized the man. His wife informed me of a situation at work where he was caught in the middle of a crossfire. She reminded him of a verse I had used at his baptism. It was the one from Ezekiel 22:30 about making up the hedge and standing in the gap. She reminded him that this was what God had confirmed for him despite the turbulence at that point in his life. She thanked me for those words that I had completely forgotten. But those were God's words, and He used them in a man's life at work all those years later. (And it ministered to me on one of my Mondays of malaise when I felt I hadn't done well the day before.)

Simply, the Word of God works! And the miracle is that it keeps working despite those who preach and teach it.

The impact of Christ's preaching and teaching is indisputable. After 21 centuries of human history, He still stands as the most influential person who has ever lived. Countless millions have confirmed their faith in Him and committed their lives to Him. The Written Word continues to be declared and demonstrated through the Living Word.

SUMMARY: The two essential elements in the preaching-teaching role are the messenger and the message. The preparation of the messenger precludes the effectiveness of the presenter. Authenticity and authority emanate from a genuine relationship thru the Living Word, Jesus Christ. The preacher is also a teacher who, along with others, facilitates the Christian education of the congregation. The weekly assignment of preparing and presenting is facilitated by God, who provides all resources needed for the sacred assignment.

Peril: Making the preparation of the messenger secondary to the presentation of the Word, accommodating what people want to hear rather than what they ought to hear, and reliance upon your own power and performance in preaching and teaching.

Privilege: Proclaiming the eternal truth of God through preaching and teaching with authenticity, power, passion, and relevance, helping people grow into spiritual adulthood.

Questions for personal reflection: Chapter 13 The Pastor as Preacher/Teacher

1. Why is the preparation of the messenger as important as the message?
2. What made Christ 'not as the scribes'?
3. How are preaching and teaching interchangeable?
4. What are the five Christian education objectives?
5. Explain Christ's philosophy of preaching and teaching?
6. Identify the methods Christ used in His preaching and teaching ministry.
7. What apprehensions could a pastor have in preparing and presenting a message?

14   The Pastor As Counselor

The Need for a Counselor:
Fallout from the Fall

Since the fall of humanity into sin, we all have fallout issues. It's not do we have baggage, it's what we do with it!

The dilemma pastor-counselors face is dealing with their own issues. Thus, it becomes a case of physician, heal thyself. We may well need healing administered to us in order to assist others.

Clergy may require assistance to face the same fear, anxiety, and denial that others face. The pastor's willingness to own and seek counsel for remediation not only provides personal healing for themselves but permits parishioners to do the same.

Our daughter earned a master's degree in educational counseling. In the second half of the course, she was required to be the counselee, to sit on the other side of the table, and deal with any potential unresolved issues which impacted her role as counselor.

Hebrews describes the priesthood of Christ. "He is able to deal gently with those who are ignorant and are going astray since He Himself is subject to weakness." (Hebrews 5:2)

II Corinthians 1:6 defines it correspondingly this way."If we are distressed, it is for your comfort and salvation; if we are comforted, it is for your comfort, which produces in you patient endurance for the same sufferings." As referenced, what we go through, we learn for two. (See 'The Supremacy of Shepherding')

Pastors are less threatening and more effective when able to identify with church members. The areas in which pastors struggle put them on familiar ground with their parishioners.

An incident in my family's past underscores this principle. I had a younger brother, deceased at age 47, from the dual causes of an unhealthy lifestyle and alcoholism, which precipitated both his early demise and death after two suicide attempts.

Upon meeting new parishioners, the topic of gay relatives surfaced; one shared with much shame, embarrassment, and fear as to my response. Sharing my experience allowed me to empathize and pray with them. Our shared experience became a source of encouragement. It also indirectly validated my family's painful experience.

Buried deep inside our brains are special brain cells called mirror neurons that fire in response to another person's situation. Neuroscientists believe that these cells allow humans and some primates to feel empathy and compassion for others.

Isaiah describes Christ, the Messiah as a wounded healer in Isaiah 53. "Surely He took up our infirmities and carried our sorrows, yet we considered Him stricken by God, smitten by Him and afflicted. But He was pierced for our transgressions. He was crushed for our iniquities, and by His wounds, we are healed." His suffering became the source of consolation to the wounded; His pain became productive. (Isaiah 53:4-5)

Pastors can utilize their woundedness to help others. Conversely, if we fail to deal with our issues, we may hurt and inflict pain on others. (See 'The Certainty of Call')

216

Avoidance in dealing with our issues is detrimental to us and others. And the price of not dealing with problems is greater than the expense of getting help.

Much of what causes us to have emotional baggage is our unresolved anger over our past. We cannot change the conditions that made us who we are, but we can change our response to them. We are responsible for making healthy choices in dealing with these life situations.

Pastors and their people must learn to observe their behavioral patterns and accept responsibility for changing them. We can choose to be victims or victors in how we view and respond to the circumstances and those who have wounded us. Our response makes all the difference.

We who are called to be healers often do not know how to set boundaries. We may have been violated by others and think we deserve what has happened to us. Or we may take out our anger on those who have hurt us.

Ironically, we often feel that if we have enough faith, we can be healed without assistance. We, in turn, teach our parishioners to respond in the same way.

Pastors may try to compensate by helping others but unconsciously make others dependent upon them. The essence of codependence is to make it appear we are helping someone else, while the real benefit is what we get out of it. Pastors easily fall prey to this behavioral pattern.

People who have not addressed their hurts tend to hurt other people. Conversely, when hurting people become healed, they can help others to heal.

The Basis of Exhortation/Counseling:
Coming Alongside to Help

The biblical base of counseling centers in the Holy Spirit, the third member of the Trinity, who is called the Paraclete. This title is taken from two Greek words, para (alongside) and kalew (to call.) The Master Counselor is one called alongside us. As pastor-counselors, we are called alongside to offer counsel through the discernment and direction of the Holy Spirit Himself.

One of the main functions of the counselor is to speak the truth. In John 16:13, Christ explains it this way, "But when He, the Spirit of Truth comes, He will guide you into all truth." This truth is based upon biblical principles. Counselors are called alongside to tell a person the truth that will bring them to wholeness and health.

In the New Testament, the synonym for counseling is exhorting, in the category of speaking gifts. It is a means of *verbal healing* that helps wounded people to become well.

The concept of coming alongside distinguishes this speaking gift from the other two, preaching and teaching. Preaching takes place in a larger group setting, worship. Teaching occurs in an environment such as a Sunday School Class, a Bible Study, or a small group. Exhortation is usually carried out in the smallest context, that of a personal interchange.

Often, a pastor has all three speaking gifts and uses them interchangeably. The Lord gifted me with these gifts, the strongest of which is the gift of exhortation in the context of a counselor-counselee relationship.

Exhortation-counseling may be defined as: coming alongside to comfort, challenge, confront, bring content, and promote change in the individual's life.

These are the five elements of exhortation-counseling.

Comfort A significant part of the exhortation-counseling process is bringing support and encouragement to someone. This initial response is simply being available to them, listening and absorbing the pain in a sympathetic spirit. Counseling is the spiritual and psychological arm around the individual.

Challenge The objective of proper counseling is not merely to give the counselee a place to vent or telling them what they want to hear. They are there because they have a problem, unable to solve it themselves. They come to someone they know and respect to help them. A person may be resistant to deal with issues initially but subconsciously hopes that someone will offer new information and help them think differently about the problem and how they respond to it. To do this, we need to get adequate information to determine the counseling process and solicit their commitment to the plan of action determined. Effective listening requires patience and allows for lapses in conversation. This permits the individual to process the information shared.

Confront The counselor must confront the individual with the right motive and appropriate methodology. The rule is: truth without love is brutality, and love without truth is sentimentality. Confrontation done in the right way is an act of caring. It is caring enough to confront. Pain can be motivational in the client wanting to get well. We are only responsible for our responses, not those of the client.

Content Our counseling must be centered on the truths and principles of God's Word. It is essential to remember that we allow the counselee to discern the problem and access the power to solve it using the right resources. Note, however, that secular resources can be auxiliary to Christian counseling in applying biblical principles.

Change The result of this process is to change, not to remain the same. Change is often difficult and threatening; it often takes place slowly and not without relapsing into old ways of thinking and behaving. Significantly, the first four elements of exhortation facilitate the desired objective. The system encourages the counselee to participate in and celebrate their progress, incentivizing them to incorporate new behaviors. The counselor and counselee should discuss mutual expectations in the counseling process. Destination will determine the direction of the journey.

We see these elements in the role and function of the Holy Spirit, the chief exhorter-counselor.

Comfort "The Spirit Himself intercedes for us with groanings too deep for words." (Romans 8:26b)

Challenge "When He comes, He will convict the world of sin, righteousness, and judgment." (John 16:11)

Confront "Instead speaking the truth in love; we will in all things grow up into Him who is the Head, that is Christ." (Ephesians 4:15)

Content "The Spirit guides us into all truth." (John 16:13)

Change "Therefore if anyone is in Christ, he is a new creation; the old is gone, the new has come." (II Corinthians 5:17)

Pastors who serve as counselors follow the mandate and the example of God the Father, Son, and Holy Spirit. We bring the truth alongside to help people apply the principles to their lives personally and practically in order to help them be healed.

We confront in a loving way that disallows judgment or condemnation; attitudes that only exacerbate the woundedness.

While there is no place in scripture for judging others (Matthew 7:1), there is a place for correction. (Galatians 6:1) *Judgment* is self-directed, negative, and punitive. It serves the needs of the one who is judging. *Correction* is other-directed, positive, and nurturing. It serves the needs of the one who is being corrected. There is a place for godly confrontation and correction in the Body of Christ. In essence, love does the best for the one loved, so we tell them the truth, which helps them change rather than stay the same.

Confrontation can be daunting for the shepherd who must live and serve amid the sheep. Sometimes sheep would rather walk off the cliff than have the shepherd's staff put around their neck to save their life. Spiritual shepherds often stand amazed to watch their human-sheep perform in much the same way. People can run from reality. They can deny problems and can refuse to seek help.

Facing, dealing with, and resolving causal factors will be painful, challenging, and constructive for the counselee. Dealing with the issues or failing to deal with the issues results in pain either way. There is the pain of changing or the greater pain of remaining the same. Facing the problem can be productive; running from the pain can be destructive.

However, while all pastors and ministers are called to counsel, not all are equally motivated or equipped to perform the task. Some pastors feel comfortable with large groups of people instead of a smaller context. I have known pastors who thought they could counsel from the pulpit believing the applied word would help people with specific needs. I chose a more personal approach because it allowed for the privacy and directiveness needed.

Shortly after I came to a new pastorate, a woman inquired about whether I did pastoral counseling, which surprised me. Later on, I discovered that the pastor I followed did not do counseling. He referred individuals to another resource person, something which we now explore.

The Necessity of Referral: Understanding Your Professional Limits

An expert told a group of pastors, "If you can't cure 'em in four sessions, then refer 'em out!" It's a bit unrealistic to think you can cure someone in just four sessions, give them quick fixes or refer them prematurely.

One of the limitations of such counseling may be that the pastor is not adequately equipped to care for the counselee, so free counseling becomes substandard, expected as gratis. Incidentally, I have often found a correlation between those with psychological issues and financial needs. Often those who need counseling can't pay for it. So, pastors get counselees by default; the client has no place else to go.

But, not every church member feels comfortable coming to their pastor for counseling. Confiding in someone who knows them well is threatening, not comforting. The thought of having to face their counselor, who is their pastor is awkward. They believe that the pastor now feels differently towards them. I told parishioners, "I respect you more, not less for seeking help." I was not affronted if a person did not choose to come to me for counseling. What concerned me was that they get the help they needed, more than its source, preferably with a competent Christian counselor. In any situation, confidentiality is imperative. To violate it builds mistrust and discourages people from seeking help.

A humorous story comes to mind to illustrate this basic premise. A parish priest was being honored at a 25th anniversary dinner. A leading local politician, a member of the congregation, was chosen to make the presentation and give a little speech at the dinner but was delayed in traffic. So, the priest decided to say a few words while they waited. "You understand that the seal of the confessional can never be broken. However, I got my initial impressions of the parish from the first confession I heard. I can only hint vaguely about this, but when I came here 25 years ago, I thought I had been assigned to a terrible place."

"The very first chap who entered my confessional told me how he had stolen a TV, and when the police stopped him, he tried to speed away. Further, he told me he had embezzled money from his place of business and had an affair with his boss's wife. I was appalled. But as the days transpired, I knew that my people were not all like that and I had, indeed, come to a fine parish full of understanding and loving people."

Just as the priest finished his talk, the politician arrived full of apologies for being late. He immediately began to make the presentation and give his speech. "I'll never forget the first day our priest arrived in this parish," said the politician. "I had the honor of being the first person to go to him for confession." (Oops!)

There are other reasons why congregants are resistant to counseling. They consider themselves not to have a problem. If so, it is not as bad as the problems others have. They are often embarrassed to have people find out they are in counseling. As Christians, they believe they should not have a problem or should have enough faith to solve it. It is surmised that at least nine other people should seek counseling for every person who does.

I have heard the myriad of excuses to which I have made the following responses:

- Which would you rather have, the pain of staying sick or the pain of getting well? There is risk, fear, and pain either way.
- What is more uncomfortable; people knowing you are in

counseling or finding out that you have a broken marriage or personal problems?

- Why is it easier to go to the hospital with a physical problem than seek a counselor or psychological specialist for an emotional issue?

It is pride and fear that keep people from getting help. So, the church needs to remove any barriers to recognizing the need for getting the help. These barriers may include stigma, cost, and discomfort.

The unique nature of the individual's need may require a referral to a specialist. Although ministers can address general spiritual needs such as anxiety, temptation, and failure, they may not be able to deal with more in-depth problems such as eating disorders, depression, addictions, or sociopathic illness.

Some churches will not refer a person to a secular, non-Christian counselor. Though I would prefer to have the person seek the help of a pastor, another team member, or lay counselor, there are many qualified secular specialists in the broader community who God can and will use to treat the individual situation.

This perspective in the church community is based on the fear that all secular psychological counseling is non-biblical, therefore non-Christian, and thus avoided. This position has moderated somewhat over the years due to the complexity of issues becoming a social tsunami. I believe people need to know that it is okay to seek counseling that best suits their needs. However, if it is a secular resource, the process should be ideally augmented with spiritual counseling.

A referral does not always imply sending the person to the counselor, psychiatrist, or therapist. It may involve offering other resources. The pastor should be appraised of books, articles, videos, etc., dealing with the specialty areas. Ideally, support groups can be a part of the total church ministry and available in the community. For example, Celebrate Recovery, Alcoholics Anonymous, Al-Anon, and Ala-Teen provide a support system that helps deal with addictive behaviors.

Again, the parish counselor needs to offer the best resources to the person who has come to them for help.

My advice is to do some pastoral counseling as part of your ministry and make referrals when necessary. When a referral becomes necessary, perhaps ask the church to supply the required financial resources to cover at least a portion of the cost. Churches often have special funds set aside for such purposes. One of our parishes called it 'The LUV Fund.'

One of the unseen benefits of providing pastoral counseling is to let people know that the church takes their needs seriously, allows them to identify, own, and seek resources to meet those needs.

Because we are whole persons, every part of us complements the other. There is a definite correlation between our spiritual and psychological health. Becoming a Christian doesn't automatically cure everything that is wrong with us. It does, however, provide the context in which necessary resources are provided. Pastors are called to be involved directly or indirectly with exhortation-counseling.

The Role of Client Accountability: Giving Homework

A critical component in the counselee getting well is giving them ownership in the process. They need to have a part in their recovery.

One of the potential drawbacks of pastoral counseling is that the counselee may have little incentive to share responsibility for their recovery. Some people expect to talk and have someone else just listen and comfort but not require change, short-circuiting the process.

Most churches require too little from their membership in general. Today's Christian consumer is often acclimated to having their needs met with little reciprocal commitment on their part; all the privileges with none of the responsibilities.

One way to increase the client's responsibility is to assign homework and tasks that correlate with the counseling process. "And if you don't have your homework done, don't come back next week!" (Well, not quite!)

When the counselor sets down homework expectations, the counselee is often surprised. (Apply the principles? What a new, novel, and unpopular idea!) But people who invest in their process enjoy the dividends!

Cooperation is especially relevant in pre-marital counseling, which employs diagnostic testing, adaptability profiles, role-comparison exercises, and temperament analyses. I have used the Taylor-Johnson Temperament Analysis and Prepare and Enrich pre-marriage tools.

In essence, we are holding the individual responsible for becoming a partner in the process. Taking responsibility facilitates our ability to challenge, confront, and help them produce change.

People get excited when the process begins to work and they begin to get well. They are incentivized to work the program, develop hope, and have a growing confidence that it will succeed.

Christ held people responsible for involvement in the process. He told the disciples to go out two by two after their basic training. He told the woman taken in adultery to "go and sin no more." He instructed the religious leaders to rid the temple of their merchandise and return His House to one of prayer.

226

However, note that Christ gives them directives to formulate an action plan. He did not carry it out for them!

The client taking the responsibility to change helps the process and protects the pastor-counselor from being held responsible if the counselee makes a wrong decision. A well-known pastor was sued by a counselee's family, who claimed that their son's counselor advocated suicide. The case was thrown out, but the danger of making decisions for people is highlighted.

Some people are professional students, and others are professional counselees; always in counseling, never cured. Professional students never graduate; professional counselees never get well. In a sense, these people become counselor-(co)dependent, and the counselor becomes the enabler, allowing them to continue with unhealthy habits. Parameters in the process keep the individual from replacing one addiction with another.

One of the unexpected discoveries I made was that many people are stuck on the continuum of personal maturity. They are much older chronologically than they are emotionally.

A young couple came to me early in their marriage with a definite problem. They were spending less time together now than before they were married. The young groom spent at least four nights a week with the guys; he loved softball and bars! And the only way the wife could be with him in the evening was to join him at the bar, a place where she didn't want to be with peers she didn't enjoy. This guy was 30 going on 17, still acting like an adolescent. If it hadn't been for the news of a forthcoming baby, he might still have been coming to counseling with no real desire to change. In this case, he represents many who have become frozen somewhere at a much earlier stage in life, with unresolved issues that stifle their development into true maturity. We need to incentivize people to change.

There are two main goals in exhortation-counseling.

- To help the counselee change their thinking and conduct and give them tools to change and sustain new patterns of behavior.
- To make them independent of you and not sign on for a long-term relationship with a counselee, also known as a professional leach.

In other words, help the individual(s) to accept responsibility to work out the problem without you. After serving as their co-pilot, let them go solo. Allow initial dependency to help them to become ultimately independent.

The parental metaphor is helpful here. A healthy parent has expectations for their children, and one is to assume more responsibility for their own choices as they get older and ultimately function independently. (Not be still be living at home at 45!)

The loving parent who attempts to do what is best for the child can be met with resistance if their child disagrees with them. Pastors confront this response in their spiritual children.

The Development of Lay Counselors:
A Spiritual Intensive Care Unit

Counseling can be provided by pastors, other professionals, and people in the congregation. One of the things I have attempted to do in pastoral counseling has been to train members in the congregation to assist in the task.

It is often assumed that pastors or paid professionals are to do everything. Translation: If you have a problem, see the pastor!

The concept of training laypeople has a biblical basis. In Titus chapter 1, Paul instructs the young pastor to appoint elders in every town to help with the pastoral ministry.

The counseling task can be shared with others in the congregation. But, ask most pastors; the laity is scared to death of talking to someone about knowing Christ, much less helping one of their own with their problem!

Church members often ask each other, "How are you?" without really wanting to know the answer. They don't know what to do if the person says something other than "I'm just fine."

Here is an amusing antidote about what happens when you ask someone how they are; they usually say "FINE". which really means *F*-rustrated, *I*-nsecure, *N*-eurotic, and *E*-xhausted!

There is biblical precedent for the **I**ntensive **C**are **U**nit to be incorporated into the local church.

I Thessalonians 5:14, "And we urge you, brothers, warn those who are idle, *encourage* the timid, help the weak."

Hebrews 3:12-13 "See to it brothers that none of you has a sinful, unbelieving heart that turns away from the living God. But *encourage* one another daily, as long as it is called today so that none of you be hardened by sins deceitfulness."

Hebrews 10:24-25, "And let us consider how we may spur one another on toward love and good deeds. Let us not give up meeting together, but let us *encourage* one another and all the more as you see the Day approaching."

We need to consider that the work of exhortation also belongs to the body-at-large and to parishioners who have the specific gift of exhortation.

The ministry of exhortation becomes more critical in the troubled time in which we live. Members of the church need to encourage one another. A counselee once gave me a cup with this saying,

"Friends are angels who lift us up when our wings forget to fly." This is the role of the exhorter.

An ICU may facilitate the role of the church congregation in the ministry of exhortation-counseling. Who could be members of the Unit? People who have the gift of exhortation. These people also have personalities and temperaments that accompany their spiritual capacity.

Others who have gone through like experiences can identify with similar problems. Simply, no experience is ever wasted; our pain becomes productive when it enables us to assist someone else to go through theirs.

To sympathize is to *understand* the same pain; to empathize is to *experience* the same pain. Both have been defined as two hearts tugging at the same load. Every pastor cannot experience every issue of their congregants; they need others in the congregation to help them understand what they can't.

The upside is that their peers can identify with other people's problems. ICU training can expand the class member's knowledge on a wide range of social issues. A possible tool to develop an ICU curriculum can be found in the eBook, Issues and Answers, referenced in Chapter 13.

The downside of lay counseling is that the congregation may not accept anyone else other than the pastor providing counseling. None the less the pastor needs to be involved in the training and advising the ICU members.

What worked best for me was a combination of pastoral and lay counseling. I took on the central role in counseling but often referred the counselee to others. Here is a winning combination. The pastor can provide *general* principles by which to deal with the individual problem. The parishioner can provide *specific* personal understanding and empathy that facilitates the healing process.

Land Mines in the Couch: The Danger of Going Deep

There are potential dangers of going deep with people in the parish for the pastor, who serves as their authority, spiritual leader, and counselor. Any relationship has its risks. These relational risks occur when one is a pastor.

One danger is that people who come to you for counsel will later resent the fact that you know too much about them; they feel embarrassed and ashamed for failing.

Another danger is and that you will not honor confidentiality. I felt that I would break confidence unless I asked permission to share information with someone else even including my wife.

Pastor-counselors can exercise too much power and control over people's life. People are often conditioned to follow any authority, be told what to do and have other people decide for them. The counselee should be encouraged to make their own choices in behavior; for which the pastor is not ultimately responsible.

The greatest danger is getting too involved with a counselee. Pastors may attempt to compensate for their own emotional needs.

Data has confirmed that people in religious occupations command a certain amount of respect and admiration by the sheer fact of who they are. People tend to deify pastors. Because they trust them explicitly, they may put them on a pedestal viewing them as God's direct representatives. This situation is dangerous for the pastor put on a pedestal. The union can become a lethal combination. The deified professional may enter into an inappropriate relationship with someone who has the same needs.

For several years I sat on a denominational board that interviewed candidates for the pastoral ministry and those in need of pastoral discipline. I remember seeing many men (only rarely a woman) who would tell stories of how they became involved with parishioners of the opposite sex in the counseling setting.

They became involved emotionally and then, most usually physically. With tears and anguish, these broken pastors would confess to infidelity and face the consequences of their choices.

Why did this happen? Because an insecure person viewed their counselor as a person of power and authority. The person in authority misused their position overstepping the professional boundaries intended to safeguard illicit behavior. It is truly one of Satan's finely-honed instruments of destruction. It also stresses the importance of the referral process.

The harsh reality is that the enemy of our souls seeks to ruin pastors in this area of vulnerability, often using unstable and scheming people to do it. There are men and women in congregations who are out to bring pastors and religious leaders down! Sadly, over-confident and under-vigilant pastors and religious leaders are complicit with the evil one in causing the downfall. They can make good choices or bad choices. Too, in the realm of infidelity, a person has plenty of time to consider their actions and ample time to stop the downward process.

Nothing gives Satan more delight and God more discomfort than having an appointed overseer of the flock misuse the sheep. The reputation of Christ is maligned, the credibility of the pastor questioned. The church's ministry is compromised, and the trust of the congregation is severely weakened or destroyed.

Pastors must be extremely cautious and continuously vigilant about relationships with members of the opposite sex, especially when counseling. They also need to exercise propriety in physical contact with members of the congregation in general. The cardinal

232

rule is never to meet with a member of the opposite sex either alone or when there is no other staff in the facility.

While serving on this same denominational board, I recall an instance where, after interviewing a fallen brother, several of us entered into a dialogue about our personal histories in this area. None of us could remember having difficulty with the issue. One astute member of the board put bluntly, "The reason we haven't is we don't have a sign that says we're available." I have never forgotten what that meant. Each of us felt secure in who we were and thus not needing to use the ministerial position for power and personal satisfaction. We all had happy marriages. One pastor wisely said, "We all had prime rib at home; we didn't need to settle for hamburger on the street!"

I have personally never had a woman come onto me. I have let my congregants know in a variety of ways that I had prime rib at home. People knew that my wife and I were committed to each other and had a good thing going; it showed. We wanted them to know that upfront. A healthy marriage is one of the best defenses against getting involved with someone else or people ever spreading rumors about you're getting involved. The best offense is a strong defense!

A pastor has to take precautions. The exhortation-counseling capacity given to those in ministry can be an asset or a liability. The counselor's contribution will ultimately not be determined only by their capacities but in how they use them. The test of our effectiveness as counselors will be decided in the lives of those we encourage and counsel.

Remember, one of the most potentially beneficial aspects of the pastoral ministry can also become hazardous. But, there are rewards as well as risks in going deeper. A thank you card from a parishioner makes the risk of counseling worth it.

It reads: "Dear Pastor Rol and Joyce, How do I begin to express to you all that I am feeling about you? You have truly stood with me during the most difficult year of my life. As you know, I was obsessed with becoming a martyr for Christ; I believed that He wanted to take my life and that I sought ways to make that happen. Few took the time to hear me and try to understand what I was experiencing. But you were there for me every time I needed you. You were available to me repeatedly, sometimes on short notice. You never scolded or condemned me; you listened and gave me godly counsel. You prayed for me and with me. You believed in my potential and gave me hope for my future, something I could not feel or imagine. You are a huge part of my becoming well. I have begun to be my old self again. Thank you from my whole heart for being God's instrument to help me find my way through the darkness."

Summary: The church must deal with the fallout of our fall into sin. The pastor comes alongside in the ministry of exhortation-counseling to facilitate restoration. Not all pastors are equipped to do counseling and thus should be aware of resources and referrals to help those seeking it. Our call as pastor-counselors is to come alongside to care, confront, challenge, correct, and promote change. This service renders great rewards for the individual and the congregation.

The counselee is encouraged to contribute to the process financially and by completing homework. Pastors are encouraged to develop a Spiritual **I**ntensive **C**are **U**nit utilizing those members of their congregation who have the gift of exhortation and experience, complemented by pastoral counseling. Pastoral counselors may encounter significant risks in this ministry area, but they also realize great rewards from helping individuals to come into health and wholeness.

Peril: To deny your own psychological needs, fail to provide counseling for parishioners, or misuse your power and position in inappropriate relationships with counselees.

Privilege: To facilitate people becoming healthy through exhortation-counseling in all dimensions of their lives, validating their need for help, and providing the appropriate resources in the process.

Questions for personal reflection: Chapter 14 The Pastor as Counselor

1. Why is it necessary for a pastor to deal with their own psychological issues?
2. When is it appropriate to refer a counselee to another counselor?
3. Why and how should the counselee be involved in the counseling process?
4. How can a spiritual Intensive Care Unit help in the counseling ministry?
5. What are the potential dangers involved with pastoral counseling?

15   The Pastor as Steward

Basis of Biblical Stewardship:
Managing the Master's Household

The writer of Corinthians defines a steward. "Let a man so account as ministers of Christ and stewards of God. Moreover, it is required in stewards that a man be found faithful." (I Corinthians 4:1-2 KJV)

Paul defines a biblical steward as one entrusted to care for something of great value and worth by the one who owns it. Pastors are steward-managers.

The background of the word steward is one who is placed in the management of another's household. In the Old Testament, Joseph would be such a person. He was placed in charge of Potiphar's home and possessions.

Key Concept: Stewardship is management, not ownership. God owns everything; we manage it.

By its very nature, the job description implies responsibility for many different things: Household, people, supplies, finances, and maintaining a daily routine.

The pastor becomes the manager of God's house and all the things that accompany it. God entrusts all these things to the pastor's care and management; theirs is a divine investment.

236

People

Ministry is stewardship of people. Caring for the oversight of sheep is the prime responsibility of the shepherd. Our most important area of accountability is that of ultimately presenting them to God as complete in Christ.

Resources

Ministry is stewardship of physical buildings, properties, etc. Physical endowments given to us are of central importance in providing both a place and supplies for the ministry.

Finances

Ministry is stewardship of money, budgeting, and acquisitions; all are part of using the financial endowments for the local church's ministry.

Daily Routine

Ministry is stewardship of maintaining the church's life, including programs, calendar-keeping, directing staff and lay personnel, advertising, recruitment, and general organization.

Preparing a pastor to become an effective steward-manager poses challenges.

Not everyone in church ministry is given the gift of administration, but all are called to the care and keeping of the church. This is a stewardship for which they are held accountable on earth and rewarded eternally.

Total Life Stewardship: Beyond the Wallet

It is common to think of stewardship as only a financial concept. But it extends beyond that single sphere.

In 1858, the hymn writer, William B. How, captures this concept in *We Give Thee But Thine Own.* "We give thee but thine own, what e'er the gift may be. All that we have is thine alone, a trust, O Lord from thee. May we thy bounties thus as stewards true receive, and gladly as thou blesses us, to thee our firstfruits give." (Old language, new meaning).

On our Annual Stewardship Sunday a message concluded with an opportunity to commit to the 4 T's of stewardship.

Time: A portion of the 168 hours a week is to be given to our spiritual life, family life, physical maintenance, vocation, ministry, and community involvement.

Talent: We are called to share our God-given capacities and abilities in the work of the ministry as well as the marketplace.

Treasure: Each of us has been given monetary and physical resources, which the Giver expects to be given back to Him in some measure. He owns it all; He only asks for a portion.

Testimony: All believers in Christ have something to share; each story is unique and is to be shared within the congregation and community.

Key Concept: The pastor and people are to tithe on those spiritual *and* physical resources placed at their disposal.

So doesn't it make sense that we owe God a measure of what He has given us? He only asks for a 10% portion. In the Old Testament, the Jewish tithe was upwards of 23%.

In the New Testament, in I Corinthians 16:2, Paul replaces the tenth/tithe concept with a new basis of measurement for giving, *"According to how each of you has prospered."* In other words, starting with the floor and moving toward the ceiling.

The average person who attends a church in this country gives roughly 2% of their income to the local ministry, although the figure may be higher for all charitable giving. But, we are talking about the work of God through the local church. The statistic is abysmal and hardly a compliment to God's most blessed people. "Blessed be the Lord, who daily loadeth us with benefits, even the God of our salvation." (Psalm 68:19 KJV)

If we are grateful for all we have, should we give just what is required or give more? Remember, Christ didn't eke out just enough for us; He gave way more than enough! (John 10:10b)

Think about it. God owns all the resources and gives us everything we have. What He asks for in return is for us to fulfill our stewardship by giving Him what is rightfully His.

The Heart of Stewardship:
Knowing and Following the Model of the Master

What is our master asking? Are we willing to give back to Him in the same way He has given to us? In other words, the master does not want stingy stewards.

Paul addresses this issue of the heart in II Corinthians 9:7 when he reminds his readers, "Each man should give what he has decided in his *heart* to give, not reluctantly or under compulsion, for God loves a cheerful giver." He asks we give not from duty but delight!

Christmas provides a correlation. You have two lists; loved ones and office staff. You shop for the first group because you know them and love them; you take time to find unique gifts; cost is not a factor. You are obligated to shop for the second group because they work with you. You don't know them well, and you are not related to them. You shop Neiman Marcus for the first group; the local Target will suffice for the second.

One of my favorite Old Testament stewardship texts is Exodus 35 within the context of building the tabernacle. The people were bringing much more than enough for the construction of the temple. Thus, the people were restrained from bringing any more. The people were motivated by God's generosity to give generously. Know any pastors who have had to tell their people to stop giving? (It's not a problem I've ever had!)

Over the years in pastoral ministry, I have approached this subject in every way possible. Yet, stewardship can always be reduced to one bottom line: Giving back to the Giver of all things out of respect for Him and what He has given us. *It is always a matter of the heart!* If we are faithful followers of Christ, total life stewardship will follow, like a caboose follows a train.

We can apply the 4-T concepts to the pastorate, which by its very nature requires the stewardship of time, talent, treasure, and testimony.

Time Pastors don't often get in trouble from working too little, but working too much. Also, pastors need to plan and use time wisely and be punctual. (See 'Self-care')

Talent This has to do with spiritual gifts specifically listed in the New Testament and other capacities not listed. The use of **T**(alents) **A**(bilities) **G**(ifts) is an essential part of fulfilling our stewardship. In addition to their spiritual gifts, many pastors are also musicians, athletes, artists, chefs, mechanics, and computer gurus. All these talents and abilities are part of the divine endowments entrusted to their care. Pastors, like their people, are multi-gifted. (See 'The Pastor as Administrator')

Treasure Pastors are responsible for tending to their finances and not be governed by the desire for wealth. It also extends to the church finances, for which pastors often seek the assistance of those with the gift of financial management.

Principles of good stewardship of our treasure are incorporated in the following:

1.   Always tithe and increase it proportionately with income.

2.   As income permits, support projects beyond the tithe, both inside and outside the church. The tithe goes strictly to the church, and the offering may go to work outside the church, such as food banks, missions, or educational causes.

3.   Attempt to live simply and not beyond your means, avoiding the accumulation of things not needed; sell or give away stuff regularly.

4.   Stay out of debt. Borrow only for appreciable things; be conservative with charging non-appreciable things. Use debit cards as often as possible.

5.   Strive to live adequately yet moderately, including housing and automobiles.

6.   Resist making money a primary focus in ministry. Instead, promote personal spiritual maturity, which engenders a focus on eternal investments.

7.   Don't try to get in with wealthy people to assure financial security.

8.   Avoid expecting that people will give you financial favors, i.e., giving discounts.

9.   Limit the use of credit cards. Attempt to pay them off in the same month.

10. Make it a practice not to know what other people give.

Christ did not personify the affluent. Instead, He preached and practiced the principle of living simply and frugally. In Mark 10:25,

He said, "It was easier for a camel to go through the eye of a needle than for a rich man to enter the kingdom of heaven."

What we qualify as necessities, most of the world considers luxuries. We have made luxuries our new necessities. Too, the hidden persuaders and merciless marketers of our time have redefined what we need to survive and succeed. Our culture can be described as having come down with a bad case of *affluenza*.

The scriptures do not teach that the believer will be blessed with health and wealth. This false doctrine stands in marked contrast to the life of our Lord in Matthew 8:20b. "The Son of Man had no place to lay His head." "He became poor, that through His poverty, you might become rich." (II Corinthians 8:9)

The Great Ambition, a video produced by my denomination, tells the story of the inception of the Evangelical Covenant Church in the late 1800s. One unforgettable frame features an early pastor wearing shoes with holes in them and holding a sack of potatoes for compensation. When his son queries him about their situation, he remarked, "Christ was always on His way to the poor house."

Even though the New Testament talks more about money than it does about hell, it does not infer that everyone who believes in Jesus will have great wealth. The love of money, the root of all evil, often creates its own hell.

Conversely, this does not mean that having wealth is wrong. There were wealthy people throughout the scriptures. (Job and Zacheeus weren't on welfare!) The problem with wealth is when it's promised to everyone as an automatic by-product of faith in Christ.

Testimony The most rudimentary definition of testimony is to give a witness to something God is doing in our lives. By this definition, a pastor often fails to fulfill this stewardship. Why? Because pastors usually resist talking too much about themselves or sharing their struggles for fear of looking weak or being too self-focused.

To share yourself in an honest, uncontrived way lets your people know you as a person as well as a pastor. They can relate to you when you have successful moments or hard times.

In a recent magazine article, the main subject was pastors sharing about themselves in the ministry. Several pastors confessed how hard it was to come to a place where they could be honest with their congregation without feeling awkward or calling attention to themselves or their family. One man shared a meaningful point of connection when meeting several of his parishioners in remedial driving school! (Well, that's a new way to do visitation!)

It is a matter of balance. Bearing testimony does not mean coming into the pulpit with a tale of woe. "This is the worst week I've ever had...just about left my spouse and resigned the church." We can share honestly and openly how to get through the tough times and maintain hope! The testimony of the pastor needs to be transparent but as triumphant as possible. Reminder: Always get permission from someone you are using as an illustration, especially your family members!

The stewardship of testimony also extends to sharing your faith with others outside the church. We who are pastors are encouraged to pray for and build relationships with pre-Christians in our lives. When we talk about sharing Christ with others, we give our people the incentive to do the same.

Key Concept: Good shepherding and good stewardship are demonstrated in both the realm of the pastor's personal and professional life.

Investors vs. Consumers: Giving or getting?

Stewardship calls for us to be continuously grateful for the Master's resources. I like to call these *life loans* for a temporary season. Yet, we have adopted many of the secular culture's attitudes when it comes to them.

Even though God has dramatically blessed Americans, we are driven by consumption to have more and often invest less in the lives of others. How much more do we need to consume? As approximately 6% of the world's population, we consume upward to 70 % of the world's resources.

Ours is a society that seems driven by satisfaction and selfishness. This is symptomatic of people who have had too much for too long and expect to have it indefinitely. (The free lunch never ends.) When someone asked John D. Rockefeller, "How much money is enough?" He said, "A little bit more." This passion for consumption begins; where else? The heart. The heart is the center of emotions, affections, and our will. It can be lured away from God; we can experience an *alienation of affection.*

Let's consider two questions:

Are we monetarily wealthy but spiritually impoverished? Someone has called it needs and greeds. Our values directly impact how we live, use our resources and our lifestyle choices.

Should not our giving be sacrificial? Our giving should not always be convenient; it needs to cost us something. It is often beyond our comfort zone, which requires faith to claim His resources in response to our giving. Christ gave sacrificially claiming His Father's provision by faith. This sentiment is expressed in David's act of worship. 2 Samuel 24:24b, "I will not sacrifice to the Lord my God burnt offerings that cost me nothing."

Key Concept: To be rich, give; to be poor, grasp; to have abundance, scatter; to be needy, hoard.

The model of proper stewardship is based on values, priorities, principles, and lifestyle which reflect the teaching and life of our Lord. If, as pastors, we espouse the importance of being contributors, not merely consumers, it will be transmitted by our thinking, living, preaching, and especially by our example. It has been said that what matters most in our life can be measured by our calendar and our wallet; how we spend our time and money.

The Benefits of Giving: What do we get out of it?

The disciples also asked Jesus about this in Matthew 19:27,29. The impulsive and outspoken Peter asks the question, "We have left everything to follow you. What then will there be for us?" Christ's answer, "And everyone who has left houses or brothers or sisters or father, mother or children or fields for my sake will receive a hundred times as much and eternal life."

Thus, the focus of His work on earth is investing in the lives of others. The Christ-follower is challenged to ask the question: What's in it for *others,* more than what is in it for *me*?

God promises that we will get out of it what we put into it. We just can't out-give Him. He will always give back in the same measure we have given to Him. If we believe in what He says, why don't we give Him more?

In 2 Corinthians 9:8, He promises, "And God is able to make all grace abound to you so that in all things at all times, you will have all you need."

If we give as He gives, we can't lose. When we give Him the *best,* the first fruits, not leftovers, He has promised to bless the *rest.* "But seek first His kingdom and His righteousness, and all these things will be given you as well." (Matthew 6:33)

And, the financial residual is not all we get out of it. We receive the blessing in a variety of ways. The New Testament indicates that the quality and even the quantity of life are derived from good stewardship of finances and all other resources. Pastors who believe in and put this principle into practice can motivate their people to do the same.

Paul puts it this way to Timothy in his first letter, "Charge them that are rich in this world, that they not be high-minded nor trust in uncertain riches, but in the living God who giveth us richly all things to enjoy; that they do good, that they be rich in good works, ready to distribute, willing to communicate, laying up in store for themselves a good foundation against the time to come, that they may lay hold on eternal life." (I Timothy 6:17-19 KJV) This portion refers to the reward in the present and in the future.

Key Concept: "You can't take it with you, but you can send it on ahead."

Thus, good stewards have an eternal perspective relative to investing their wealth in the needs of others who are impoverished physically, educationally, spiritually, and financially.

Today's church needs to re-discover that everything we are, have, and do is a temporary means to an eternal end.

Jim Elliot, the famous missionary who gave his life trying to reach the Auca Indians of Ecuador, put it this way: "He is no fool who gives what he cannot keep to gain that which he cannot lose."

As steward-managers of our Master, Jesus Christ, how we fulfill our stewardship will have lasting implications for others and ourselves, now and forever.

The story is told of a rich man who commissioned one of his servants to build a house while he was away on a long journey. The man developed a stealth plan to build the house, substituting

246

inferior materials for quality ones, and using unskilled rather than quality labor. He completed the project in only half the time.

Upon his master's return, he was greeted warmly with accolades as to a job well done. The master then said, "In gratitude for what you have done for me, I want you to occupy the house you have built."

Summary: Pastors and their people are stewards entrusted with the care and management of their Master's resources of time, talent, treasure, and testimony. These are divine endowments given for a brief time on earth for which they are accountable and will be rewarded eternally. God asks for a willing heart that prompts us to give Him what is rightfully His because we want to, not because we have to. We are motivated to give in the same way our Master has abundantly given to us. In an age of self-centered consumers, we are called to be contributors. The scriptures remind us that we glorify God and do good for ourselves when we use His resources wisely and share them generously. Our Master gives us resources that are a means to a greater end, making investments in His work and the lives of others.

Peril: To mismanage the resources, fail to teach and model good stewardship in our lives and ministry

Privilege: To help others view and use total life resources for the cause of Christ and the good of others.

Questions for personal reflection: Chapter 15 The Pastor as Steward

1. What is the basis of biblical stewardship?
2. How do the four T's of total life stewardship apply to pastors?
3. Why is our response to stewardship ultimately an issue of the heart?

4. What is the difference between a consumer and an investor?

5. What are the lasting benefits of biblical stewardship?

16   The Pastor As Evangelist

Christ in the Market Place:
The Impact of a Contrasted Life

In surveying the chapter title, your natural inclination might be to ask what program the pastor should promote, what training seminar should be conducted, what guest evangelist needs to be brought in, what kind of tracts should be used to witness to others?

Integral to evangelism is our life and walk with God. In its simplest and purest form, evangelism emulates the Master's model in the marketplace, where we live, move, and have our being. It is the Living Good News.

The pastor is called to live a transparent, consistent, and exemplary life in modeling Christ in their behavior, precipitated by having a heart to see lost people found.

Early in my pastoral career, I had people tell me that I had an unusual excitement and passion when preaching about evangelism. Although I do not consider myself to have a special capacity for evangelism, I do indeed have the heart of an evangelist. More importantly, I have a responsibility to bear witness, as does every believer.

I believe that many pastors would share this sentiment. They may not be gifted in evangelism, but they have a heart for reaching lost people. They evangelize primarily by the way they live; their contrasted life draws people to them who want what they have. In his first letter, Peter encourages early followers of Christ to live so that people could know what they believed and see how they behaved. (I Peter 3:15,16)

As part of my community connection in one of my pastorates, I frequented the local grade school near the church, often dropping by for lunch. Upon the conclusion of that ministry, the faculty gave me a send-off; we had become good friends. I had no other agenda than befriending the school and finding ways to serve the community. One of the teachers, in conversation with the principal, made a comment I have not forgotten. When describing me and my involvement with the school, she said, "If I met that man and weren't a Christian, I'd sure be working on it." No higher tribute could have been given me than to think that someone would consider coming to know my Jesus because they caught a glimpse of Him in me. Herein is the heart of the pastor as an evangelist.

The late Dr. Win Arn, Youth for Christ Director, would close every Saturday night rally with this challenge: "Lord help us bear witness of you by lip and by life." Our actions needed to match our words.

The contrasted life is distinctly different from the world; it is where the Lord can be seen and draw people to Himself.

I don't always live the kind of life I want. For instance, I tend to speed under the guise of having to stay on a tight schedule to help Jesus help people! (Uh, huh!) Try telling that to the police officer, which I have tried to do on more than one occasion. It is also the reason I don't have Christian bumper stickers on my car! In these moments, I am not imitating the model of my Master or drawing people to Him!

By lip also means to talk naturally about what the Lord is doing in our life and taking the opportunity to share the plan of salvation. But remember: The life precedes the lip.

The pastor-evangelist is called to flesh out the gospel. "You are our letter written on our hearts, known and read by everybody." (II Corinthians 3:2)

True story: A few years ago, a group of salesmen went to a regional sales convention in Chicago. They assured their wives that they would be home in plenty of time for dinner on Friday evening. In their rush to make it to the gate on time, one of these salesmen inadvertently kicked over a table that held a display of apples. Apples flew everywhere. The men all managed to reach the plane in time for their nearly-missed boarding without stopping or looking back. All but one. He paused, took a deep breath, and experienced a twinge of compassion for the girl whose apple stand had been overturned.

He told his buddies to go on without him, and waved good-bye. Then he returned to the terminal where the apples were still all over the floor. He was glad he did.

The 16-year-old girl was blind. She was softly crying, tears running down her cheeks in frustration, and at the same time helplessly groping for her spilled produce as the crowd swirled about her, no one stopping and no one caring for her plight.

The salesman knelt on the floor with her, gathered up the apples, put them into the baskets, and helped set the display up once more. As he did, he noticed that many of them had become battered and bruised; these he set aside in another basket.

When he had finished, he pulled out his wallet and said to the girl,

"Here, please take this $20.00 for the damage we did. Are you okay?" She nodded through her tears. He continued with, "I hope we did not spoil your day too badly." As the salesman started to walk away, the bewildered blind girl called out to him. "Mister." He paused and turned to look back into those blind eyes. She continued, "Are you, Jesus?"

He stopped in mid-stride and wondered. Then slowly, he made his way to catch the later flight with that question burning in his soul.

The essence of evangelism is a contrasted life where people can see Jesus in us and ask about Him!

Intentionality in the Life of the Church: Non-accidental Outreach

Coupled with the heart for the lost and a contrasted life, however, is the intentionality of bringing lost people to find Jesus. Intentionality comes from the word intentional. It means to do something on purpose.

Being intentional in this area as a pastor or lay leader is central to carrying out the Great Commission. In Matthew 28, upon Christ's send-off of the disciples, He identifies them as those under His authority and operating by His power. The imperative "make disciples" is followed by a participle: "while going through the course of everyday life." Significantly, Christ said, "Go," literally "while going," implying that bringing our world to Christ takes place *wherever* we walk, play, work, go to school, in the whole sphere of life.

Yet, sadly today, for the most part, the Great Commission has become the great omission.

One church we served surveyed the congregation to determine which programs would suit the people's interest and involvement level. They were proud of the fact that they come up with 45 programs.

Significantly, the survey reflected little or no evangelistic outreach. It was not part of the people's thinking to use these same efforts as potential bridges of personal friendship or creating opportunities to share the gospel.

In the Dallas area, a large downtown church operates on the premise that people should come to the church rather than the church coming to the people. The focus is on people hearing the gospel through their pastor. The church spends large amounts of money on their building and their advertising budget. They are the church gathered more than the church scattered.   (See 'The Pastor as Worship Leader')

Understand, I am not discrediting evangelism seminars, evangelistic techniques, or big churches. Yet, systemic to the church reaching its world for Christ is each person going into their world who shares Christ by lip and by life. This concept is especially relevant in a culture that puts more of a premium on how we live out our faith than the faith itself.

A former church we attended and served in the North Texas area has this mission statement: *Come as you are, Be transformed, Make a difference.* The church encourages people to feel comfortable coming, finding new life in Christ and then allowing others to see the difference Christ had made in their lives. Intentionality in evangelism involves these elements:

- Caring about the lost.
- Wanting to reach the lost.
- Expecting to reach the lost.
- Planning to reach the lost.
- Praying to reach the lost.
- Reaching the lost.

- Integrating the lost into the life of the church.
- Discipling the lost.

Over the years, evangelism styles have changed from the more assertive and direct presentation of the gospel to the less confrontational and more of an indirect approach.

There is an accelerated emphasis on building a trust relationship with a person as a preface to sharing our faith personally. The (event) passing out tracts on the street corner, taking surveys on the beach, and reciting a pre-written testimony has been replaced by the (environment) of demonstrating Christ in our life and winning the right to be heard.

Two terms have become more significant to the whole of Christian Evangelism: My non-Christian relationships and My story.

Non-Christian Relationships

The impact on our peer relationships is called the *circle of influence.*

For most Christ-followers, the circle starts with a higher percentage of non-believers at the time of their conversion. Gradually it is made up of more of their fellow believers. Thus, the field of non-Christians recedes.

There is now an accelerated effort to help Christians gain a new understanding of how to relate to people in their circle of influence.

Ministries such as *Alpha* and the *Truth Project* explore the fundamentals of the Christian and secular belief systems. This helps the Christ-follower have meaningful interaction with people from a non-biblical background while articulating a rational defense of the Judeo-Christian belief system.

My Story

Since the inception of the Christian faith, the scriptures have constituted the basis of the Christian witness, the central core of the gospel.

The Bible has been called, His-Story, based on the history of salvation centered on the prediction and actual coming of Christ. For all practical purposes, the church has been telling the ancient story, one that has taken on new meaning in today's post-Christian culture.

Modern society's focus has gradually changed from the historical and theological approach to the Christian faith. (Is it true?) Now it is a pragmatic approach. (Does it work?) The challenge has been to remain faithful to the historicity and theology of the Bible and express the Christian faith in terms that the modern culture can understand.

A third element is the place of prayer in the evangelization process. My particular denomination has instituted an emphasis called *Bringing My World to Christ*. Each year the church sets apart two Sundays for presenting the program. The first week calls for the presentation and distribution of personal prayer forms. People make a list of others they are praying for. These lists are then collected and brought forward at the annual congregational meeting so that all those present can rejoice in the ingathering. This past year, for example, some 15,000 people were being prayed for regularly.

This transferable concept is implemented as people pray for the opportunity to share the gospel with others and their receptivity to it. The Spirit of God goes before us. Prayer prepares the environment for telling our story. This is the blending of sharing the truth (lip) and living the truth (life). The soil has to be prepared for the planting.

Sometimes we aren't intentional about outreach and evangelism. It's not that we are cavalier about sharing the message of Christ; after all, it has changed our life. Usually, it is a feeling of inadequacy, fear of not knowing what to say, not wanting to be rejected, being regarded as a zealot, or accused of proselyting. It is not so much a lack of intentionality, but the intimidation stifles our bearing witness.

For us, a new approach to evangelization is positive and helpful. The environment is one where trust can be gained, dialogue encouraged, and a person accepted regardless of their belief system.

Getting Beyond the Walls:
Interfacing with the Contemporary Culture

Christ made it clear that He didn't come to heal the healthy, but the sick. By His example, He did not remain isolated within the synagogue, spending all His time in the Temple reading the Torah to His disciples. More often than not, Jesus went out to the highways and byways to interface with the lost.

We have often become too influenced by the world we are sent to reach. Our conformity to the mores of the world impedes the impact of our witness; we have compromised our distinctiveness. When we get beyond the safety of the sanctuary, we have little to say.

Again it could be argued that Christ was able to be in the world but not of the world; we can't. He could get close to the world without being sucked in from the under-current of contemporary culture. Although we cannot maintain His balance, we are still responsible for bearing witness through a contrasted life.

Christians can be fearful of associating with people who are different from who they are and with whom they have little in common. It's funny how often the modern church members circle the wagons to protect themselves from people with whom they are uncomfortable; a retreat mindset. The implication is that we don't like to leave the comfort zones of our fellowship. We become uncomfortable and resentful when a new person tries to break up the ol' gang, which affords security and familiarity. Sadly, I recall frequently walking through the church foyer and noticing people conversing only with those they knew. They were unaware of the new people around them.

We have created our own Christian sub-culture, which allows us to withdraw from the world we are called and commissioned to reach for Christ. Christian radio, schools, and publications allow the church to remain incubated from the cultural mainstream.

After all, going into all the world does not mean that the task would be nice and comfortable. Jesus established the evangelism paradigm of going outside the walls. He realized something that we commonly misunderstand.

More than ever, people seek spirituality, but not necessarily through Christian belief, coming to church, or through organized religion. They are waiting for the church to come to them.

Jesus challenged people to risk beyond what they considered reasonable, get out of the box, meet people on their turf, and relate to them where they live. He modeled His methodology. (See 'The Pastor as Vison Caster')

He didn't only hang around with people with whom He felt safe. No Sir! Jesus was often criticized for spending His time with people who had dubious lifestyles and questionable backgrounds. People gossiped about why He wasn't acting like the Messiah. He was! He didn't hobnob with the rich but with the poor. They came to Him because He first came to them. A short-sighted church loses its focus when it becomes what I call a social club for the saints rather than a hospital for the hurting. Stepping out of the security of the synagogue cost Him His life! By doing this, He saved our lives.

Taking advantage of special occasions to contact neighbors and friends is effective. We can become involved in a neighborhood association, host a block party or use the holidays as an opportunity to invite people to our home for an informal gathering. These are trust-building overtures, which can lead to friendship-building. (Our pastor and his wife just had a Halloween gathering for 35 of their neighbors!)

Upon moving into our new neighborhood in Santa Fe, New Mexico, we wrote a letter introducing ourselves to our neighbors, accompanied by a plate of brownies. We got to know them, greet them by name, and prayed for them.

Involvement in a local mission effort is an important entry-level contact with people in the broader community. We could adopt a senior adult in a care center (visiting them regularly and remembering their birthday), become involved in a scouting program, PTA, cancer fund drives, or Meals on Wheels. All these are natural ways of connecting with people who may be different from us, people who need to be loved, prayed for, befriended, and reached. They are connected initially by our presence and through our prayers before our presentation ever reaches them.

In one of our pastorates, we linked up with a local shoe store through an effort called Hearts and Soles. We supplied shoes for low-income families at the beginning of the school year. We became known as the *shoe church*. (After all, we were into saving souls!)

One of my community connections was serving as a police chaplain. Although a chaplain's primary task was to assist in special crises, there was the option of attending briefings and doing a ride-along with officers. More than one officer expressed their surprise in seeing a pastor willing to invest time in a community activity. One of my primary reasons for taking on this extra-curricular activity was to meet people outside of my usual circle.

My wife and I came to know a couple through my involvement in a community-based radio program that featured reading to the blind. The woman I read with was a declared atheist, her husband a self-proclaimed agnostic. They were people searching for meaning.

They were a rather unlikely couple to be socializing with, but it happened. Our adult children were both amazed and amused by this unique friendship. Yet, this couple became two of our closest friends. We spent time together often; they were an essential part of both of our children's weddings. What was most interesting; they almost always brought up something spiritual in the course of our conversations.

One of the things I remember most was a statement the woman made during one of our times together. She said, "You know; if you were trying to convert me, you wouldn't be here!" I knew what she said was true. And it was true. We weren't trying to convert her; we were simply there to befriend and accept the two of them and let them see a difference in our lives. To this day, we don't know the outcome of that friendship. Perhaps the outcome was the friendship itself, one through which God would do things that would never have taken place otherwise. At our farewell service, she gave public testimony how through knowing us and coming to our church a couple of times, she had begun to open her mind to the possibility that there might be a God. It was a significant moment in our lives and the life of the congregation. The people actually applauded. And our model had communicated a message about reaching out to people.

Definition Through Demonstration:
Turning the Church Inside Out

I have discovered four criteria that may measure the health of a local church:

- How it prays.
- How it worships.
- How it gives.
- How it reaches out.

These four criteria happen simultaneously and progressively build on each other. In a healthy church, they culminate in outreach.

One of the critical factors in evangelism is to make every church member aware that their job is a ministry. From the CEO to the postal carrier, the pre-school teacher to the boy scout leader, the government official to the waitress; every person's job provides an opportunity for ministry. All are placed there by God to bear witness of Christ and to take the gospel of the good news to those outside the walls in the marketplace of their world.

We taught our people to think locally. We encouraged our church members to pray for neighbors, begin prayer-walking on their block, pray for their schools and government officials.

On the evening before completing this manuscript while walking our dog, I was approached by three individuals I'd never met before. They asked how they could pray for me. I proceeded to tell them about this book and asked them to pray for its publication. I walked home, overwhelmed by God's timing and grateful He had provided special prayer for this project.

We promoted our congregation's involvement by working with food banks, donating blood, reading to grade school kids, providing scholarships for a latchkey kid to go camping, and offer free child care for a single mother during the Christmas shopping season.

Sister Act One is the story of nuns under the Reverend Mother's leadership. Sister Whoppi Goldberg unites them to get beyond the walls of the church to change their community. (A must-see for anyone intentional about evangelization.)

Many people have been hurt by the church, whether those hurts are real or perceived. The fear of being hurt again can affect a person's trust. No church is perfect. It's made up of imperfect people, but the ideal is to see a congregation growing into Christ to demonstrate how we should respond to each other before a world that watches.

Often, like the Ephesian Church of the Revelation, we have lost our first love. Our flame needs to be re-kindled. (Revelation 3:14-20) This need for renewal is based on the reality that we can quickly become stagnant and lethargic in our spiritual development. Thus, renewal becomes a necessity for evangelism.

Evangelism is its simplest terms, is based on these specific characteristics:

- Showing Christ-likeness in the marketplace.
- Being intentional about building bridges of friendship within our circle of influence.
- Creating arenas for connection with those different than ourselves.
- Building credibility and trust.
- Praying regularly for specific people we seek to reach.
- Telling our stories that relate faith to everyday life.
- Interfacing with a culture in a spirit of authenticity and hope.

The Marriage of Local and Global:
The Mission at Home and Abroad

The church getting beyond the walls, touches both the local and global community. Each person is divinely called, placed, and given a specialized capacity to carry out their mission, whether at a local food pantry or a freshwater pump in Nairobi.

The characteristics were evident in the early Church, as paraphrased in Acts 2:42-47. They devoted themselves to the apostle's teaching and fellowship. All the believers were together and had everything in common. Selling their possessions and goods, they gave to anyone as they had need. Praising God, they enjoyed the favor of all the people. Then the Lord added to their number daily those who were being saved. Their *local* effort extended to the *whole* of the world.

Keep in mind that this mission was launched at the birth of the Church in Jerusalem, which extended to Judea, Samaria, and the uttermost parts of the world. The followers of Christ were given the great commission to go and make disciples of all nations.

Ours is an age described by Daniel, "There will be a time of distress." "Those who are wise will shine like the brightness of the heavens and those who lead many to righteousness like the stars forever and ever." (Daniel 12:2,4)

In Matthew 24, Christ foretells the mission to the whole world in the last days. "And this Gospel of the kingdom will be preached in the entire world as a testimony to all nations, and then the end will come." (Matthew 24:14)

These Old and New Testament texts correlate. Technical advances in global communication will allow the gospel to be preached to the whole world.

The mission becomes both the cause and effect of renewal and

262

revival in the church. It renews the purpose of the church. It validates the potential contribution of its members. It is a charge led by the leadership of the church that is committed to the mandate lived out in practical ways.

- Praying for the church's foreign missionaries regularly.
- Teaming up with missionaries abroad by correspondence and featuring them in a service via live video or Skype.
- Hosting international students studying in this country.
- Participating in Operation Christmas Child.
- Sponsoring a child through World Vision.
- Sending a mission team abroad.
- Starting a new church plant in a foreign country.

When we extend help and assistance to others, often different from ourselves, we develop a hunger for doing that *anywhere*.

Carrying out our mission across the street or across the sea answers the question: "Why are we doing this?" The answer, "For Christ." The message has been validated through clean-up efforts in the wake of devastating tsunamis, hurricanes, and other tragedies. Relief workers have won the right to be heard, establish trust, and create opportunities for witness by the compelling love of Christ.

The influx of the world's nationalities has brought a host of ideologies, philosophies, world views, and belief systems that have challenged the traditional Judeo-Christian religious mindset. Ours is a global village, one in which people of diversified backgrounds tend to be less tolerant of Christian beliefs while at the same time expecting us to be much more tolerant of their own.

The challenge is to present the gospel message in a pluralistic world. It is a world characterized by a lessening of absolutes and moral values, moving away from traditional Christianity, and one that embraces the claims of New Age thought, Eastern religion, and Islam.

We are dealing with a seismic shift in belief systems, world views, and life priorities. Our on-going challenge is to equip believers to understand and share their faith in these changing times.

What if past generations had turned the church inside out, with each member having the single purpose of reaching the world for Christ. How many Christ-followers would there be today? Statisticians tell us that the whole world would have been reached for Christ by now!

Hopefully, we who have the privilege of leading the church at the end of the age will accept the challenge of reaching our world for Christ. In so doing, we follow our leader, the world's first and most significant missionary who fulfilled His commission to reach us.

A church in Portland, Oregon posted this sign as a visual reminder at each of its exits:

YOU ARE NOW ENTERING YOUR MISSION FIELD!

God's people are *sent* as missionaries into their world to declare a unique message through distinctly different lives.

For such a time as this, individual believers and Christian communities are commissioned to transform the world, which rightfully belongs to the One who created and redeemed it.

Summary: The pastor-evangelist is called to model and encourage the church to live a contrasted life. When the followers of Christ live no differently than everyone else, why would people want what they have? Outreach, however, must be intentional. It must focus on the **ultimate calling** of the church. Reaching the lost must be kept at the forefront of the life of the church. Getting beyond the walls requires an outward focus on people both locally and globally. We are called to interface with people of diverse belief systems, offering truth and hope unique to the gospel message in these final days.

Peril: The church becoming self-serving, retreating from its mission and being reclusive from the world.

Privilege: Exciting our congregation to realize we can evangelize wherever we are by living out our faith and learning to interact effectively with people different from ourselves.

Questions for personal reflection: Chapter 16 The Pastor as Evangelist

1. Why is a contrasted life fundamental to evangelism?
2. Why does outreach need to be intentional?
3. Identify ways the church can get beyond the walls both locally and globally?
4. What are the challenges of relating to a multi-ethnic and multi-religious world?
5. How does investment and involvement in local and global missions impact the church?

17 The Pastor as Warrior

Ignorance of the Enemy:
The Balance Between Apathy and Obsession

Today there is a great fascination with angels yet so little understanding of Satan and his ungodly associates. The agents who introduced sin into the world are ever hell-bent on accomplishing his sinister purposes.

The Person of Satan (Isaiah 14 and Ezekiel 28)

Satan goes by several names in the scriptures. He is called the Devil, the Prince of Darkness, Lucifer, Star of the Morning, and Beelzebub. His name literally means 'The Accuser.' This is referenced in Revelation 12. One of his main activities is to accuse believers when they fail. He is also described metaphorically as Serpent, Lion, Dragon, which reveals his character, power, and the intensity of his attack.

Contrary to modern theology, Satan and God are not equal. God is the Creator, and Satan is a created being. He is totally subservient to the Creator. However, Satan attempts to present himself as the true God to deceive and control people. Satan is under God's control, even though it doesn't always feel that way.

Here is an analogy between our old enemy and my dog, Buster, a ten-pound Shih-Tzu. Buster could only go as far as the leash let him go; I controlled how much freedom he had. Thus, God has

Satan on a leash; God controls how much freedom the Devil has and restricts him accordingly. Twice in Buster's 15 years of life, he got out of the leash, and I didn't know it. (Look at that silly man walking a leash!) God never has that problem; Satan never gets out of his leash. God is ever in control of what he does. (Job:1-2)

There are four possible reactions to this evil enemy.

Apathy: To dismiss the possibility of a devil, believing it to be the product of an over-active imagination.

Avoidance: To refuse to acknowledge, study, or discuss the subject.

Obsession: To have a fixation with Satan and his forces, attributing everything to their activity and believing them to be invincible and their strategies indefensible.

Informed: To seek out the truth, being educated and warned about Satan's threats and strategies and how to deal with them.

Apathy and avoidance are marked by willful ignorance and an absence of fear. Obsession is marked by addictive curiosity and paralyzing fear.

Awareness of the evil one and his operation is critical for the pastor. The pastor-warrior, called to further God's holy cause, is an obvious threat to the work of the Devil, who attempts to short-circuit our effectiveness in ministry.

Our Chief Commander has told us that we would have conflicts with a real opponent, a vociferous enemy. We are informed as to his whereabouts, as well as how he operates. We are to be prepared for conflict.

When pastors are neutral on the subject of evil in the world and the one who perpetuates it, they will more than likely downplay the topic in their preaching-teaching. This communicates to the congregation that evil is no big deal and the Devil is not a big problem. But, in this case, ignorance isn't bliss!

On the other hand, if we give an inordinate amount of attention to the Devil, we provide him with more publicity than he deserves; and make people hypersensitive to his reality. For instance, they will attribute everything terrible that happens to him. They tend to find Satan everywhere, under the towels, the hood of the car, in their desert. (Devil's Food Cake, of course!)

Leaders who are asleep to the reality of an opponent and his warfare will fail to be alert and prepare the troops for battle. Winning this unseen but real war may be jeopardized by pastors and congregations who need to be awakened.

What is the pastor to do? I studied this subject for one entire year before editing a seminar entitled *Standing Firm in Christ*. (A guide to spiritual warfare.) This is available upon request. (rolboyce@theultimatecalling.com) The finest book I have read on the subject is: *Know Your Real Enemy* by Michael Youssef. It is urgent at this hour!

The Devil and the D's: The Timeless Strategy

General Strategy

- At first glance, we cannot help but notice that dEVIL is a part of his name. This term defines him: he who is evil does evil. (Revelation 12:9)
- He pretends to be something he is not. (II Corinthians 11:14-15)
- He lies to people to destroy them. (John 8:44)
- He attacks and misleads individuals to make them ineffective in discovering and living out their faith in Christ. (I Peter 5:8)

- He seeks revenge on God for kicking him out of heaven and takes it out on God's people. (Revelation 12:10)
- He accelerates his attack against God and the world as the end of the age approaches. (Revelation 12:13)

Specific Strategy

The Devil used the 'D' strategy with Adam and Eve then, and he continues to use it now with us.

Deception: He appeared to be something he wasn't.

Doubt: He convinced the first couple to question what God had told them and disregard what they knew to be true about Him.

Desire: He exploited the natural thirst for knowledge, power, and control to tempt them to be like God.

Distraction: He focused their attention on what they didn't have rather than what they did, creating unthankfulness, discontent, and a want for more.

Division: He helped create a rift between God and each other.

Depression: He caused them to experience guilt, remorse, fear, and rejection due to their self-caused condition.

Death: He told them they would not die immediately. But he omitted to tell them that based on the choices they made, they would ultimately die. The process of dying would affect all aspects of their lives.

Here's what his strategy might look like today. A seasoned member of a church was asked what Satan's strategy might be to capture the American culture. He responded:

"Gain control of the most powerful nation in the world by deluding their minds into thinking they had come from man's effort instead of God's blessing."

"Promote an attitude of loving things and using people; instead of the other way around."

"Dupe entire states into relying on gambling for their state revenue."

"Convince people that character is not an issue when it comes to leadership."

"Make it legal to take the life of unborn babies."

"Make it socially acceptable to take one's own life and invent medicine to make it convenient."

"Cheapen human life as much as possible so that an animal's life is valued more than the life of human beings."

"Take God out of the schools where even the mention of His name would be grounds for a lawsuit."

"Get control of the media to pollute all family member's minds for his agenda."

"Attack the family, the backbone of the nation."

"Compel people to express their most depraved fantasies on canvas and movie screens and call it art."

"Convince people that right and wrong are determined by a few who call themselves authorities and refer to their agenda as politically correct."

"Persuade people that the church is irrelevant and out-of-date, and the Bible is for the naïve."

"Dull the minds of Christians and make them believe that prayer isn't essential and that faithfulness and obedience are optional."

From my observation, it pretty much sums up where we are today!

This strategy is timeless because it keeps on working and renders the desired result. As goes the old saying, "If it ain't broke, don't fix it." Satan has no need to change it. It works because we let it!

Consider the place of volition in Satan's strategy against us. We have been created with a will and the power of choice. Like our parents in Eden, we can make good or bad choices that determine self-caused consequences. The aftermath of the choices made in Eden has affected everyone on earth.

What was the purpose of his strategy? Ultimately it is to dethrone God, the evil one's motivation in rebelling against the one who had created him. The consequences of his being thrown from heaven are described by another one of his names, diabolos (diabolic), which means the one thrown down. The results of God's reaction are irreversible. (Isaiah 14:12-15, Revelation 12:7-12)

Satan knows that nothing will hurt God the Father more than when His children disobey Him and live apart from His power in their lives. Satan robs them of all that God has promised them.

What is a pastor to do? I encourage you to do a survey of your own life concerning Satan's strategies and have your people do the same.

Our Spiritual Arsenal: Fighting the War

The person of God

In addition to being omniscient, all-powerful, and everywhere present, He is also known as a Warrior in Exodus 15:3, the

271

Commander and Chief of the forces of heaven and earth/Lord Sabaoth in Isaiah 31:4.

The war

Wars are a part of life. There have been 14,400 wars throughout human history with a mere 297 years of peace. The toll of human life is 3.6 billion people.

The war we face in the spiritual realm began with Satan's expulsion from heaven. It will not end until Christ casts the Devil and his fallen forces into Hell permanently. "For our struggle is not against flesh and blood, but against rulers, against the authorities, against the powers of this dark world and the spiritual forces of evil in the heavenly realm." (Ephesians 6:12)

Each of us battles with our enemy. Warfare is part of the Christian life. Pastors are especially vulnerable to attack. Psalm 110:3a.

A pastor relates his experience in doing warfare with the enemy. During his first months in a new and very challenging assignment, he identifies his struggle. "You should know that every Sunday afternoon and all day Monday are a battleground for me. No matter what happens on Sunday morning, I feel as though it was awful. And Mondays are even worse as I correct and critique myself all day because of the previous day's message. I'm sure the enemy has something to do with that, but I am just as sure that I cooperate with him with a sort of self-absorption that is every bit as unhealthy as being beaten with a stick, maybe even more harmful."

Although Christ's conquest has won the spiritual battle at the cross, the ongoing battles still have to be fought.

The themes of warfare are reflected in this hymn of the church. *Onward Christian Soldiers* Imagine soldiers going to war with

Jesus leading them under a banner that reads VICTORY, which results in Satan's army retreating in defeat.

Weapons of war and winning the war

We can only withstand Satan by the power given to us. "Be strong in the Lord and the power of His might. Put on the full armor of God that you may be able to stand against the schemes of the devil." (Ephesians 6:10-11)

To understand the nature of the spiritual war, we need to define the word *scheme.* The word translated means a well-thought-out strategy. Paul speaks to the Corinthian Church about this, "So that Satan might not outwit us, for we are not unaware of his schemes." (II Corinthians 2:11)

The schemer uses *tailor-made temptations.* They are customized according to the individual, their temperament, weaknesses, and vulnerabilities.

One prominent example of this strategy is in the temptation of Christ recorded in Matthew 4. The evil one uses tailor-made temptations to trip Christ up. He used both overt and less obvious means to accomplish the objective of rendering the Savior of the world ineffective. Christ and His potential work on the cross was a direct threat to the power and purposes of Satan himself.

The strategy of Satan was to tempt the Lord to make bread out of stones. After 40 days of fasting, it would fair to say that Christ was tempted to fulfill the human need for food. The second strategy was to lure Christ into misusing His power by forcing God to catch Him if He jumped from a high place. The third strategy was to offer Christ the rule of all the kingdoms of the earth by bowing to Satan himself. Let's take a look at Satan's strategy of attack and Christ's counter-attack.

Throughout Christ's life and ministry, He won the war over evil by resisting and overcoming the temptations. He met them with *tailor-made truths,* mandatory for victory. They were directly connected to the sword of the Spirit, which is God's Word; literally God's specific principles applicable to each temptation.

Attack: "Command that these stones become bread." (Temptation)

Counter Attack: "Man shall not live by bread alone but by every Word that precedes from the mouth of God." (Truth)

Attack: "If you are the son of God, throw yourself down." (Temptation)

Counter Attack:" You shall not tempt the Lord your God." (Truth)

Attack: "Fall and worship me." (Temptation)

Counter Attack: "You shall worship the Lord your God and Him only." (Truth)

The great opponent knew exactly what he was doing. He used a well-thought-out distraction strategy, attempting to short-circuit God's eternal plan. The stakes were high. Satan had much to gain, and Christ had much to lose.

Part of the temptation narrative records that angels came and ministered to Him during the ordeal. Angels are mentioned 273 times in the Bible; every author in the Bible refers to them except James. One-third of the angels, called demons, fell from heaven when Lucifer was expelled. They do the Devil's dirty work, bringing destruction to believers. Two-thirds of them are good angels who carry out God's work of bringing deliverance to believers. So, remember, in doing spiritual warfare, good angels outnumber the evil angels two to one!!

We cannot outwit Satan with our own power. One thing we observe in our Savior's strategy is His absolute reliance upon God, His Father, and His Word by which to overcome the evil one. The observation teaches us that we must do the same.

To deal with the evil one, we must do as James suggests. "Submit to God, resist Satan, and he will flee from you. Come near to God, and He will come near to you." (James 4:7-8)

We cannot successfully resist on our own. But as we submit, we can win our war over sin. "Because the one who is in you is greater than the one who is in the world." (I John 4:4)

Paul emphasizes this practical approach to winning the spiritual war in Ephesians 6:10-11, where he states: "Finally, be strong in the Lord and in His mighty power. Put on the whole armor of God so that you can take your stand against the Devil's *schemes*."

He lists the spiritual arsenal necessary to win the war in Ephesians 6:14-17.

The helmet of salvation: The intellectual and personal knowledge of salvation; fact over feeling.

The breastplate of righteousness: The protection of the heart, which is the center of the intellect, emotion, and will.

Loins girded with truth: The protection of the Word surrounding the most vulnerable part of the anatomy.

Feet shod with the preparation of the gospel of peace: Bringing the Gospel of Christ wherever we go and promoting peace in our relationships with others.

The shield of faith: Moving forward in confidence of the Lord being able to go before and overcome any obstacles that oppose His people and His purposes.

The sword of the Spirit, which is the Word of God: The specific principles of God which defeat the opposition; the tailor-made truths which come against the tailor-made temptations.

Example: Taylor-made temptation: to swear. Taylor-made truth: "Let your conversation be always full of grace, seasoned with salt so that you know how to answer everyone." (Colossians 4:6)

Example: Taylor-made temptation: losing your temper. Taylor-made truth: "In your anger do not sin: Do not let the sun go down while you are angry, and do not give the Devil a foot-hold." (Ephesians 4:26-27) Note: Anger is a human emotion that must be expressed, but in a way that is not harmful, resolved as quickly as possible, and not allowed to foster bitterness and unforgiveness.

Prayer: The petitioning of God individually and corporately in a spirit of perseverance, claiming power and protection.

One of the essential aspects of fighting the battle is the final offensive weapon in our spiritual arsenal. It is prayer. It is no coincidence that the words prayer and warfare rhyme!

Prayer is imperative, not optional. The connection between prayer and warfare is mandatory; it is the key to spiritual survival! Paul included it in the spiritual arsenal. "And pray in the Spirit on all occasions with all kinds of prayers and requests. With this in mind, be alert and always keep on praying for all the saints." (Ephesians 6:18)

Yet, the whole area of being engaged in warfare with a real enemy is perplexing and troublesome. We can't understand why God allowed evil to exist in the first place. God allows us, just as He allowed Satan to have free will. The existence of evil did not catch God by surprise. Satan did not circumvent His plan for man. God both anticipated and provided a way to save us. God said to the serpent, "And I will put enmity between you and the woman and between your offspring and hers; He will crush your head and you will strike His heel." (Genesis 3:15)

Though we still fight the battles, we can be confident that the war has been won and the ultimate victory is assured.

I Corinthians proclaims the victory. "For since death came through a man, the resurrection of the dead comes also through a man. For as in Adam, all die, so in Christ, all will be made alive. Then the end will come when He hands over the kingdom to God, the Father after He has destroyed all dominion, authority, and power, for He must reign until He has put His enemies under His feet. The last enemy to be destroyed is death." (I Corinthians 15:21-22,24-25)

The themes of victory are reflected in this hymn of the church. *Faith is the Victory* God promises that we will be overcomers through the power of the risen Christ.

The ultimate statement of victory is found in Revelation 12:10-11. "Then I heard a loud voice in heaven say: Now has come the salvation and the power and the kingdom of our God, and the authority of His Christ. For the accuser of our brothers, who accuses them before our God day and night, has been hurled down. They overcame him by the blood of the Lamb and by the word of their testimony."

Practical application of the promise: *When the accuser reminds you of your past, remind him of his future!*

What is the pastor to do? I preached a series on winning the war, especially at Easter and on July 4th. I asked members to share their victory stories to encourage believers and as a witness to non-believers.

Victory in Everyday Life: Living Triumphantly in the World

Walking in spiritual freedom

The scriptures explain the concept of freedom of the believer. Isaiah 61:1, Psalm 146:7, John 8:32, Galatians 5:13, and Revelation 1:5.

Christ came to bring people out of the bondage of their old life into the freedom of their new life. Christ died to make us different; He did not die to let us stay the same! Satan wants us bound, but Jesus sets us free.

Tragically, many people in the pews today have faith but no freedom. They live imprisoned by the habits and encumbrances of the old life, not experiencing the emancipation promised them. How sad to see so many believers in churches today living in self-imposed bondage at a level of mediocrity. As a seasoned believer once said, "Christians are living below their privileges."

The enemy has neutralized their effectiveness; they have become less of a threat to his purposes. He keeps them from being different and making a difference.

One of our prime responsibilities as pastors is to lead our people into the deeper life in God, out of bondage into freedom, out of darkness into light. To be free in Christ is our spiritual legacy, the emancipation given at God's expense.

God stresses that when it comes to our life-long struggle with sin and the life of bondage, we have other options and alternatives.

I John 3:9 amplifies this truth. "No one who is born of God will continue to sin because God's seed remains in him. He cannot go on sinning because he has been born of God." It doesn't say we won't sin, but rather, we don't have to give in; we can win over sin!

An Eskimo boy became a Christian and was asked how he was doing in his new life. He gave an unusual answer. "I have two dogs, a white one and a black one; they are both trying to tell me what to do. The black one tells me to do the wrong things. The white one tells me to do the right things. They fight with each other. He was asked, "Which one wins?" The boy paused, then said, "The one I feed the most!" Galatians 5:16-17.

Impacting the Political Arena

A pastor is called to engage in the battle mounted against society and the church. They are called to make up the hedge and stand in the gap in an evil day. Ezekiel 22:30-31.

Pastors must realize that they serve as modern-day prophets. In a sense, the pastor-prophet is the embodiment of a watchman; one who functions to alert the church of impending evil and challenge them to be God's chosen people in this age. Ezekiel 3:16-21.

To exercise the prophetic gift is to both fore-tell and forth-tell the truth, both essential to the church's life. The first is to explain what is happening in the future; the second is to explain what is happening in the present.

The prophet has always been a lonely and unpopular role. Isaiah, Jeremiah, and Amos, among others, all faced the rejection and ridicule of their peers. In the New Testament, Christ Himself said, "Truly I say to you, no prophet is welcome in his home town." Modern-day prophets are not always welcome in their home church. (Luke 4:24)

It could be said that the modern pastor is called to comfort the disturbed and disturb the comfortable. Part of what makes people uncomfortable is becoming involved in the political arena.

The threat to religious liberty and the inherent rights of believers is mounting. The secularized culture is characterized by an intolerance of and censoring opposing views, marginalizing the Christian faith, and open opposition to religious freedom.

In a land where freedom of speech is a right granted to its citizens and our religious rights guaranteed, it seems that the rule of intolerance now prevails. It is enigmatic that the law does not allow us as Christ-followers to do what others can do.

Example: A coach was fired from his job. Reason? He had a short prayer with his team after the game!

Example: A pastor was told that he could not mention Christianity as the only religion that led to God in deference to those in the convalescent home who could be offended by what appeared to be an exclusive position.

The antagonists to the Christian faith espouse humanism religiously. But they claim that it does not violate any wall of separation. They preach the legality of such things as abortion on demand, free distribution of contraceptives, same-sex marriage, the legitimacy of homosexuality, the right to trans-gender, and the naturalness of pedophilia. They claim that humanism *is not* a religion, but they sure do have a belief system they perpetuate!

The separation of church and state only intended that the government not dictate or interfere with the people's religious life but rather support religious freedom. Americans would have freedom *of* religion, not freedom *from* religion. Religious activities and symbols are called into question as illegal in a society where the right has become wrong, and wrong has become right.

In the modern arena, traditional beliefs are met with increased antagonism to the counter-cultural message we proclaim. Because of this tension, many churches have compromised their biblical teaching and their stance on critical issues. Such is the case with several denominations aligned more with social mores than biblical norms, giving sanction to liberal agendas.

As pastors, our voice is needed in the political realm. We are to stand for truth and righteousness; there is a consequence for remaining uninformed and disengaged from the political process. The church has been told not to be engaged with politics. As a result, we have forfeited our influence in the political area. This tactical error has contributed to Christianity's demise and its influence on politicians, policies, and practices. It has silenced the collective conservative voice needed to be heard irrespective of those who oppose it.

Thus, it is not a stretch to declare that pastor-prophets are to be warriors; they are called to enlist in a battle to fight a war against the encroachment of evil and the mounting assault against a democratic society. What was once unthinkable is now possible. Our beloved country, the noble experiment, is under a spiritual siege fighting the war that rages from within. The evil one, the enemy of our souls, wants to see our great nation under God collapse under the weight of atheistic Socialism. Yet, going against the trend of popular political thought is to do so at significant risk; but it is one the pastor-warrior and congregation need to take. To not take the risk is greater.

How can the pastor and congregation respond to politics?

1. Organize a Christian Action Committee led by people in the congregation interested in political and social issues. The purpose of the effort is two-fold: Keeping people aware of what is happening and being proactive in the political process.

2. Mobilize the Christian community to be educated on issues and candidates. Voters guides and online resources are available for this purpose.

3. Plan pre-election prayer times as an individual congregation or in concert with neighboring churches. Encourage your people to pray for the governmental leaders.

4. Provide contact information on legislators encouraging your people to write, email, or call their leaders, especially on critical issues.

Withstanding Persecution

Statistics confirm that more people have died worldwide for their Christian faith in this last century than all other centuries since the coming of Christ combined!

The scriptures clearly identify persecution coming upon God's people. Matthew 5:11-12, "Blessed are you when people insult you, persecute you and falsely say all kinds of evil against you because of Me. Rejoice and be glad because great is your reward in heaven, for in the same way, they persecuted the prophets before you." II Timothy 3:12, "In fact, everyone who wants to live a godly life in Christ Jesus will be persecuted."

The direction of the world and our country indicates that persecution of Christians will increase. Therefore, the Church of Christ is called to unite around these three things. To uphold the basic tenants of Christianity, to pray collectively for our country and its leaders, and become more involved in the political realm. This will require courage and persistence.

Often this group of people is referred to in scripture as the remnant. The remnant is a small cadre of righteous people who stand for truth and what is right in perilous times. The metaphor of yeast illustrates the function of the remnant; it is a small element that permeates the whole. This is the task of the church in our culture. In the Old Testament, the remnant is referred to in Isaiah 10:20-23, Isaiah 11:10-12.

In the New Testament, a remnant is to be a restraining force holding back the onslaught of evil in the end times. Such is the role of the church in today's world. II Thessalonians 2:7.

What is the pastor to do?

I have preached on these subjects and encouraged people to intercede for national and world leaders and those persecuted for their faith.

I use the following guides for my own intercession:

- Every Home for Christ: United States Prayer Map/World Prayer Map available from www.ehc.org
- Intercessors for America: Praying for Government Guide www.ifapray.org
- Voice of the Martyrs: Praying for Persecuted Christians Guide www.persecution.com

As the end of the age approaches, may we be set-apart believers who shine brighter as the world grows darker. Philippians 2:13-16. In these end times, let us come against our opponent who battles the church, which Christ said the gates of Hell would not overcome. Matthew 16:18.

The story is told of a young man who visited a world-renowned art gallery, and was enthralled by a large portrait entitled **Checkmate**. The artist had created a giant chessboard, a man seated on one side, the Devil on the opposite side. The young man sat for hours, mesmerized by the contest. At the end of the day, the guard informed the spectator that the gallery was closing and that he would have to leave. As he got up to go, the guard heard him whisper, *"Sir, there is one more move you can make."*

In our battle with the Devil and his evil forces, we are not checkmated. The war has already been won. Thus, we can win our war against all evil forces. This eternal truth is a fitting conclusion to this chapter. The battles the church must engage in will conclude with ultimate victory. It is our faith that will ultimately overcome the world. "You, dear children, are from God and have overcome them because the one who is in you is greater than the one who is in the world." (1 John 4:4) "For everyone who is born of God overcomes the world. This is the victory that overcomes the world, even our faith. Who is it that overcomes the world? Only he who believes that Jesus is the Son of God." (1 John 5:4-5)

Summary: The pastor-warrior is called is responsible to educate their congregation about Satan, his person, and his strategies in the war against us. They also instruct them about our God, the greater power, and how to fight the battles, knowing the ultimate war has already been won. Our victory enables us to walk in spiritual freedom, impact the political arena and withstand persecution as victors, not victims.

Peril: Not taking Satan seriously or failing to help believers know that they are at war with evil powers that attack pastors and churches.

Privilege: Serving as pastor-warrior and pastor-prophet who assures the church of victory already won in the daily battles of life and stands with the church in positively impacting the culture in the last days before the Lord's return.

Questions for personal reflection: Chapter 17 The Pastor as Warrior

1. What is the balance between apathy and obsession regarding the Devil?
2. What is the Devil's timeless strategy?
3. How can we win the war against the Devil?
4. Why are believers in bondage instead of walking in freedom?

5. How can the church be effective in impacting the political arena?
6. What is our response to the persecutions of Christians?

18   The Pastor as Lifelong Servant

Biblical Background on Retirement:
Those Who Didn't Hang it up

Finding people who retired in the pages of the scriptures is difficult.

Included in the line-up of great non-retirees; Moses (120), Caleb (85), and Joshua (110). Jehoiada, the high priest (130), and Daniel, who lived long enough to serve under four kings.

The historical records don't indicate that these men were taking it easy at home, living off their pension or spending their days golfing at the Jerusalem Country Club. They weren't winding it down; they were just getting wound up!

I saw seven truths about growing old the other day that made me chuckle. Growing old is not optional; growing up is a choice. Forget the healthy food; you need all the preservatives you can get. When you fall, you wonder what else you can do while you're down there. You're getting old when you get the same sensation from a rocking chair you once got from a roller coaster. It's frustrating when you know all the answers, but nobody bothers to ask you the questions. Time may be a great healer, but it's a lousy beautician. Wisdom comes with age, but sometimes age comes alone.

Our culture fixates on being done. We run through the hoops, and pass through the cycles of life: Get through school, get married,
286

get our family grown, receive our gold watch. (We now have time on our hands in more ways than one!)

When we think we're about done, it can be when we've just begun! A conclusion becomes a commencement. Danger, wilderness, and conquest are yet set before us. And most likely, we are better able to take them on now than ever before. It's never too late to risk, to become all that God has designed us to be!

Too often, those who retire trade the thrill of the quest for the status quo of security. They have all the resources with no place to expend them but on themselves.

A friend of mine, a financial advisor, asks a standard question of new retirees. It is not what are you retiring *from,* but what are you retiring *to*? Every person considering retirement would do well to ask themselves the same question.

Many people live to retire to travel, sleep late, do gardening. While there is nothing intrinsically wrong with these things, the list may omit one vital thing, ministering.

There is one instance where retirement from the ministry is mandated in Numbers 8:23-26. It applied to the Levites, who took part in the Tent of Meeting. The men had to be at least 25 years old to work but were commanded to retire at age 50. However, the retirees were allowed and encouraged to assist the younger men in the performance of priestly duties. God did not want older priests to retire from doing something to doing nothing. And note, there was no time limit on how long the senior priest could co-minister with the younger priest.

Let's look at this from a practical standpoint. Why should we *not* 'hang it up?

First, retirement is usually a drastic change in routine. To go from a routine of time clocks and deadlines to the absence of a regular schedule and unlimited free time can be detrimental physically and mentally. It can cause people to age prematurely. Breaking the rhythm and routine can be a shock to our entire system.

A couple in Minnesota announced their retirement. At their reception, they had made it clear that they were not retiring but *re-treading*. They had many miles left on their life odometer.

Retiring should not mean that something alive and well becomes dormant. A completely sedentary life robs us from enriching the lives of others and might even shorten ours!

Some in ministry may withdraw from it just when they may well be at a point of having more to offer than ever before. They have the resources of experience, wisdom, and even more material means to invest in God's work.

The withdrawal mindset is evident in the proverbial call for workers to help with infants and children in the church. More than once, I have heard the argument, "I've raised my kids, I put in my time." They forget that someone older once helped care for their kids. But more than that, they overlook what they have to offer the parish children.

Back in the day, families took an annual vacation, which meant they would be gone once a year, usually in the summer. Pastors could pretty well expect attendance and offerings to be down for a season.

However, with the increase of affluence and mobility, that has all changed; it has been traceable during my pastoral career. The traditional pattern prevailed into the mid-80s. After that time, people's travel began to extend beyond two weeks of summer vacation. Now, they travel all year. It has become harder to rally the troops and utilize their time, money, and other resources in ministry.

Investing yourself in ministry for an extended time is confirmed biblically.

Gospels: "But seek first His Kingdom and His righteousness and all these things shall be added to you." (Matthew 6:33)

"Do not lay up for yourselves treasures upon earth but lay up for yourselves treasures in heaven." (Matthew 6:19)

Epistles: "Set your mind on things above, not on the things that are on earth." (Colossians 3:2)

In Paul's first letter to Timothy, he captures the essence of the argument. May I paraphrase? Those in the prime of their lives and a place in life to have maximum resources are in the best position to share them with others. (I Timothy 6:19-20)

At this prime time in their lives, people in the church decide to retire from everything. Why? Retirement in modern social circles is considered a reward for working all your life; you've earned it, take it.

There are legitimate reasons why people do retire: Health issues, the need to care for elderly parents, the care of grand-children. All of these represent situations in which retirement is natural and necessary.

However, I choose to use the term *'modulation,'* a transition from one phase of ministry to another without termination.

Doing Ministry Better: Wisdom Works Smarter Not Harder

Modulation allows us to expend less time and energy than in the

past. The pastor may do the same work, but maybe more effectively.

In the second half of our life, we can also *re-invent* ourselves. We are the same people with the same capacities, but perhaps we can begin using them differently.

Coming into this season, I have learned invaluable lessons in the laboratory of life. What are some of these lessons?

Not all things have to be done by *me!* The whole Body of Christ is not the head. Maybe those who were the head in pre-retirement become hands and feet in the period of re-treading and re-invention.

I learned that I am not in the ministry for bolstering self-esteem through performance. I am secure enough to share the limelight with another and receive their acclamation by supporting and promoting another's success. I don't have to be the center of attention or take credit for everything that happens; I've learned that the one who receives the compliments also gets the criticism. When we are on top, we are more likely to be in the line of fire; in retirement, I am finally free from having the buck stop with me.

As I pondered retirement-modulation, I thought about things I would love to do that previous positions had not allowed me to do; sing on the Praise Team, be the cook for retreats, or assist with the Boy Scout program. I could contemplate travel, compose music, and maybe even write a book! To modulate may also mean developing unused gift areas.

By the way, what prevents mid-life crisis in the pre-retirement years also makes for a healthy, active, and productive life in modulation.

The older pastor can also bring their experience and correspondent seasoning to bear on the parish ministry in various ways: Transitioning to the role of consultant, counselor, or coach. They can be available to people because they don't have to do all the regular stuff. This happened when I concluded full-time pastoral ministry and became lead pastoral Counselor at our home church for six years; I loved doing one thing!

We never graduate from the school of experience. Thus, the pastor is a co-learner at every point in the process. This makes it more comfortable for the younger to come to the older for prayer, counsel, and support without feeling threatened.

One paradigm of leadership is: In the early years, we lead by *perception.* (What we believe we know.) In the middle years, we lead by *performance.* (What we can do.) In the later years, we lead by *presence.* (Who we are and what we have become.)

By virtue of their occupation, pastors always have a ministry of presence. Pastors have a different kind of presence in the new era, based more on being, less on doing.

The secular world confirms this concept. Everyone from ex-presidents to retired football coaches, emeritus seminary deans, and former CEO's are people of presence. They elicit admiration and respect by the very nature of their experiences, good and bad, which have resulted in wisdom. Theirs is a seasoned presence. There are no short-cuts to this level of experience.

We can only arrive at this station by attempting to travel the straight path, survive the perils and detours, and surmount the obstacles.

Such a man in my life was the president of my seminary, Dr. Earl Radmacher. At first, he appeared to be a much older man simply because of his stature. In actuality, he was a young father of four and an active churchman. He epitomized all that I would purpose to be as a man, a pastor, and a leader in my lifetime. His qualities included a keen and seeking mind, a zeal for truth, deep loyalty to his wife and family, a rollicking sense of humor, and a deep concern and compassion for people.

Two events in my life underscored his presence and influence. As the only seminarian senior who was neither engaged nor married, I was subject to a certain amount of teasing with people trying to play God, either finding a wife for me or enrolling me in a monastery! At my seminary graduation, I announced my engagement to Joyce Saint. The president remarked, "Since Roland could never be a saint himself, he's decided to marry one!"

In an incident several years later, I heard the sound of a car door opening in the street behind my backyard. I noticed none other than my president retrieving a lost child that had somehow wandered off unnoticed. Fixed in my mind is the picture of this man of high rank and national notoriety taking the hand of a small bewildered child and leading him to safety.

His was the influence of a seasoned life characterized by authenticity and accessibility. It seemed there were no years between us.

Several distinct qualities of seasoned pastors become evident when they show up: An aura of genuine godliness, a gentleness of spirit, easy to be around, not taking themselves too seriously, and a sense of humor; they have learned to laugh at themselves.

Their ministry is more indirect and less within the church's confines; it takes place more often at Starbucks, Barnes & Noble, and Home Depot.

Getting Ready for Modulation:
Knowing When to Pass the Baton

We've all have vivid images of Olympic relay race teams failing to win gold due to dropping the baton and failing to execute the handoff efficiently. Hundreds of hours, multiple practices, yet at the most strategic moment when the handoff counted most, something went wrong, and the gold was forfeited.

Perhaps few of us do an adequate job of working ourselves out of a job and preparing someone else to continue in the race after us. Most of us in ministry don't have the chance to pick our successor. Pastors usually leave their positions before the next pastor is chosen. Few of us are in the same church for the entirety of our careers.

There are exceptions. In one situation, the Associate pastor simply became Senior pastor at the behest of the man he followed. In my fifth pastorate, I witnessed a pastor who began modulating at age 63 and groomed the man who would follow him. We rarely have a chance to pass the baton to our successor, but all of us as pastors can prepare team members and laypersons for on-going ministry.

Perhaps this is why the scriptures exonerate the gray head. Samuel, at the installation of Saul, the first king of Isreal, said, "And now, a king is walking before you, but I am old and gray, and I have walked before you from my youth even to this day." (1 Samuel 12:2)

David makes this assessment in Psalm 71. "O God, thou hast taught me from my youth, and still I declare they wondrous deeds. And even when I am old and gray, O God, do not forsake me until I declare thy truth to the generations to come." Here is the passing of the biblical baton.

Two biblical illustrations confirm this principle, one secular and one sacred. During Nebuchadnezzar's reign, two kings were reigning at the same time, confusing historians. The second was Nebuchadnezzar's successor, a king in training, assuring that there would be no lapse of leadership in the event of the first king's death.

The other setting was that of David and Solomon. God had forbid David to build the temple because of his involvement in wars. David then gave the assignment to Solomon.

In both these situations, modulation took place, the older preparing the younger to carry on the mission.

We attended a church where the founding pastor chose a young man with exceptional capacity to succeed him. He had intentionally invested himself in the new pastor and carefully prepared the church for his leadership. The modulation was seamless. The older pastor let go of controlling things, and the younger heir was entirely respectful and appreciative of his mentor's contribution to the work of the church they led. The Pastor Emeritus has stayed on the staff and developed a radio ministry into his eighties.

Part of preparing to pass the baton and entrusting the future to another is realizing a smaller role. We who are called can continue in the pastoral ministry for life. Yet, the God who calls us to the **ultimate calling** will re-define our ministry. Some do make this transition smoothly; some don't.

How you leave your post will impact you, your successor, and the life of the congregation. It is essential to know when to pass the baton and how to pass it.

The person epitomizing this process is renowned evangelist Billy Graham. How many times did we think that the next crusade would be his last? In actuality, it wasn't. Billy was preparing the way for those who would come after him. Schools of Evangelism have trained hundreds of young pastors to continue the tradition, including his son, Franklin, and other team evangelists. One of them was my dear personal friend and prayer partner, the late Dr. Lon Allison, who was also the director of the Billy Graham Center for Evangelism.

Certainly, Billy Graham is a legend in his own time and was the dominant voice of crusade evangelism for over a generation. He could have held on tightly to power, disallowed things to be done differently, and competed with any under-study who would succeed him. But he was indeed an older modern-day Joshua who prepared a younger Caleb to minister in his stead. When the time came, God and Billy made sure that the baton was passed, and the race continued.

Upon leaving the White House, former President George W. Bush left this letter for his successor, President Bill Clinton.

Dear Bill,

When I walked into this office just now, I felt the same sense of wonder and respect that I felt four years ago. I know you will feel that, too. I wish you great happiness here. I never felt the loneliness some Presidents have described. There will be tough times, made even more difficult by criticism you may not think is fair. I'm not a very good one to give advice, but just don't let the critics discourage you or push you off course.

You will be our President when you read this note. I wish you well. I wish your family well.

Your success is our country's success. I am rooting hard for you.

Good luck,

George

An evangelist and a president passed the baton well! We who are called to a yet higher calling are mandated to do the same.

The Art of Finishing Strong: Running Well Until the End

The sports metaphor emphasizes that one who would pass the baton must make it through *their* portion of the race.

Paul warns about this potential problem in I Corinthians 9:25-27, "Everyone who competes in the games exercises the self-control in all things not simply to run the race but to run and complete it well. They do it to get a crown that will not last, but we get a crown that will last forever. Therefore, we run in such a way as not without aim, as not beating the air, but we buffet our body so after we have preached to others, we are not *disqualified*."

The Principle: It's not just being in the race, but how you run and complete the race.

Few things bring more disgrace to the cause of Christ or discredits Christianity as the downfall and disqualification of one of His shepherds.

James reminds us that those who teach are held to a higher standard and thus subject to a greater judgment. Satan is resolutely committed to bringing about the downfall of those who lead the church. (See 'The Pastor as Warrior')

There is a correlation between keeping the rules, running, and finishing well. Paul admonishes Timothy. "And also if anyone competes as an athlete, he does not win the prize unless he competes according to the rules." (II Timothy 2:5)

What are the rules? Let me share what I consider to be the essential requirements of the race:

- To strive to be always honest, self-disciplined, dependable, trustworthy, and maintaining a reputation above reproach.
- To guard the integrity of all areas of life, especially finances and morals.
- To guard confidences and information entrusted to you.
- To maintain a priority of self-care and the care of your family as an even greater priority than ministry.

- To not indulge in any on-going sin; to guard all relationships with the opposite sex.
- To maintain a strong connection with an individual or group who can hold you accountable and responsible for your choices and actions.
- To remember that you are ultimately accountable to God and your church for how you live your life and run your race.

None of us run the race as well as we could or would like to. No runner avoids tripping and falling or even dropping out for a season. But there is a difference between a runner's motivation to run well or merely wanting to get through the race.

Both the Old and New Testaments record those who were called of God to lead His people but broke the rules and dishonored the one who called them. They ran the race, but they finished it poorly. They were not disqualified as believers but as runners whose poor performance hindered a strong finish and harmed God's people.

Two men come to mind, one from campus ministry, the other from pastoral ministry. The first became involved with a high school student while married. The second man embezzled money from the church's capital fund drive. These two situations are illustrative of not running the race well. There was a significant fall-out from their fall. (See 'The Imperative of Integrity')

God not only wants us in the race; He wants us to do well in the race. He wants us to cross the finish line in the best form possible, which others may emulate as they run their race.

To finish strong, we play by the rules, exercise self-discipline, and work with others in the race. We are to fix our eyes on the goal and the finish line. This focus is central to every runner's life; it is only Christ who can enable us to be in the race and complete it. He has promised that "Having begun a good work He will bring it to completion at the day of His returning." (Philippians 1:6) The Christ who completed the course set before Him enables us to run our race as He did His. Hebrews 12:1-2.

As I come to my 55th year of ministry, I recount with humility and abject thankfulness for God's patience, mercy, enablement, an incredible help-mate, and many indispensable people enabling me to stay the course and hopefully complete it well. My ultimate goal: to finish strong with a whole host of other runners for whom I have provided the incentive to follow me to the finish line, one of the main objectives of this book.

It should be every pastor's goal to run and finish the race well and lead others to do the same. Such was the goal of one of the most outstanding pastors who ever lived, the Apostle Paul. "I have fought the good fight, I have finished the course, I have kept the faith. Now, there is in store for me a crown of righteousness which the Lord, the righteous judge, will award me on that day and not only to me but also to all who have longed for His appearing." (II Timothy 4:7-8)

How to Know You Have Reached Your Goal:
Going for the Gold

Paul anticipates reaching his goal, as confirmed in the book of Acts. "However, I consider my life nothing to me, if only I may finish the race and complete the task the Lord Jesus has given me, the task of testifying to the gospel of God's grace." (Acts 20:24) The context is the imprisonment of the once antagonist who had become a proponent of the Gospel of Christ. There is no indication that Paul ever retired or even slowed the pace of ministry, for that matter. Paul gave it all he had, all his life.

Paul confirms this truth again to his understudy, Timothy, that fighting the good fight, finishing the course, and keeping the faith extends throughout his lifetime. Since his post-conversion entrance into pastoral ministry, Paul determined to follow Christ without reservation; the only interruption was death.

At the end of his life, he concludes, "For I am already to be poured out like a drink offering, and the time has come for my departure." He knew when his time was up and when his ministry would be completed. (II Timothy 4:6-7)

One of the remarkable factors in ministry throughout our life is that God apportions the energy and vitality required for the task, especially in the later years. God gave divine allotments to Abraham, who became Isaac's father when he was 100 years old, and Noah built a floating zoo at age 600.

In the New Testament, the apostle John was still going strong at the end of his earthly ministry. According to the historical record, John was banished to the Isle of Patmos and wrote the legendary book of Revelation; no small feat for a 90-year-old man. We can deduce that God intends for His followers to continue to serve Him for a long time. He gives them what is necessary to carry out their ministry.

We can also conclude that those who served well beyond retirement age served better because of the qualities acquired and the lessons gained from those additional years of life. They worked smarter, not harder. They were better equipped to train those who came behind them because they didn't hang it up.

Having run for a long time, pastors can understand life more clearly and what it takes to run the race successfully. They are qualified to help other runners do the same.

The words of the apostle Paul echos the sentiment. "Not that I have already obtained all this, or have already been made perfect, but I press on to take hold of that for which Christ took hold of me. Brothers, I do not consider myself to have taken hold of it. But one thing I do: Forgetting what is behind and straining toward what is ahead, I press on toward the goal to win the prize for which God has called me heavenward in Christ Jesus." (Philippians 3:12-14)

Peter puts it this way, "And when the Chief Shepherd shall appear, you will receive a crown of glory that will never fade away." (I Peter 5:4) It is the promise to under-shepherds.

The pastor can adopt a Jimmy Carter post-presidential mindset, maybe building houses, always re-constructing lives. The possibility is natural because our giftedness is never terminated. A person who would fulfill their calling never outgrows the need to use their spiritual capacities.

As those called to the Christian ministry, we are called to serve out our days in the present to produce eternal results. I am not convinced that we should measure the days of service based on how short life is but on how long eternity is.

Whatever the design of our calling, the pastor will always be a coach, administrator, vision caster, worship leader, preacher-teacher, counselor, steward, evangelist, and warrior.

The story of two non-retirees concludes this final chapter.

The first centers on a man named Roberto Goizueta, the Chairman and Chief Executive Officer of The Coca-Cola Company, who said, "Retirement is not on my radar screen. As long as I'm having fun, as long as I have the energy necessary, as long as I'm not keeping people from their day in the sun, as long as the board wants me to stay on, I will stay on."

The second story is about a woman, Bea Crow. She was the Food Service Director at Alpine Camp in Mentone, Alabama, for 69 years, starting when she was 17. When someone bought the camp in 1958, they asked her to stay on. When her husband died in 1976, she stayed on. When she turned 65 and then 70, she stayed on. As she turned 80, she stayed on. The camp manager recalls her pie crusts, small biscuits, and yeast rolls as legendary with children and adults across America who grew up at Alpine Camp. And speaking to another element in her legendary leadership, he commented. "Mrs. Crow taught me and others the meaning of the word integrity, doing what you said you would do." When a doctor decreed that at age 86, Mrs. Crow could no longer face the stress of feeding 350 people a day, she reluctantly left the kitchen. (But to show that the doctor was wrong, she went out and planted the most extensive vegetable garden in the whole country!)

Two different people, a man and a woman who didn't retire. They realized the goal of staying the course and completing their calling of making a difference, of leaving a legacy to all who would come behind them. They didn't make the mistake of hanging it up too soon!

As we look to Christ, we observe the shortness of His ministry and the age of His death; to cite His life as an example of serving a lifetime without retirement seems irrelevant. Yet Christ could have asked the Father to give Him the right to end His ministry after death. But Christ did not do that. *What seemed like an end of Christ's ministry was only the beginning. Jesus has never retired!*

Can we who call ourselves His followers, those called to full-time ministry, not serve Him at least for a lifetime?

"Jesus, undeterred, went right ahead and gave this charge: God authorized and commanded Me to commission you: Go out and train everyone you meet far and near, in this way of life. Then instruct them in the practice of all I have commanded you. I'll be with you as you do this, day after day, right up to the end of the age." (Matthew 28:18-20 The Message)

The **ultimate calling** to pastoral ministry carries with it the perils and privileges of serving the One who served us all the days of His life on earth and who now serves us in heaven. It is He who has called us to serve Him all the days of *our* lives!

Summary: Great biblical leaders didn't hang it up; they weren't winding down so much as getting wound up, retreading, and re-inventing themselves. Ours is a time of modulation, of taking on different tasks and allowing others to utilize their gifts in complement to our own. We are wiser from experience, more secure in who we have become, and lead by presence. We purpose to run the race faithfully, taking care to avoid side roads that would deter us from running well and finishing strong. We need to pass the baton to others who come behind us in the race. We are called to run the race until our earthly life ends, or the Chief Shepherd returns. Until then, He will guide us through the transition as we go for the gold, the crown of life which awaits us!

Peril: Retiring from the ministry too soon and forfeiting the chance to make even greater contributions to the calling or disgracing the one who has called us to run the race.

Privilege: Re-inventing and re-investing ourselves, making the second half of our life and ministry the best in our pastoral career.

Questions for personal reflection: Chapter 18 The Pastor as Lifelong Servant

1. What is the biblical background of retirement?
2. What are the benefits of non-retirement?
3. How does the pastor prepare to pass the baton?
4. How does the pastor finish the race well?

The certification of The Ultimate Calling Isaiah 49-50

*"Listen to me, you islands; hear this you distant nations: Before I was born the Lord **called** me; from my birth He has made mention of my name. He made my mouth a sharp sword, in the shadow of His arm, He has hidden me: He made me a polished arrow and consealed me in His quiver. I, even I have spoken, yes I have **called** him; I will bring him and he will succeed in his mission. The soverign Lord has given me an instructed tongue, to know the word that sustains the weary. He awakens me morning by morning to hear like one being taught. The soverign Lord has opened my ears and I have not been rebellious; I have not drawn back."*

Endorsements

You have provided a holistic, nuts and bolts guide to the pastorate that is sure to be a resource to pastors for years to come. Your years of experience and practical wisdom come through on every page, hitting deep at times but always full of grace. If any young pastor had ever wanted to sit down over coffee to have a deep dive into all aspects of the pastorate, here is the chance. It is truly an incredible work!

Craig Rush Former Lead Pastor,
Chase Oaks Wood Bridge Church

Roland Boyce is a model pastor. For my entire life, his godly character and dedication have inspired and influenced me. As a pastor, he is gifted with the skill of a surgeon and the wise, loving care of a shepherd. The Ultimate Calling zeros in on the primary principles that forged Roland's character and the pragmatic practices that have yielded 50 years of God-glorifying results. For the novice it is a primer. For the more experienced it brings clarity and inspiration. In either case, this book is a resource to be treasured.

Paul Fleischmann, President Emeritus
National Network of Youth Ministries
Founder, Better Together Resources

I hear your voice thru-out this work. A Welcome voice!

Dr. John Johnson Retired Pastor, Author, and Professor
at Western Baptist Seminary, and former Associate Pastor
at Milwaukie Covenant Church with the Author

Roland, your book is engaging and inspiring. You continue to teach and model for me how to live into this pastoral calling with greater excellence.

Rick Lindholtz, Pastor and former staff member
at Milwaukie Covenant Church with the Author

I love your book. It should be required reading for every seminary student.

David Lindfors, retired Senior Pastor of Broadway Covenant Church, Rockford, Illinois

You have many years of wisdom and teaching this work which is of much value. What I read in the book is what I have seen in you.

Dr. Ron Marrs. Former Pastor, Professor at Western Baptist Seminary who served with the Author in Campus Ministry

It's phenomenally you in every way, so full of rich ministry perspectives.You have lived it so well, and others like myself will continue to benefit from HIS transformative work in and through you over many significant years. This is a book that every person considering ministry should read. It is a book that takes an honest and practical look at the many joys and challenges that go hand in hand with pastoral ministry. His writing and life are Jesus-centered and drenched in grace. I commend this book to you; be ready for a God-chiseling to occur in your relationship with Him and the ministry He prepares you for.

David Ahrens, Former Associate Pastor who served with the Author at the First Covenant Church, Rockford, Illinois

Rol Boyce is a pastor in the fullest sense of the word. He is a theologian who cares deeply about the Word of God. But he is also a practitioner who has gotten into the trenches of ministry, journeyed with people through thick and thin (including me), and provided caring hope and wise guidance. I'm thrilled he put this wisdom down in written form so that others can glean from his experiences through his kind, charming and grace-filled style. You're in for a treat!

Eric Torrence, Groups Pastor Chase Oaks Church, served on staff with the Author

Decades ago, when I began pastoral ministry, I wish I'd had a book like *The Ultimate Calling*. More than a book, it reads like a conversation with an older and wiser pastor who is so well-read and experienced as he offers timely help in every aspect of pastoral ministry. Whether you're looking for guidance leading people or to think deeply about who the pastor is or what they do, the call is clarified here. A pathway to discovery spreads out before the pastor. Grace from seasoned wisdom and loving God's people is a helpful, caring friend when this book is in one's hand. Culture may be changing rapidly, but the need for this kind of friendship with the pastor will never change. Nor will the imperative of a clear calling in the task.

Dwain Tissell Senior Pastor at Eastridge Covenant Church and former School of Prayer Associate with the Author

After reading *The Ultimate Calling*, my reaction was WOW! It is the most comprehensive book on pastoral call and ministry I have read, by a lot.

Bill Anthes, Senior Pastor, Redeemer Evangelical Covenant Church, Liverpool, New York and Former School of Prayer Associate with the Author

Your work is very well organized, and I deeply appreciate the story of your own call.

Steve Pitts, retired Pastor In the Evangelical Covenant Church, served in Campus Life Campus Ministry with the Author

The greatest affirmation I can give to this work is the Holy Spirit working in me as I read *The Ultimate Calling*. This is truly God's work!

Alan Eagle, Senior Pastor who served on staff at Milwaukie Covenant Church with the Author

If you want honest and thoughtful writing, you'll find it here. Rol Boyce knows of what he speaks. Having served students for many years and their families in Youth for Christ and several decades as the always-praying-down-the-walls Pastor, he has had a long ministry journey. Do yourself a favor and give yourself the gift of his insights.

Dr. Art Greco, Retired Pastor and former Director of Prayer and Evangelism, Evangelical Covenant Church

Made in the USA
Monee, IL
31 August 2022

12909362R00187